The Powe

My Experience in a U.S. Immigration Jail

by Ana Amalia Guzmán Molina

Translation to English
Marilu MacCarthy

Foreword
Rev. Robert McChesney, S.J.

EPICA
Washington DC

The Power of Love: My Experience in a U.S. Immigration Jail

Ecumenical Program on Central America and the Caribbean (EPICA)
1470 Irving St. NW, Washington, D.C. 20010
(202) 332-0292; fax (202) 332-1184
Email: epicabooks@epica.org
Website: www.epica.org

Translation: Marilu MacCarthy
Cover Art: Rosa Lozano and Zoila Elias
Editing and Coordination: Kathy Ogle
Spanish Proofreading: Mario Bencastro
English Proofreading: Siobhán Dugan
Translation of Introduction: Alex Taylor
Layout and Design: Scott Wright

Library of Congress Cataloging-in-Publication Data
Guzmán Molina, Ana Amalia, 1955-
The power of love: my experience in a U.S. immigration jail / by Ana Amalia Guzmán Molina; translation to English, Marilu MacCarthy; foreword, Robert McChesney.
p. cm.
In English and Spanish.
ISBN 0-918346-33-9
1. Guzmán Molina, Ana Amalia, 1955- 2. Immigrants--California--Los Angeles--Biography. 3. Immigrants--Government policy--United States. 4. Alien detention centers--California--Los Angeles. 5. United States-Emigration and immigration--Government policy. I. Ecumenical Program on Central America and the Caribbean. II. Title.
JV6926.S26G894 2003
365'.4--dc22

Contents

This book is dedicated with deep love and affection to my children, Diana, Amy and Gilito. Their love, courage, and strength in the face of the things they had to go through at such a young age were my incentive to not lose hope. For sixteen months, they suffered the absence of their parents, financial scarcity, and the anguish of not having a stable place to live. They had to pretend they were living a normal life in order to keep from being reported as minors without adult supervision. They are my inspiration.

Acknowledgments

I give thanks to God for being with me during those 16 months in jail and for giving me strength and love to help my companions.

I am grateful to my children for being my companions in suffering without ever a word of reproach.

I am thankful for Gil, my husband – may he rest in peace – who during our 24 ½ years of marriage, taught me the value of family and the importance of working for a better future.

I thank my family, on both the Molina and Guzmán sides, for all of the efforts they made for us and for all their moral and economic support. Thanks especially to my sisters-in-law, who were on the front lines for us in our absence.

I am grateful to all of the Church volunteers who visit the San Pedro Detention Center and are like a ray of light in the darkness: Fr. Robert McChesney, S.J., Fr. Pete Neeley, S.J., Fr. John Galvan, S. J., Sr. Molly Mertens, Pastor Ron Bayer, Alice Amaro, the Congregation of Mother Teresa of Calcutta, Albert (the man with the guitar), Ken Auyeng, Vicente and Josefina Zepeda, Donald Frederick, and many more who are not mentioned here. They have made a difference in my life by showing love and compassion during the most difficult of times.

I thank all of my fellow prisoners who opened their hearts and shared their stories, allowing me to know of their joys and sorrows, their defeats and failures.

I would like to also thank the guards who did their jobs professionally and with a good heart – the ones who followed rules and maintained discipline without humiliating, demeaning, or mistreating the prisoners. Special thanks to Mrs. Davis, Harper, Willeby, Jackson, McCaughin, and Mrs. Franks.

I am grateful to Alice Linsmeier who read my story and began to knock on doors to make its publication possible.

Thanks also to the EPICA team for their professionalism and support in making this book a reality.

Foreword

by Rev. Robert McChesney, S.J.

"I ask myself if the American public knows what's going on in these jails." In this remarkable book, Amalia Guzman Molina presents an insider's haunting narrative of 16 months inside the walls of a federal immigration detention center near Los Angeles. In so doing, she opens the curtain to ensure that the American public does, indeed, know what is going on.

The Power of Love succeeds on several levels. It is the finest first-hand account to emerge from the detained noncitizen population that, since 1996, has exploded in the United States. The noxious impact of recent legislation on family unity and stability is just one piece of the broader story so well told here.

Subsequent to Mrs. Molina's release from custody, the tragic events of September 11, 2001 resulted in even more arbitrary and inhumane treatment of noncitizens. As the war on terrorism escalates, immigrants and asylum-seekers predictably, if sadly, are being scapegoated. The publication of *The Power of Love* should prove timely as the debate intensifies over federal detention policies and procedures.

The narrative also succeeds as a grueling, roller-coaster, page-turning story of human survival. In this regard, the book is a superb addition to the prison literature genre. Students of ethnicity and migration will be fascinated and moved by the human drama of more than 100 women, from as many as 40 countries, confined 23 hours a day in a space less than half the square footage of a football field. Here is a fresh, if bittersweet, take on the American Dream.

Finally, Amalia's story is a testament of robust religious faith, an epic 21st century lament. She is Job, mysteriously tested by God to the limits of endurance only to emerge as prophetic witness to the power of love. Her husband Gil, detained in the unit on the other side of the wall from Amalia, is Abraham. In the wake of a violent attack on his father in El Salvador, Gil heard Yahweh's call in the Book of Genesis to "Leave your country, your family and your father's house for the land I will show you."

The difficulty of being cooped up in such a foul setting under such stressful conditions was sometimes exacerbated by conflicts among religious denominations and volunteers. Intolerant, self-righteous fundamentalists – Christian and Muslim – occasionally preyed upon this vulnerable group of prisoners. One of Amalia's notable contributions was to lead her unit through this ecumenical and interfaith minefield, always faithful to her own religious tradition but respectful of the others.

Amalia and I arrived around the same time to the San Pedro Federal Service Processing Center, as the then Immigration and Naturalization Service (INS) called the detention facility for noncitizens. It is located on Terminal Island in Los Angeles Harbor, alongside a deepwater channel through which we regularly watched the Carnival Cruise ships depart for the Pacific resorts of Mexico.

During the 1920s and 1930s, Terminal Island was home to a thriving fishing colony of Japanese, many of them American citizens. After Pearl Harbor the federal government forcibly removed and detained most of them, and their land was confiscated. Many years later, the federal government formally apologized for its errors, and even paid some reparations. A monument to these Japanese "Terminal Islanders" was recently erected by their descendants to honor their patriotism, dedication, and sacrifices, and is located in the public parking lot outside the first security gate into the present-day detention center.

I had been asked in 1997 by the Jesuit Refugee Service (JRS) national office in Washington, D.C. to establish a program to serve the San Pedro facility, as well as several others in Los Angeles County. In that capacity I began visiting San Pedro regularly as a volunteer chaplain in 1998, and came to know Amalia, Gil, and their three lovely children quite well.

The Power of Love is a story by an unusual woman about a shadowy world, a hell which she decided to "redecorate" – to use her colorful language – rather than be victimized by its ugliness. Gil, likewise, found a way not only to survive and attend to the children, but to provide leadership to the other detainees.

Though this couple stands out, in my five years of experience, I remember others who had memorable stories to tell, and who similarly found the resources to not merely survive but even find meaning and purpose in solidarity. Noncitizen detention, sadly, brutalizes too many individuals and families; yet there are others who overcome and grow through the experience. *The Power of Love* is valuable in painting a lively picture of a complex experience that has for too long remained hidden, and demonstrates the gifts a new generation of immigrants and asylum-seekers brings to the United States.

Who are the People in Noncitizen Detention?

On any given day at the Hotel San Pedro, as I liked to call it, one encountered approximately 500 noncitizens, from as many as 50 different countries. These were men and women 18 years of age or older; minors under 18 were held separately. The majority were from Mexico and Central America, with a large number as well from China. When I first arrived I worked in all seven units, or "Pods," but as the program developed I came to accompany the women exclusively.

Some were traditional asylum-seekers, who had been picked up at Los Angeles International Airport as they tried to enter the United States using falsified documents, doctored so as to escape an authoritarian or dictatorial regime. I think of a Nigerian small businessman who had been active in the democracy movement during the 1990s when repression was common in his country. After spending a year under tortuous conditions in a Nigerian prison, he managed to escape the facility and, hiding his identity with a false passport, leave his country. This honorable gentleman spent more than a year in two Los Angeles County detention centers before winning political asylum on appeal.

A second large group of detainees was in fact *legally* in the United States This surprises most Americans to learn. The INS (now broken up and partially reorganized into the Bureau of Immigration and Customs Enforcement within the Department of Homeland Security) calls this group "criminal aliens," by which they mean to suggest that those identified are not citizens and had criminal records. But so-called "criminal aliens" are neither, at least as ordinary people understand those terms.

The "criminal" reference highlights correctly that these folks had been convicted of a felony in the United States, typically a nonviolent offense. What it doesn't say is that they had subsequently completed their time in state prison, successfully paid their dues to society, and been released.

However, as the "alien" reference suggests, there was another issue. These people were not citizens, but were green card holders, legal permanent residents of the United States Many, in fact, were married to U.S. citizens, had citizen children and substantial equities in Los Angeles or other U.S. communities. Many had been in the United States for years. Legislation passed in 1996 mandated that this population who had legally entered the United States be detained by the INS after completion of their time in prison, processed by an Immigration Judge and then, in most cases, deported.

Had these folks taken the initiative to naturalize, they would have been free to return to their families and workplace. One of the more important lessons learned by those of us accompanying the detainees was how vulnerable to the law are legal permanent residents. Significant legislative changes have been made since 1996, and the climate is even worse since 9/11. It is imperative to make this fact more widely known.

In my estimation, the most difficult aspect of the ministry for religious volunteers was accompanying the female legal permanent residents, as they prepared to be separated from their children via deportation (the INS calls it "removal"). Celebrating Mother's Day at the Hotel San Pedro, as *The Power of Love* recounts, could be a painful experience.

A subset of the so-called "criminal alien" population included those born in Cuba, Vietnam and Cambodia. They were typically green card holders who had run afoul of the law in the United States and done time, often for possession of drugs or infractions related to drinking and driving. They included many Vietnamese boatpeople who had come to the United States as infants or children during the 1980s, received their green card, but made the huge mistake of never becoming citizens.

For longstanding political reasons, the governments of these select countries have refused to accept back their "nationals," reasoning that they are the responsibility of the United States because they were granted legal permanent residency here. The result has been, tragically, that these individuals are equivalently "stateless" throwaway people. Consequently, they can sometimes languish for years in noncitizen facilities. Despite a Supreme Court ruling that the INS could not hold people indefinitely, Attorney General Ashcroft has enforced a narrow interpretation of this court ruling, and many of this group remain in limbo inside the walls.

Another substantial population encountered inside Hotel San Pedro was the economic migrants, frequently from one of the Latin

American countries. They are people driven by the often dire economic situations of their families to come to work in the United States. It is nearly impossible for poor people to obtain legal documents to do this. So the majority arrives without documentation and does not have legal work authorization.

In addition to their own needs, economic migrants are responding to the needs of employers in many sectors and industries of the U.S. economy who seek hard-working, low-paid employees. Their situation is precarious, however. On the one hand they may be working in substandard conditions for very little pay. On the other hand, they can often be picked up in workplace raids by the INS and sent to noncitizen detention for deportation.

The United States exhibits historic ambivalence towards immigrants, denigrating them politically while relying on them economically, for example to keep food, hotel, and restaurant prices down and provide otherwise scarce employees. One of the casualties of the 9/11 attacks was that the warming conversation between President George W. Bush and President Fox of Mexico, which was scheduled to address the issue of normalizing the work and perhaps even immigration status of many of these workers, was put on hold.

The story of Amalia Guzmán Molina, like many I met at San Pedro, defies easy categorization. Her father-in-law was a victim of the wartime violence. She and Gil were seeking a new economic start. And, as her story tragicomically narrates, Amalia and her husband were assigned the uniform colors of criminals. When detainees would ask me why this or that had happened at San Pedro, I would sometimes answer "because the moon was full," as a light-hearted way of suggesting that there was no coherence to the whole process. Amalia's case highlights why the noncitizen detention system can only function well via individualized legal determinations for each detainee, represented by counsel, before an immigration judge.

Amalia and Gil were unusual for their relatively advanced education: Amalia was a graduate in accounting from the Jesuit

University of Central America in San Salvador, and successfully operated small businesses there. Gil was a graduate of Louisiana State University and similarly had successful business experience in El Salvador. The Molinas were among only a small percentage of college graduates encountered at San Pedro, and were further distinguished by a modest proficiency in English. A woman and man for others, they viewed their gifts in a spirit of solidarity, for the benefit of their brothers and sisters in need.

Some Statistics on Noncitizen Detention

Noncitizens detained by the INS have been the fastest growing segment of the huge incarcerated population in the United States, quadrupling from 1996 to 2003. According to federal statistics, there were 22,716 INS adult detainees as of February 2003. During the course of FY 2002, there were 182,738 persons in detention. The numbers highlight the basic reality that most of those detained are rapidly removed to their countries of birth.

Noncitizen detention is a revolving door that typically exits in deportation. Federal statistics reveal that approximately 150,000 noncitizens were removed during FY 2002, and the number will likely increase substantially for FY 2003. These numbers are in addition to the nearly one million who chose voluntary return in FY 2002, and do not include those turned away at ports of entry like the border.

As of September 30, 2002, the INS (together with the U.S. Marshals Service) housed detainees in 1,072 facilities nationally. Of these, 123 were federal facilities; 915 state or local facilities; 22 private facilities; and 22 other facilities such as hospitals and non-secure facilities. The growing trend is towards privatization.

The number of unaccompanied children detained in the United States has more than doubled over the past six years, rising from 2,375 in 1997 to 5,385 in 2001, according to a recent report by Amnesty International. On any given day it is estimated that 500 children are held in U.S. detention. Many of these children come by themselves from Central America or Mexico, making the journey north to reunite with one or more parents. Many are the victims of abuse at home and flee seeking a more humane life as well as family reunification.

What Can Be Done?

Amalia refers to the positive impact of the Detention Watch Network (DWN) on the lives of detainees. DWN is a loose national network of religious, legal, human rights, community and popular agencies and organizations that provides a forum and organizing mechanism for anyone who wants to learn more and improve the present morass of noncitizen detention. DWN members also address many related refugee, asylum and immigration issues.

One founding organization of DWN is the Baltimore-based Lutheran Immigration and Refugee Service (LIRS). From their web site (www.LIRS.org) one can review a variety of useful internet links. The DWN link, for example, includes useful self-help legal materials, in English and Spanish, which will be of interest to noncitizen detainees and their loved ones.

The LIRS website also publishes many timely updates in the area of refugee resettlement, asylum protection and immigration law. The specter of 9/11 hovers here, as everywhere, over U.S. migration-related policies.

Nine months into fiscal year 2003, LIRS reports in a recent "Washington Update" feature, the crisis in the U.S. Refugee Resettlement Program continues. Fewer than 18,000 have found new hope in the United States this year – just 25% of the 70,000 the White House said would be resettled. The number admitted in FY 2002 was the lowest in 25 years. It would be tragic if the federal government allowed fears over terrorism to undermine this signature program, as there is no more improbable path a would-be terrorist might take to reach U.S. shores.

In a recent "Legal Update," LIRS reports on continuing assaults on the traditional regime of asylum protection. One report relates to the use of falsified documents in order to escape persecution at home and win asylum once in the United States. Immigration law has traditionally understood that falsified documents sometimes must be used for people to escape from persecution to safety. Since 9/11 however, new enforcement policies are undermining this legacy.

To cite just one example, federal prosecutors in Florida have begun charging asylum seekers who use falsified papers with document fraud. Those who have been convicted could still apply for asylum upon release from prison, but their chances of success would be greatly impaired with a criminal record.

Another founding member agency of the Detention Watch Network is the Catholic Legal Immigration Network, Incorporated (CLINIC), a subsidiary of the U.S. Conference of Catholic Bishops. With national offices in Washington, D.C., CLINIC (www.cliniclegal.org) maintains affiliates in many dioceses around the country, and is a major provider of pro-bono legal services to detained noncitizens.

While CLINIC is present on the front lines, it is also a significant player within the Washington network of organizations advocating for more humane immigration, asylum, and detention policies.

CLINIC is one of several significant agencies and nongovernmental organizations which continue to press the federal government to distinguish between immigrants, refugees and asylum-seekers on the one hand, and terrorists on the other. As Executive Director Donald Kerwin points out in a recent article, "The government has justified its immigration enforcement measures based on contested theories of national security. . . Few idealize the presence (or treatment) of the several million undocumented persons in the United States, but the undocumented do not present a heightened security risk. Nearly 80 percent come from Mexico and Latin America, not nations with a strong Al Queda presence." Investigators have concluded that Al Queda operatives implicated in the 9/11 attacks overwhelmingly entered the United States legally.

In the important crackdown on terror, the federal government needs to be tougher but also smarter. Immigration policy should not be used as a proxy for good intelligence and traditional law enforcement, which remain the most effective investigative mechanisms to locate those associated with terrorism. Are immigrants, including economic migrants, being scapegoated for colossal failures of the Central Intelligence Agency and Federal Bureau of Investigation? As exemplified by the experience of the Japanese "Terminal Islanders," U.S. history teaches how tempting a target immigrants make when the government moves to a war footing.

Concretely, what needs to be done in the area of noncitizen detention to address the shortcomings that *The Power of Love* highlights? Amalia calls the religious volunteers the real "heroes" of her story. My own experience confirms the importance of this unsung group, which is the only one able to gain official approval to directly serve detainees inside the walls. This is a ministry of presence and accompaniment. The main purpose is to be there, not to proselytize but to lend dignity to the experience, and to support in solidarity all who desire a sympathetic smile or small act of human kindness. Within this context, of course, the volunteers worship and pray with the detainees according to what the latter find helpful.

Unfortunately, the federal government has been very slow to respond to the recommendations of the Jesuit Refugee Service and other faith-based agencies and their partners. Funds should be appropriated to hire chaplains at all federal Service Processing Centers like San Pedro, as well as at facilities like Mira Loma in Los Angeles County which is run by the local sheriff under contract with the federal government.

It is past time for the government to fully fund and institutionalize the role of chaplains in noncitizen detention. Under existing, excellent federal guidelines, they would work to monitor deleterious religious fanaticism and ensure that detainees of all religious faiths and denominations have access to their religious leaders, volunteers, and necessities for worship.

One doesn't want to become sick as a noncitizen detainee, as *The Power of Love* painfully documents. The government, in dialogue with nongovernmental health, medical and human rights groups, needs to bring its care to a minimum of humanity and professionalism. Decent guidelines for medical care are in place but lack the force of law. Without better oversight, these guidelines are followed in an arbitrary or spotty fashion, if at all.

Another area of concern is the predatory pricing arrangements which gouge detainees out of scarce funds. As the noncitizen detention population has exploded since 1996, a network of local governments, for-profit prisons and prison contractors has emerged with a financial self-interest in the detention system. Localities and for-profit prisons benefit handsomely from contracts for phone services, for example, as companies charge exorbitant rates to the detainees and to parties called collect from detention. This inflicts untold hardship on families like the Molinas.

Even under current law, CLINIC notes that thousands of detained noncitizens could be released under supervision. Yet, historically INS has refused to adopt effective supervised release programs. After years of demonstrated success of alternative model programs, the federal government has yet to institutionalize detention alternatives for people like Amalia and Gil Molina who represent neither a threat to the community nor a flight risk.

CLINIC and its partners make two other key recommendations in areas of concern that predate 9/11, but are now coming to light via a recent internal investigation by the Department of Justice into the treatment of those held on immigration charges in connection with the investigation into the 9/11 attacks.

1. Each noncitizen detainee should be afforded an individualized bond hearing before an immigration judge. Individuals should be released from custody on a reasonable bond unless they are found to be a flight risk or a danger to the community.

2. Noncitizens face many "right to counsel" barriers, once detained. For example, a communications blackout was placed on many 9/11 detainees, who were essentially "disappeared" from their families. It is chilling to know that at the Metropolitan Detention Center in New York the first legal phone call by a 9/11 detainee did not take place until October 15. Even after the blackout was lifted, detainees could make one legal call a week but busy signals and answers by voicemail were counted as a call.

Additionally, the INS did not consistently provide a list of pro-bono attorneys to the 9/11 detainees, as they are required to do. And attorneys were regularly told their clients were not in a facility, when in fact they were.

But this was Amalia's upside-down world on a regular basis, as *The Power of Love* suggests. The federal government should move expeditiously to ensure that noncitizen detainees receive regular access to court-appointed counsel, regardless of their classification. Finally, there are legislative efforts underway to put an end to the inhumane practice of putting unaccompanied noncitizen children in detention centers. It is my hope that readers of this book will be moved to support this kind of legislation that moves towards a more compassionate and just immigration policy.

The Power of Love will break its readers' hearts but also, paradoxically, inform and inspire them. Many recently arrived in the United States will read this story as their own. In this sense the book makes an original contribution to the literature of harrowing first-person immigration narratives, as it shines a light on the growing phenomenon of noncitizen detention.

Longstanding citizens, perhaps especially those with little personal association with immigrants and asylum-seekers, will be fascinated to meet Amalia and her family, and to spend 16 months inside Amalia's world. Her compelling story speaks for itself in terms of the many gifts this immigrant family brings. I hope many citizens will also take to heart Amalia's prayer to join her in rebuilding what is broken in her new land.

I, I am your consoler. How then can you be afraid of mortal man, of son of man, whose fate is the fate of grass? You have forgotten Yahweh who made you, who spread out the heavens and laid the earth's foundations, why still go in daily dread of the oppressor's fury, when he sets out to destroy you? What has happened to the fury of oppressors?
The captive is soon to be set free; he will not die in a deep dungeon nor will his bread run out. I am Yahweh your God who stirs the sea, making its waves roar, my name is Yahweh Sabaoth.

(Isaiah 51: 12-16)

Introduction

This is a book that tries to illustrate in a simple way: 1) the reality of life inside an immigration jail, 2) the consequences of unjust laws that were created without taking into account the devastating impact on families who are broken apart, 3) the contribution of volunteers from religious communities who do their work quietly without expecting anything in return, 4) the realization that in helping others one helps oneself, and 5) the power of faith and love.

It is a personal story lived out in an immigration detention center located on an island in the city of San Pedro, California. Even though they call it a detention center, it is in fact a maximum-security prison with the capacity to house around 500 people. Due to changes in the immigration law, at times this number is much greater.

I come from a strong religious background and in 1990 I joined the charismatic movement in the Catholic Church. There I was "born again" and learned to truly live my faith. I consider myself a practicing Catholic and I've been blessed to feel God's love for me in the most difficult moments, through His messengers, some Catholic and others Protestant. All of them without exception brought comfort, faith, and hope in a better future. We were brought together in our pain and sorrow, and were not divided by different religious beliefs. We were One Body, One Church with One Pastor in a valley of tears, pain, desperation, injustice, and death.

Journey to the Unknown

It was a Wednesday at 7:10 in the morning. My children were hurrying to leave for school, so I threw on a sweater and a pair of gray slacks that belonged to my son. I drove them to school – first dropping off Gil and then Amy. It was a beautiful sunny, winter morning with clear, blue skies and a slight chill in the air.

On my way home, a block before my house, the car behind me put on its flashing lights for me to stop. They were flashing lights exactly like those of a patrol car, but I was suspicious because it was a luxury car and didn't have license plates. I stayed calm and a tall man asked to see my driver's license. He wasn't wearing a police uniform but I obeyed and showed him the driver's permit that I was carrying.

He asked me to step out of the car and I, baffled and disconcerted, obeyed. Suddenly a woman police officer approached me from out of nowhere and proceeded to pat me down to make sure I wasn't carrying any weapons. Then she handcuffed me. The man who had stopped me asked if my husband was at home and if he had a gun. It struck me as funny when he asked that question, since Gil is actually frightened of guns and we've never had one in the house, not even a machete. Anyhow I told him that "yes," my husband was at home and "no," we did not have any type of weapon in the house.

They put me in their car, drove the last block, and parked in front of my house. Two other similar cars appeared then. About six men got out wearing black jackets with FEDERAL POLICE written on the back. They were all armed and they surrounded the house. One of them rang the bell. My oldest daughter, Dianita, who is nineteen, answered the door.

What happened then, I didn't see, but my daughter says that the policeman asked, "Is there an adult in the house?" "Yes," she answered, "my father. I'll go get him."

Suddenly they burst into the bedroom, arrested my husband, searched everything, and confiscated his passport.

I was still in the car while all this was going on. A man approached the car and identified himself as an immigration official and asked me for my passport. I handed it to him and he said then that I had violated immigration laws by staying in this country past the allowed time. I remembered that I had proof that we had applied for a certain Law #245 that allows you to negotiate your residency without leaving the country if you have a family member who is an American citizen. I showed it to him, but he acted as if it didn't mean anything and told me that I would have to go with him.

Before we left, another car with two well-dressed men showed up. I noticed the jewelry they were wearing: big, thick bracelets and expensive looking chains, just like the watches they had on. Before taking off, one of them made the victory sign with his fingers to the guy behind the steering wheel, and then they left. It was then that I realized it had been a well-planned operation. It was as if they had thought that they would find weapons and dangerous people.

The immigration official in charge of my arrest seemed polite. When he realized that I couldn't get comfortable in the backseat because my hands were cuffed behind me, he undid the handcuffs and recuffed me with my arms in front. I asked him if I could give my daughter my purse and he let me. Poor Dianita, I could see such fear in her eyes. I told her, "Darling, don't worry. Take care of your brother and sister and everything will be all right." The official gave her his card with the address of where they were taking us and we left.

* * * * *

We were heading toward Los Angeles but I didn't have a clue where we were going. Besides, my mind was on my kids, wondering how they would manage on their own in such a large city – one they had just arrived in a few months ago – without family to take care of them and without the kind of friends you can count on in such difficult circumstances.

It seemed like less than 20 minutes had gone by when we arrived at a building and parked in a basement garage. They took my mug shot right away and did a complete fingerprinting on me. This took place in a closed room without a window – like a fort or a bunker. There was a lot of activity going on with lots of people being detained and officials in civilian dress running all around.

I asked the official about my husband Gil and he told me that he also was in the same building. I asked to see him and he said I could for just a few minutes. They had him in a cell by himself and the poor guy was feeling alarmed and confused just like I was. In reality we hardly spoke, I just asked him if he was okay and he said he was. Then the official told me I had to go.

* * * * *

They put me in a cell with other people, all women and children. Most were Mexicans, but there was one Chinese woman, a Salvadoran, and myself. We were 12 in all. The cell was an enclosed room with a metal door that had one small window no larger than "eight by ten" inches and metal benches along the walls, two metallic toilets, and two tiny sinks. The room was filthy with orange peels on the floor, fruit flies, and small roaches everywhere. I saw that there were two public phones, an empty water thermos covered in a film of dirt as if no one had ever washed it, and security cameras watching your every move. The air conditioning was on full blast and I felt like I was in a deep freeze.

Some of the detainees were lying on newspapers on the floor. Others had blankets they were lying on, while others sat on benches.

Lots of attitudes were evident. The ones who'd come from jail or prison were upset because they'd expected to be released after serving their time. Since they had paid their dues, they thought they could join their families again, but then immigration officials had gone after them and detained them. They were the most aggressive. They were cursing and were in such a bad mood that they were really scary. Those who'd been wrenched from their homes with their children were drowning in a sea of tears. They expected to be deported with just the clothes on their back and no money. They would be taken to Tijuana or Mexicali and dumped, left on their own to figure out how to get back to their homeland. Those who were picked up at their workplace for being undocumented were worried about their children, and they cried as they thought about being deported and leaving their children behind.

So this is how your Calvary starts: you only hear negativism, anger, swear words, and frustration. This, along with the uncertainty you feel, is damaging because fear is contagious and you reach a point where your body feels like a time bomb. Your heart is racing, anguish and alarm rise, your stomach feels like it is shriveling up and you can't stand the thought of food. Even if you eat something, it has no taste and you feel like throwing up.

* * * * *

Two hours had gone by when the door opened and I heard my name called. It was the same official who'd arrested me. He asked me if I wanted to voluntarily leave the country and said I should sign the paper he gave me. I immediately answered him that I wanted to speak with my husband first and then speak with my lawyer. Without another word, he returned me to my cell.

I realized I needed to talk to Diana but since I didn't have any money I had no choice but to borrow some. I asked the Chinese woman since she had a coin purse filled with quarters that a relative had brought her. She was good and kind and she lent money to those of us who didn't have any. I spoke with Diana and asked her to call the lawyer and see what she could do to help us.

Exactly at noon the door opened again. It was an officer who had a box full of bologna sandwiches, milk, and oranges. Each of us got one. The milk and oranges were fine but not the sandwiches. The meat was kind of green. I didn't eat anything. I wasn't hungry so I gave my food away. At two o'clock in the afternoon, they called me again. I saw Gil and we decided to see a judge. In the meantime, Diana had contacted our lawyer, the same one who'd helped us fill out papers months earlier for permanent legal residence through my sister-in-law Tita. Tita is an American citizen and has been a lot of help to us.

The deportation officials tried to pressure me to sign the deportation papers and agree to voluntarily leave the country, but I'd already made up my mind. Only my lawyer's counsel would have validity for me. In the meantime, I'd face the INS monster (Immigration and Naturalization Service).

That afternoon was an eternity. I prayed the rosary, sang praises to God to give myself some hope, and tried to practice what I'd preached for so long. . . If your troubles have a remedy, why do you worry? And if they don't, what do you gain by worrying? It seemed to me that in taking this attitude I wouldn't be adding undue importance to the problem. In the first place, what would be gained by worrying about something that didn't have a solution? If that's the case, the best thing is to accept reality, turn myself over to the will of God, and get on with it. In the second place, if the problem has a solution, the worst thing I can do is waste my time worrying. Instead, I have to take action to forge ahead and find the solutions. Fear causes worry and despair and doesn't let even the tiniest ray of hope shine through and so it destroys faith.

* * * * *

Hours later an officer showed up and directed us all out into the hallway, telling us to sit on some metal chairs there while they cleaned the room. As soon as we stepped into the hallway, we heard cat-calls, laughter, and men's voices. That's when I realized that there were three more cells next to ours full of men of every shape and color.

They were asking us our names, making flirtatious remarks, offering to be our boyfriends, and in general acting like men who'd been in jail a long time and who went crazy when they see a woman. The officer was annoyed and ordered them to be quiet. But of course there were women in our group who ate up all the attention and gave it right back, calling out answers to all their questions. This bit of entertainment lasted about ten minutes and then we were returned to our cell.

A little while later they brought us our dinner. It was about 5 p.m. and the menu consisted of tasteless, sticky white rice, boiled carrots, and two round slices of turkey ham, along with some milk. I ate the carrots and that was all. I needed to drink some water but there wasn't any in the jug. We were all so thirsty that finally a brave soul asked the guard for water.

The officer was clearly annoyed and answered, "When you come into this country crossing the mountains, you probably drink water out of the rivers, and here you complain about everything. If you're thirsty, drink from the tap." Then he shut the door.

Fine, then. Better to drink from the sink than to be thirsty. So out of necessity I drank water from the tap, even though most of the women wouldn't because they said it was dirty.

* * * * *

Around 6 p.m. more women and children were put in the cell. The children were crying a lot, clearly exhausted and frightened at being put in with so many strangers. Everyone who had arrived that afternoon was to be deported to Mexico that night. Nobody knew what border crossing they'd be taken to, so they couldn't notify relatives to meet them on the other side of the border, to give them money, or help them find a safe place to spend the night. They talked about how dangerous it is for a woman to be alone because of the chance of assault or even rape, so they decided to stick together. Most of the women didn't have a penny on them but they'd heard about some safe houses that would shelter immigrants and let them spend the night safely. In the morning they could contact their families and see how to get back home.

* * * * *

At 8 p.m. a guard showed up and began calling off women's names, one by one. Six of us weren't on the list and stayed behind in the cell. I was totally exhausted – tired and hungry. I was feeling absolutely awful, filled with anxiety about what would happen next, when at last another officer came and called off five names. I was one of the five. By then, it was ten o'clock at night.

They led us to a bus and sat us in the first two rows of seats. We waited there for about ten minutes until they brought on the men. I was so happy to see Gil was among them. He wasn't put right behind me, more like two rows back, but while the guards weren't looking, he changed seats and we were able to hold hands and talk.

Although some of the men seemed happy singing anti-INS songs, telling jokes, and calling out compliments to the women, I asked Gil if it wasn't kind of dangerous to be with those men. Some of them really looked like criminals. They were scary, and you could see the anger and frustration in their faces. Gil didn't think so. "The prisoners are punished by being put in seclusion if they act coarse and rough with the officers," he said. I asked him if he knew where they were taking us and he said we were being taken to a detention center in San Pedro. We would spend the night there.

* * * * *

We arrived around 11 p.m. They lined us up. The women were processed first. They took our photos, fingerprinted us, and then put us in a cell again where we waited for an hour until another officer showed up. It was a Latino-looking woman, a little overweight with dark skin and short, curly hair. She wore a uniform with a nametag that said "Officer X." She was carrying some yellow uniforms and some plastic bags.

What followed was the most humiliating and denigrating experience of my life. The officer told us to put our clothes in the bag, all our clothes, including our panties and bra. She made us line up, asked each one of us to shake loose our hair, open our mouth, stick out our tongue, lift up our breasts, turn around and bend over, spread open our butt cheeks, and cough three times.

I truly could not believe this was happening to me. I'd seen stuff like this in the movies. I remembered the movie Papillon when they made prisoners strip naked and then issued them their uniforms when they were put in jail. But this wasn't fiction or a dream. . . it was my reality. I was very afraid, and the minutes seemed like hours as the strip search proceeded. What made it even worse was that it was all caught on a camera that records your every move. I guess this routine is to prevent anyone from hiding drugs or cigarettes. The men go through the same thing.

It got very late and it was past midnight before she was done searching us. After giving us two sheets and a bedspread like the ones I'd seen in the INS cell, we were finally led away to Pod 6 which is the women's section of the jail. A Pod is like a group jail cell. It has a common bathroom and two large rooms: a dayroom for all the daily activities and a dormitory full of bunk beds.

* * * * *

We stood in line while we waited for the door to open. It was metal door with a small window. We heard a key turn, and a black officer appeared. She was tall and strong and had thick lips and long hair braided in an African style. She asked the officer who accompanied us if we were the last group for the night. The officer said yes and gave her some yellow cards. She took them and started reading them. She proceeded to call us by our last names like in the military, using a strong, energetic voice.

Then we walked one by one into a dayroom with tables and chairs. There was a television that was on, of course, and there were several women watching. Some were dressed in red, others in blue, and others in orange. I sat down at a table and after about ten minutes, the officer called each of us to come get a blue, plastic platform-like bed that was as hard as the floor. She gave us a towel, a small bag with shampoo, a small bar of soap, a short toothbrush, and a small tube of toothpaste.

My cellmates went to wash up, but I didn't have the strength so I lay down. I felt really tired; it was one in the morning and I usually go to bed at ten at night. I tried to go to sleep but I was bothered by all the lights that were left on, the noise from the television, and all the voices of everyone there. I closed my eyes and began to pray. I don't know when I fell asleep, but I felt like it had hardly been any time at all.

* * * * *

At five o'clock in the morning, I felt someone kick the "bed" and heard in English, "Get up!" I got up and hurried to wash up because they only give you 30 minutes to stack the beds, hand in your blanket, sheets and towel, and wait for an officer to come and take you to the cell where you were the night before.

When we were put in that common cell, most of us laid down on the floor because we were tired. At that moment, I felt like one of the homeless people who sleep on the street, the only difference being that they, at least, have some cardboard to put over themselves and they don't sleep directly on the floor. I didn't even have that.

Around 6:30 a.m., an officer handed us the plastic bags that held our clothes so that we could change back into them. I saw that one of my cellmates had rolled a small blanket around her waist. She put on her clothes but she left her shirt out, untucked, so the officer wouldn't notice what she had on. My clothes smelled bad and were dirty. I had to put on my same underpants and the same dirty socks and I felt very uncomfortable. They quickly brought our breakfast: two small boxes of cereal, an orange, and a carton of milk. Once again I didn't eat, but I had no trouble giving my food away since there's always a big eater in any group.

At around eight o'clock, we boarded the buses again and they took us to Los Angeles. I saw Gil again. He had deep, dark shadows under his eyes, and I guessed I probably looked the same or worse. He mentioned that he'd hardly slept and that he felt very tired. I told him I'd call Diana to bring us some clean clothes, especially sweaters and clean underwear, and to find out what the lawyer had told her.

* * * * *

We arrived at our destination – again the room that was freezing cold. We were surprised to see the woman who'd been left behind the night before. It looked like they just forgot to take her to San Pedro. The poor thing was tired and very cold. They'd already brought in more people too, and I noticed a lady with a baby girl who looked about six months old. The little girl was sick. She had a wheezing cough and a fever, and she cried and cried without stopping.

I called Diana and asked her to bring a change of clothes and some coins so I could call her. I asked her about her brother and sister, and she told me they'd gone to school and were fine. I knew she'd never do anything to make me worry, but I asked God to give the children the strength to be able to deal with this misfortune. Diana also told me that the lawyer was coming to see us today. I felt a little calmer and we hung up.

I invited my cellmates to pray the rosary, and some of them prayed it with me with great devotion. The majority were indifferent, though, talking foolishness. At ten in the morning they brought us some potato burritos, milk and oranges. I couldn't stand to look at the oranges and milk anymore, but from the look of things, they'd be my constant companions.

At 11 a.m. they said I had a visitor. It was my daughter Diana with the clothes and the money I'd asked for earlier. We just had a few moments to speak. I tried to give her faith and trust that all would be well, and I told her I'd call that night to talk to her brother and sister. Most of all, I asked her not to miss school and to go on with things just like always, even though her Dad and I weren't physically present at home. Then we said good-bye.

Back in the cell, the baby continued crying. She was hungry, her diapers were dirty, and she had the rest of us at our wits end because there was nothing we could do to help the mother. We called out to the officer explaining the problem, but he didn't even bother to answer us.

It was 11:30 a.m. and the baby continued crying. The mother didn't have a bottle to give her, or diapers to change her. It was awful! What an injustice to that baby! So we started kicking the door and shouting loudly. This small riot produced results, and finally an officer showed up. We explained that the baby was sick, without food, medicine, or diapers, and that to make things worse, the air conditioning was on maximum! I think the officer talked with a superior because not five minutes had gone by when they came to get the mother and take her and the baby to the doctor. Thank God, at least we'd accomplished something. It seemed so unfair what that baby was enduring. The officers' indifference was incredible! They see you and treat you like animals.

Then it was noon and they brought lunch. It was the same menu. I didn't have any appetite and I felt awful. My stomach felt like it had an ice cube inside it. I tried to eat something and I lay down on one of the wall benches. I slept a little when sleep and exhaustion finally overtook me. I woke up when the door opened. It was around two o'clock in the afternoon. It was the woman and her baby. She told us they'd taken her to the doctor. They'd given her medicine and diapers and told her they would be taking her to another place where they detain mothers with small children.

* * * * *

Then they told me I had another visitor, my lawyer. I was so happy to see her. She brought with her a black man who she said would take our case. He didn't speak Spanish but he was more experienced in taking our kind of case through the courts. I asked her how she saw our situation, and she said she couldn't tell me anything for sure right then. But she said not to worry because she was going to try to get us out on bail so we could all work on it together. She said she'd let me know what I needed to do. She sounded so sure of herself that I felt very calm. At least I knew we had someone really working for us. I signed some papers so her associate could present himself to INS as our lawyer and be able to get all the information about our case.

The hours passed slowly and people were filling the cell. It tore my soul apart to see so many tears and cries of misery from women who'd been yanked from their homes, leaving everything in their lives behind . . . their children (American citizens), their belongings, their life partner. In short, they'd lost everything. Never in my life had I seen so much pain and suffering from so close. As a mother, I felt a solidarity with their suffering. It was truly difficult to know what words of comfort to say under these circumstances.

Then it was 4 p.m. and I knew my children would be home so I called them. Amy, my 16-year-old, was, of course, worried. She wanted to know how long we'd be in this place and what I thought would happen. Unfortunately, I didn't have any answers for her but I begged her to just be calm and continue her studies. That it was important now more than ever. I told her I loved her very much and that I was so grateful to God that the INS agents had come when they were in school because otherwise the problem could have been much more serious.

Then she gave the phone to Gilito, my youngest child who is 14 years old. He just asked how I was and whether I was with his dad. From then on he just listened to all the admonitions that I gave him: take care of your sisters, don't open the door to anyone, especially at night, please eat well, and don't miss school. When I hung up, I sobbed. My children were the most important part of my life, and it terrified me to think that something could happen to them now that they were alone. I called back and told Diana to take the bank cards out of my purse, and I gave her my PIN number so that at least they could buy food. It was already Thursday, and Friday was the day we usually did the shopping. I told her I'd call every day at 6 p.m. when all three of them would be at home.

* * * * *

That day they took us to San Pedro earlier, at around 7 p.m. Gil and I talked the whole way about what might happen to us. The thing that worried us the most was the kids. How would they be able to support themselves? So many questions and doubts passed through our minds. What would happen to our house? We had bought it barely a year ago and we made the mortgage payments only with a lot of sacrifice. How would we make the payments? What would we tell them at our workplaces to explain our absence? We needed to decide whether to notify our family right away in El Salvador. It would be a great hardship for my in-laws, and we didn't want to cause them such great distress. There were so many decisions to make and since we were feeling so much anguish and uncertainty about our future, it was very hard to make them.

We arrived at San Pedro. We went through the same process as the day before, but thank God, this time the officer who checked us in told us to do it quickly. Since it was still the same five of us, it was less difficult. We got to Pod 6, and I took the opportunity to wash up. I washed my hair and decided to wait awhile to let it dry before going to sleep.

I took this opportunity to ask one of the other detainees why the uniforms came in different colors. She told me that the red uniforms identified dangerous criminals, like murderers or people found guilty of violent crimes; the ones dressed in blue were robbers or drug pushers; and the prisoners in the orange suits were people without criminal records who were detained at airports or on the border trying to enter the country illegally.

I lay down to go to sleep and this time I didn't care about the noise or about the lights being on. I felt practically dead. I covered my eyes with the same towel I'd used to dry off with, said my prayers, and fell right to sleep. They woke us up early the next morning. It was the same routine as the day before, but this time I took two small bars of soap with me to wash out my underpants and socks, taking advantage of the fact that I had one change of clothes.

* * * * *

It was already Friday, payday. As soon as we got to the main INS building, I called Diana and told her to go pick up our paycheck and to tell the office that we had had to leave suddenly because of an emergency in Miami with my sister-in-law, Tita. I couldn't think of any other excuse, and I was sure that this horrible nightmare wouldn't last more than a week.

Back in the cell, I saw they had brought in an Iranian woman and her three year old daughter, and an Indian woman and her ten-year-old son. I talked with the Iranian woman who spoke perfect English, and she told me she'd already been in detention three months, locked in a motel room at the airport. She'd arrived from Iran with her husband but when they were detained at the airport, the two of them had been separated. Now they only saw each other when they were brought to this building to see the judge. They were asking for political asylum, but they never dreamed they'd have to go through this nightmare. Her daughter seemed to be affected psychologically.

She told me that the Indian woman had been arrested at the airport also, along with her husband and another son who was 14 years old and that they, too, had been separated. Both said they never dreamed they'd be treated so inhumanely in the great land of democracy and respect for human rights.

A very well dressed woman who was brought in also caught my attention. She wore high heels and her hair was fixed all nice. She was from Armenia. The poor thing cried inconsolably. Her husband is an American citizen, and she had received a summons for an interview with INS to arrange for her permanent residence status. She'd gone with her husband and her lawyer. But when she got there, they handcuffed and detained her. They said she had a deportation order. Even her lawyer couldn't do anything to help her. They'd simply tricked her.

It seemed like every person I spoke with only had negative things to say. Nobody had anything positive to tell me or anything to say that could give me comfort. On the contrary, all I heard was frustration, resentment, and a lot of pain.

* * * * *

In the afternoon, I talked with the children and it seemed like everything was okay. They'd gone to school but were feeling very anxious to know when we would get back home.

It was 9 p.m. and they hadn't called us out to take us to San Pedro. I was desperate. There were only three of us left and that included the Armenian woman whose name was Flo. The rest had been taken away. Finally around 10 p.m., they called us. This time we didn't go in a regular bus, but rather in a minibus together with six men. Gil was one of them. Everyone's face showed exhaustion. It was so late. This trip was different from the others; nobody told any jokes or sang songs. A total silence fell over the group indicating that everybody's mind was somewhere else. Some had a lost look in their eyes, others were almost asleep, but all were aware that it was Friday. It meant we'd spend the weekend in detention.

When we arrived, we expected the same officer as before, but instead it was a different one. She was tall and fat, and she wasn't in a blue uniform like the others. Instead, her uniform was green and her jacket said INS. She had three prisoner's uniforms in her hands – a red, a blue and an orange one. What happened next was truly a nightmare. I felt like it was happening in slow motion. Flo was having her period, and she refused to undress. She hadn't been through this humiliating experience before. The officer said we could just spend the whole night there if we needed to, unless we obeyed her. In the end, poor Flo gave in as tears ran down her cheeks.

We all felt bad, but finally we were done around 1 a.m. The officer gave out the uniforms: Flo got the orange one, the blue one was for me, and the red one went to the other lady. I felt terrible because I thought I'd get the orange one. But the most traumatizing thing for me was when I saw that Gil had a red uniform on. Oh God, that was when I hit bottom. I've always been a very protective wife and mother, but here I couldn't do anything to help my husband. There had to be some terrible mistake. Gil couldn't be dressed in red! Just the dangerous criminals wore that color! I couldn't take it anymore and I started to cry in total distress. There had to be a mistake, a terrible, horrible mistake. I didn't understand what was going on.

* * * * *

We got to Pod 6 and the officer told us to go to the sleeping area and take whichever bed was empty. The room was dark and I was afraid I'd wake someone up. I took a top bunk in the first row right next to the guardroom. That night I understood that being assigned a specific uniform color meant that I would have to stay in this detention center until I was brought before the judge and my case was resolved. It also meant that Gil and I wouldn't be able to talk and continue to make decisions together as a couple. We were held completely incommunicado.

For a moment I felt like I was in a different country. I'd seen so much pain, so much injustice, and so much disrespect for human rights. This reality didn't fit with the majestic image that I had of this great country that I admired so much. It bothered me a lot. But in that moment the most important thing was to get some sleep and to get in touch with Diana the next day to let her know where we were.

Confronting Reality

I awoke to the loudspeaker announcing breakfast was ready. Most of the women sprang out of bed to be one of the first in line. I waited a while and was the last to get my food. A blond officer who always had an irritated look on her face and who never bothered to say "good morning" was in charge of giving out the food that day. She gave me a tray with a donut, some milk and some cottage cheese. When I went into the dayroom I took the first available chair at a table with two Cubans, a woman from Belize and a Guatemalan. As soon as the Cubans figured out I wasn't going to eat my breakfast, they asked for my food and divided it up between them. The only thing I wanted right then was to have some coffee, but I didn't have a cup. So Dor, the Guatemalan woman, gave me hers and that was my breakfast.

We had to return to the sleeping area while the dayroom was being cleaned and so I went back to my bunk and started talking to the young woman in the bottom bunk. She was from Sri Lanka and her name was Pria. She was 18 years old. Her mother, who everyone called "Mama," was also in the cell. They'd been arrested at the airport during a layover while changing flights on the way to Canada to join the rest of the family who'd been given political asylum there.

When the cleaning was finished, I went to use the telephone to call Diana. In this prison, we were only allowed to make collect calls. When I got through to the house, I gave Diana the address and told her visiting hours were only on Saturdays and Sundays, from 8 to 11 a.m., from 1 to 4 p.m., and from 6 to 9 p.m.. I told her to look at a map to see how to get here. I also told her to call my friend Ceci and tell her what had happened. Ceci lived in San Diego, but they could call her if they needed something. Diana said she'd come the next day, and we hung up.

* * * * *

I stayed in the dayroom because from there I had a beautiful view of the ocean. I started to pray the rosary and think about my children. I was so worried for their safety. They were inexperienced and naive teenagers and they'd just arrived in the States about seven months earlier. I would have to work hard with them even if I had to do it from a distance. Now more than ever, I needed for them to be strong and caring and supportive of each other. Most of all, I needed them to make good choices for themselves even though they were alone and unsupervised.

* * * * *

Lunchtime was at noon. I sat at the same table as before. Laz, one of the Cubans, a black woman, was short and overweight and dressed in a red uniform. Mar, the other Cuban, was tall and stocky, and loved to eat. She was also dressed in red. Laz asked me what jail I'd come from. I told her that I hadn't come from another jail and that I didn't know why they'd given me a blue uniform. Both of them smiled, doubting my answer. "You can change the color of your uniform if you don't like it. Right, Mar?" Laz quipped. Mar answered, "Of course! All you have to do is fill out an application, write down the color of the uniform you want, and give it to the guard."

To be honest, it sounded like a terrific idea to me. I have a dark complexion and blue just doesn't look good on me. After lunch, I asked the Cubans where to get an application and they told me to go and ask the officer in charge. I could feel Dor, the Guatemalan woman, stepping on my toes under the table and making gestures with her head for me not to move.

When the Cubans left, Dor explained that INS assigns the color and that the color showed the seriousness of the case. She said the

Cubans liked to pull tricks like that on new people. The time before, they'd told a Japanese woman she could ask to spend the night with her boyfriend and that all she had to do was ask for them. So the innocent girl filled out an application, turned it in, and for some time she was the laughingstock of Pod 6.

* * * * *

At 2 p.m. the guards changed, and the morning shift went home. I spent the rest of the day in the dayroom until I heard the loudspeaker blare, "366 Guzmán." I went to the guardroom and was told that they were issuing me some clothes. They gave me a sweater, a pair of shorts, a pair of pants, two T-shirts, two towels, three pairs of socks, three pairs of underpants, two bras, one pair of canvas shoes, a pair of plastic sandals to shower in, a toothbrush and a small comb, and a plastic box to keep it all in. Oh, and I also got a bag for my dirty laundry.

I organized everything in my box, put it under my bed, and lay down again for a little while. I tried to sleep but my mind was a whirlwind of desperation and anguish. At 4 p.m. we were counted to make sure no one was missing. There were 70 of us, women of all ages and races. The youngest was my bunkmate Pria, who was 18, and the oldest was her mother who was about 52 years old. Forty percent of us were Hispanic and the rest were from China, India, Sri Lanka, Iran, Ethiopia, Nigeria, Sierra Leon, Taiwan, France, Armenia, Jamaica and Syria.

At 5 p.m. they served dinner. I changed tables and so I got to meet two Salvadorans. They were both dressed in orange and I learned they'd been detained on the same day in different places. They helped each other out and were fast friends. Both were married and had children. I asked them how long they'd been in detention and they answered, "Three months."

I was completely demoralized! How awful! I never expected that one could be detained as long as three months. They tried to cheer me up and invited me to play cards with them. They warned me to be careful with the Cubans because they were terrible, especially Mar who had AIDS, and they said I should always check the bathroom to make sure there wasn't any blood around. They also warned me about the Syrian girl who could be aggressive and about the man who'd had a sex change and become a woman. "There's a woman who used to be a man? Who's that?" I asked. "That's all I need," I thought to myself. They pointed her out to me; she was a Jamaican woman, tall and black with huge hands. She wore blue prison uniform and a bitter expression. I thanked my companions for their advice and from then on I kept close to them because I felt like I could trust them.

* * * * *

That night I called home. The children sounded good. They were hopeful that everything would turn out okay, and they promised to be strong, to study, and to take care of each other. They told me that Gil had already called them and told them not to worry because at least we were now in one place and didn't have to make the inconvenient daily trip back and forth between the jail and the INS central office.

At 8 p.m. they lined us up again. We were given a snack, and at 10 p.m. they did the count and changed shifts. What a difference you see in the guards from shift to shift. The guards in the morning are mean and disrespectful; they maintain order by shouting at the top of their lungs. The ones in the afternoon are the opposite; they greet you, treat you like a real person, chat with you, smile, and maintain discipline without abusing their authority. The night guards are like sergeants in a barracks; they shout and intimidate you.

I asked some of the women if they wanted to pray the rosary and three of them accepted. We made a commitment to say the rosary every night to ask the Virgin Mary to watch over our children. We all shared that same terrible concern. When we were done, I went to bed immediately. Others stayed up writing letters or watching television, but I didn't want to do anything. I wanted to go to sleep and wake up in my own home with my husband and my children. I wanted this all to be just a bad dream. I didn't want to accept that what was happening to me was reality. I wanted to go home. I wanted to hug my children, kiss them good morning and tell them how much I loved them.

* * * * *

The next day was Sunday. I found out that would they let us go outside at 9 a.m. if we wanted to get some fresh air and some sun. This recreation time lasted an hour and it cheered me up. I was desperate having nothing to do. Outside, there was a basketball court and a ping-pong table, and two vending machines – one for sodas, the other for snacks. There was also an exercise machine and there were tables around the perimeter.

I had started to walk around the exercise yard when I noticed a priest had arrived. He was tall and thin and carried a briefcase. He invited us to participate in a mass. We cleaned off a table, and he opened his briefcase and took out a clean, white tablecloth, a crucifix, a small container with hosts, and some missals to say the mass. He also took out a white cassock and a beautiful green stole with woven designs that I recognized immediately as being from Guatemala. We celebrated mass and I cried when I received communion. It feels wonderful to cry when you're talking to God.

When mass was over, I went up to the priest who had introduced himself as Fr. Robert. I asked him if the stole was from Guatemala. He said yes and asked how I knew. I told him I was Salvadoran and that I was familiar with that kind of cloth. We talked a bit and he told me that he was a Jesuit and that he'd spent some time in Guatemala and El Salvador. When he said that, I felt a ray of light in all the darkness. He spoke perfect Spanish and his homily had been wonderful, very thoughtful. To top it all off, he was a Jesuit familiar with my culture!

I felt such a connection to him and my country. I had been educated at the Jesuit University in El Salvador, and throughout my childhood and teen years, I'd gone to boarding schools and had come to trust the nuns and priests. We talked about all the Jesuits martyred during the 12-year civil war in my country and how their deaths had galvanized people and eventually brought about positive changes. Before leaving, he mentioned that he came every Sunday to celebrate the mass. He gave us each a rosary and a Bible. After that, I invited all my cellmates to form groups to pray the rosary every night. Three groups were formed: a Hispanic, a Philippine and an English-speaking group. According to the guards, this had never happened before.

It was very transforming to know a priest like Father Robert. He didn't give me a big lecture on the gospel and repentance, he just said, "Amalia, there is great need here. Remember that your spirit is free."

The truth is that those words were the inspiration I needed not to feel defeat, but instead to feel liberated, free in spirit. My body was in prison, but I was alive. I could laugh, dream, and fight for the day when I would be free to create a better future for my children. Until that time came, I'd have to learn to live with dignity in prison. This would be my new home, one that was decorated with pain, frustration, rage, anger, evil, injustice, indifference, and hatred. It was a terrible environment, so "redecorating" it would not be easy.

But I was ready to take on that challenge. I wouldn't let the system wipe out the most precious thing I had at this moment – my spiritual freedom. I believed in a God that does not abandon His children, and in a hope that "this too shall pass." This was my new world. It was a hostile world full of injustice and pain, not a world that God had created. No, it was a world that human beings had made to destroy a person's spirit. It was a system I would struggle against, helping the other prisoners to overcome their fear, strengthen their faith, and find God's love in this place.

* * * * *

In the afternoon they told me I had a visitor. I was anxiously awaiting Diana and you can imagine my surprise when I saw her brother and sister with her. I was so happy, but I wanted to cry at the same time. I couldn't hug or kiss them because there was a glass barrier between us. I put my hand on the glass and they automatically put their hands on mine wanting to touch me. We stayed like that for a few minutes; no one shed a tear. Then I started to talk to them with as much positive energy as I could muster. Only I knew how much I was suffering inside in those moments.

I didn't want them to worry. I thought it would be worse if they realized they couldn't help me. So the "performance" had to be perfect! I told them the jail was a very nice place with a great view of the ocean, and it even had an exercise room. I told them the food was really good, and I told so many other lies that I couldn't even keep track of them all. But I thought I'd achieved my goal. They promised me they would study hard, not miss school, and behave themselves as best they could. I told them that that was the best encouragement I could possibly have. We said goodbye and left it that they would visit the following week.

When I returned to the Pod, I went directly to my bunk. I was devastated. I felt so uncertain about how long I'd last in this place. The situation of the children was what tormented me the most. How would they manage in our absence? The little money we had would last a month at most. But we also owed the bank the mortgage payments on our house so it seemed that we had to decide between paying the mortgage and buying food. In addition, some expenses had doubled. Telephone calls, for instance, were expensive because Gil and I could only call collect. And you don't just pay higher rates, taxes are higher, too! Gil and I talked to the children every day to make sure everything was all right. Who knows how much just the telephone bill was going to be!

There is nothing to compare with the pain you feel when you can't help the people you love the most. There are no words to describe the agony when they are your own children who you've sacrificed your whole life for – to educate them, love them, discipline them – when you've done everything you can so they could have a better childhood than the one you'd had. It's a gnawing pain that presses against your chest, tears at your soul, and feels like a slow death because you have absolutely no options. I wrestled with myself daily to remember that I had to be strong to bolster their strength. I had to speak very positively with them so they would have faith that all this would soon pass. I had to let them know I had complete confidence in them that they wouldn't let me down. I knew they loved me as much as I loved them, and it was then that I realized that love would be my greatest ally.

Beginning the Battle

My Salvadoran cellmate got me some work. They paid me $1.00 a day to clean. Keeping busy helped my anxiety a lot. Even though it was only a half hour, at least my mind let go of all worry during that half hour. I took the opportunity to fold clothes even though I wasn't paid for that. I just wanted to be doing something. Most of women spent their time laying in bed asking for medicine for their anxiety and being drugged up the whole day. They only got up to eat. They were a mess. They preferred to self medicate rather than deal with their problems and look for solutions.

On Monday I noticed that a group got together to sing and do Bible study at 6 p.m. and so I joined them. It helped a lot to spend the hour in reflection. We prayed for each other – especially for the ones who were due in court the next day – and we shared our problems and looked for ways to support each other.

I felt strong and positive when I read God's promises to His children. I especially loved reading the first seven verses of Isaiah 43 – I clung to that passage. I'd read the Bible and proclaimed the Word many, many times in my prayer groups in the past, but now I felt God so close. It's not something you can explain; you have to live it. God was there with me. When I felt alone and abandoned, when I felt so afraid of what might happen to my children, in all my moments of uncertainty and suffering, He was there.

* * * * *

That week I was given a piece of paper notifying me that my court date was in two weeks. I told Diana so she would get in touch with the lawyer. I was very happy to get that notice. But the days passed slowly and it was a constant struggle to not let the depression and anxiety get me down. I threw myself into being useful because it was inconceivable to me to be locked up and wasting time when there was so much need among the women.

I'd worked all my life. I'm a very active person and the confinement and inactivity was destroying me. I decided to offer my services as an interpreter with the guards since most of them didn't speak Spanish. When anybody needed anything, they asked for my help – filling out forms, trying to see a doctor, whatever. I did it happily. Because of this, a lot of the women started calling me Mother Teresa. My cellmates didn't understand why I helped so much when I got nothing in return, but I really needed to be myself and not lose my identity.

I needed to feel useful even in those precarious conditions. We were all suffering. We shared our sorrows and frustrations. We were all happy when one of us was released, and everyone felt the anguish of our confinement. The truth was that I needed them more than they needed me. As I helped and consoled them, I found a reason I could hold onto for being in that place. To give of myself gave meaning to my struggle. Anything else would have been hell for me.

* * * * *

One week before our court date, our lawyer visited Gil and me separately in jail. She explained in detail why we'd been taken into custody. The officers who had seized us were from INTERPOL (International Police) and INS (Immigration and Naturalization Service). They had a warrant for our arrest charging us with swindling someone out of $650 million *colones* back in El Salvador. I couldn't believe it but I knew right away who had accused us of this.

Before coming to the United States I had my own business and Gil had worked as an architect. I had owned several small clothing boutiques. When I closed my business, there was one unscrupulous moneylender in particular who wouldn't negotiate my debt payment. The payment plan that I proposed didn't suit him even though I'd been paying him 5% interest monthly for 5 years and he'd already collected three times the amount on the original loan. He showed me no mercy and we had had to leave the country without paying him everything he wanted. He must have been the one responsible for alerting the authorities.

But to my surprise, it wasn't only him. My husband's former secretary was filing the claim with him jointly. They'd put this whole scenario into motion together. They'd made a whole slew of accusations against us, and denounced us to the American Embassy in San Salvador, and that was it! Finding out about her involvement just added to my suffering because, at one point, this woman had almost caused the end of my marriage. Gil was really devastated, but the truth was we were the ones responsible for what was happening. We had been too trusting when we negotiated the loan.

The lawyer told us we'd have to prove these accusations were false in order to have the criminal charges dropped. But there were also problems with our immigration status, and she counseled us to apply for political asylum because we'd been affected by the civil war in our country. She said it would be a difficult case and that we'd have to gather and present all the evidence needed to clear ourselves. Time flew by and the meeting couldn't have lasted more than 15 minutes when a guard told our lawyer she had to leave.

On the way back to the Pod, my feet felt like lead. My mind was blank. My hopes of reuniting soon with my family had gone up in smoke. I felt so helpless. I was so worried about the future of my children. My thoughts went around and around futilely trying to find some answers, but they were blocked at every turn. I had to resign myself to confront the situation and be ready to endure whatever happened. We were also going to have to tell our family in El Salvador what was going on. That would cause them a lot of pain.

When the children came to visit on the weekend, I asked Diana to tell her aunt Musi what was happening. Why her? Every time I've needed her, she's been there for me. She encourages me and always reminds me that there is no problem too great for God to solve. I missed her very much and wished I could have her by my side at that moment.

* * * * *

Time passed slowly, but finally my day to appear in court arrived. I could hardly sleep the night before. I got up early to be sure to be ready. My heart raced and I was really feeling afraid. I didn't have any idea what to expect. I felt extremely nervous and my hands were sweating. The officer called out the names of those who had to go to court that day. All of us were anxious and nervous. I started whispering to myself the comforting prayer of St. Teresa of Avila, "Let nothing disturb you. Nothing frighten you. Whoever has God lacks nothing." I kept repeating this litany all the way to court until I calmed down and wasn't as nervous.

The courtroom was a small room in the same building. They sat us women in the front benches, and after awhile they brought in the men. I could see my husband out of the corner of my eye. You're not allowed to look directly at any of the men, even if he's your husband, father or any other family member. There were about twenty of us immigrants, all in different colored uniforms.

When the judge walked in, we all stood up. It was an orderly, respectful environment. No one said a word. The judge was young. She had the files of everyone who was in court that day on her desk. First, she asked for everyone who wanted to be deported back to their countries to raise their hand. Many people, especially the men, raised their hand. They took down their names and then took them away.

When it was our turn, they called us to the front of the courtroom. They asked us our name and if we needed an interpreter. We were then asked, "Do you swear to tell the truth and nothing but the truth?" They read us our rights, and then the judge exchanged some words with our lawyer. I didn't understand what they were saying because it was "legalese" but then, to my great dismay, they said that court was adjourned and that we should come back in two weeks.

I couldn't believe it! I'd waited so long for nothing. I was so upset. It had to be a joke. Oh my God, I was so frustrated! All of us who'd gone to court that day returned in worse shape than when we'd gone. Some were crying. Others were upset because their lawyers hadn't appeared and their families had already paid them large sums of money.

Only bad things happened that day, nothing good. I got back to the Pod and the first thing I did was head straight to my bunk. I didn't want to talk to anyone. My anger and frustration continued to build inside me. I didn't even want to think about what explanation I was going to give my kids that would make any sense for why we still had to remain separated. How was I going to explain that I was just another number and that no one was in a hurry to settle my case?

That night when I broke the news to the children, they were very sad, as expected. I'd been consoling them all along with positive and optimistic words about how this separation wouldn't last long. Now it seemed that all signs pointed to a long and difficult road ahead.

* * * * *

The days following my court appearance went by very slowly. On Wednesday of that week at 9 a.m., an elderly man and woman visited our cell. They invited us to a Bible reading. The man, Donald, formed an English-speaking group. I joined the group led by the woman since she spoke Spanish. Her name was Alice.

We began by praying, reading, and sharing the scriptures. At a certain point, Alice asked me why I was so sad and what was worrying me. In a faltering voice and holding back tears, I told her how worried

I was for my children, and how tormented I was by the idea that something really bad might happen to them while I was in jail.

She took my hands and in a very sweet voice, looking me straight in the eyes, said, "Has God taken care of you all these years and worked miracles in your life?" "Sure," I said, "God performed the most wonderful miracle for me when He saved my daughter Amy's life. And He's done many more miracles like that." She answered, "Then why are you worried? Don't you realize that when you need Him the most is when He is closest to you and your family? Don't focus on the hurt. Trust in Him! Turn your children over to His care and watch. He will not leave you."

Her words worked magic in changing my attitude. From then on my time in the jail took a different course. I dedicated myself fully to working with all the different religious groups that visited us. It didn't matter which denomination they were from. They did their best to bring us encouragement and consolation to try and fill that great void of love and understanding that we were feeling. Those were the only times when I didn't feel alone and abandoned. It was pure enjoyment. I felt loved and supported. I felt like a real human being. I came to believe strongly that evil would never triumph over good.

* * * * *

Finally, it was time for me to show up in court again. I was a little nervous but not like the first time. I was sure that things would get cleared up now. But I was wrong. My lawyer told the judge that we were applying for political asylum and that was it! The judge fixed the next court date for within one month.

Again I couldn't believe it. It definitely looked like this was going to be a long, drawn out process. Who knew when I'd get out? There are too many prisoners and too few judges. They can't spend much time on any one case since there are only two judges for over 700 detained immigrants.

I did get to see Gil up close, but I wasn't allowed to talk to him or look directly at him, much less touch him. I could tell he'd lost a lot of weight and he looked depressed.

* * * * *

I felt more and more apprehensive about the situation with the kids. One night when I called home, Amy was crying. She said she couldn't stand it anymore. She felt so alone. Diana had a boyfriend who went to the same university and it seemed that things between them had gotten a lot more serious. She spent lots of time with him, and her brother and sister felt like they were playing second fiddle.

This was really a difficult situation for me to handle. I couldn't expect Diana to play the mother role, but I understood how important it was to Amy and Gilito to feel supported and cared for by their older sister. She was the life preserver they clung to in these "stormy seas" of insecurities, fear, and frustration as they realized their parents wouldn't be coming home anytime soon.

But there was nothing I could do to change the situation. I asked them to do their best to keep on going and to stick together as best they could because being divided or alienated from each other would only make things more difficult. I told them to take care of one another and that the best gift they could give me would be to act as if their father and I were still at home.

It was really hard not to be able to talk things over with my husband. I had to resign myself to the fact that, at least for now, my children were not under my care. They would have to fend for themselves and learn to solve their own problems.

I had to accept reality. Not only was my children's future not in my hands, I wasn't even in control of my own. I had to learn to live day to day, with no expectations. INS had taken my freedom, children, work, and my husband. I'd lost everything.

It's like you're dead but instead of reaching paradise, you're confronted with a hostile world – one without love, hope, privacy, and resources – a world created by INS to make you feel undesirable and worthless. It's a world set up to break your spirit where you're treated like a common criminal. It's hell.

Here's where the toughest battle began. I had to carry on for my children. I didn't want them to see me as a failure with no hope for the future. If they were going to struggle to keep going on the outside, I'd have to do the same here in jail.

A Sad Story

And so time passed. I started drawing pictures and learned to color them in using M&M candies. I found this very relaxing. We had Bible study every afternoon at 6 p.m. where we sang and shared our stories. We prayed for each other and even though we sometimes had our differences – the Catholics and the Protestants – we remembered that the Bible was there to bring us together not to separate us.

Above all, we had to help each other keep our spirits up, believe we had a future, and remember that our children and families were waiting for us. They were striving on the outside with or without resources and if we failed to keep up our spirits, it was just one more problem for them. It was unfair to them to cry when we phoned home because there was nothing they could do to help us. We just added to their suffering. This was my belief.

* * * * *

Once, an immigration officer asked me to talk to a new detainee, who was refusing to enter the Pod willingly. I had to convince her to come in so they wouldn't use force on her. She was scared to death because she thought the Pod was full of "dangerous criminals" and was sure she'd be harmed. She was out of control and crying hysterically. Finally, she agreed to go in as long as I promised not to leave her side.

We talked and she told me her story. Her name was Luci. She was Peruvian from Arequipa, a province distant from Lima. She was about 50 years old. She had decided to leave Peru because her husband was an alcoholic and she'd had some problems at work. She borrowed the money to go to the United States but went first to Bolivia with the help of a *coyote.* There she joined up with another woman and the three of them flew to Los Angeles using the passports of people who looked like they did. The passports were stamped with valid tourist visas.

When they arrived at LAX airport, immigration figured out what they'd done and apprehended them along with the *coyote.* They were taken to jail and were held until they said they were willing to testify against the *coyote.* They were promised that if they testified against him they would be let go. They were in for over three months but had to hire a lawyer and post bail. For economic support, Luci had to rely on her sister who lived in Maryland.

They finally released her. When she tried to reclaim her suitcase at the jail, they told her it was back at the immigration office. Since she needed her belongings, she went to her lawyer's office and asked him to inquire about it. He called INS to find out about it and told Luci to wait there because INS was going to bring it by.

She waited patiently. But to her surprise, instead of delivering her suitcase, immigration officers arrested her and took her off to San Pedro. She handed them papers showing she had posted bail but they just told her it didn't matter.

That explained Luci's nervousness and anguish. I tried to calm her down assuring her that no one was going to hurt her and that the best thing she could do for herself was to get a hold of herself to be able to think clearly. She needed to contact her sister and explain how she'd been detained again. That day Luci joined our Bible study group and felt welcomed and supported right away. Most importantly, she realized that she wasn't the only one going through hard times. She would have to find strength in her weaknesses.

* * * * *

The situation with my children kept getting worse. We'd been in detention three months. There was no money left. The phone service was cut off when they couldn't pay the bill and so we couldn't be in regular communication. The only way to talk to each other was at our weekly visits together, which they never missed. Sometimes they had to stand in line for up to two hours to see us for only 10 to 15 minutes. I also used these visits for communicating with my husband – exchanging letters. It was the only way.

There is a system for sending mail in the jail. They have a mailbox right there and you don't need stamps; somehow they get sent anyway. The first time I sent a letter to Gil, he got it. They didn't realize it was internal mail. The second time, they called me on it and told me that no correspondence between detainees was allowed. They said it was for security reasons – it didn't matter that we were married. "What if you were planning to escape?" the officer queried. I could hardly believe it but that was the rule. From then on we got letters to each other through the children.

Diana had to leave her university studies to find work to make some money. The kids were living in the house but we didn't know how long the bank would let them continue to live there before evicting them. In letters back and forth, Gil and I agreed we'd have to find ways to make money so we could give the kids at least fifty dollars a week for food. We needed to find for new ways. I designed and drew greeting cards for all occasions, like birthday wishes, congratulations, etc., and I sold them. Gil learned to make a kind of wallet. Diana bought him the thread and took it to him when she visited.

That's how we started our little businesses. I'd measure and cut out the paper for the cards when I finished my cleaning. I'd take a break for lunch and then continue. I didn't work much at night because I couldn't see well enough, so I'd go to bed at ten o'clock. It was a good, satisfying feeling to give the children the little I was able to pull together. Every week, they left with the fifty dollars that Gil and I had promised them.

* * * * *

Finally my court date arrived. The truth is I didn't know what to think or hope for anymore. My nerves were a wreck. "Let nothing disturb you. Let nothing frighten you. Whoever has God lacks nothing," I kept repeating to myself. This is such a powerful prayer! I didn't want to give myself or my children false hopes. I adopted a new strategy and asked them to be patient and wait for the outcome.

That was my happiest court appearance. When I entered the courtroom, I saw one of Gil's brothers there. He had come to testify. It felt so good to see him. It killed me not to be able to talk to him or give him a hug, but it was enough just to see him. He explained to the judge the oppression and economic losses we had suffered during and following the war and basically pleaded with him to grant us political asylum. The judge asked Gil's brother lots of questions about our situation. Then court was adjourned and we were given another date about a month later.

When I got to the Pod everybody asked me what happened, but once again I had no answers, nothing concrete anyway. I had to continue with all the uncertainty. It was very disillusioning to see that some of the women, even some really tough ones with criminal backgrounds, were able to get out on bail. They could fight their cases from the outside – in freedom. But if I learned anything it was that you never know how a case is going to come out. It seemed pretty clear that those applying for political asylum didn't get bail. There were some who'd been there a year waiting for resolution of their cases. On the inside, I clung to the hope that that would not happen to me. Everything would get cleared up and we'd get our asylum.

* * * * *

As time passed, the number of women increased; a lot of them coming from prison and you could feel the tension level rise. It was really hard to endure. There were a lot of fights and obscene language. The law of the jungle prevailed and some weren't strong enough to withstand it.

I especially remember Martha, a Salvadoran woman who was 36 years old. She had lived in the States for 12 years and had a work permit. She'd won her political asylum case. She was like so many other thousands who were victims of the war; her husband and two sons had died, their bodies riddled with bullets by armed men who'd broken into their home. Only she and another son who was badly wounded survived.

Getting back to her story. . . she got news that her mother was very sick back in El Salvador and, since she was an only daughter, she asked INS for permission to leave and go visit her. She had to ask permission even though she had won her political asylum case because she was still waiting for her legal residency to go through. INS gave her permission to leave the country for 60 days. Before leaving, she inquired about what would happen if she didn't return within that time frame. They told her that she would have two weeks, at the most, after the expiration date to go to the American Embassy in San Salvador to ask for an extension.

She went to El Salvador and took care of her mother. Her mother didn't improve and the time expired. When she went to the consulate to ask for an extension, they told her there was no procedure for such a continuance. They told her that if she let her permission expire, that was it. She couldn't return to the United States. She didn't accept this answer, so she traveled to Honduras but got the same answer there at the consulate there. Desperate because her only surviving son was in the United States, she tried to get a tourist visa. She was successful and when her mother got better, she flew back to Los Angeles. Martha was detained as soon as she arrived at the airport. She was arrested and sent to San Pedro. She cried a lot. She'd been traumatized by so much violence in El Salvador so she was very affected by the atmosphere in the cell, especially when there were fights. She suffered from heart problems.

One time there was an incident at lunch. A fight broke out at the table next to ours and although it may have only lasted a few seconds, it felt like a riot because the space was so small. Lots of the women like to see a fight; they enjoy it. Others, like Martha, are emotionally affected and get very upset. They get especially distressed when the guards arrive to separate the prisoners because they use force and handcuff them. In that particular incident, Martha fainted and was hospitalized for three days.

When she got back from the hospital, she was more desperate than ever to get out of here. She hired a lawyer to get the quickest court date possible. Her lawyer claimed her case was cut and dry and he gave her 90% odds to win. So she agreed to fight her political asylum case. Her court date came and it was the same story as the rest of us – they postponed it for two weeks. Her desperation grew and she lost a lot of weight.

Her second court appearance brought no resolution either. She had to wait another month for them to finally tell her that her political asylum request was turned down. They gave her voluntary departure and said she had the right to appeal the judge's decision to a higher court. But she gave up her rights because she just couldn't stand the atmosphere in the jail.

She was one of my best friends. She was quiet and reserved. When you talked to her you could tell she was a wonderful woman – but a woman who had suffered a great deal and carried a terrible wound inside her. That's probably why she always wore such a sad and melancholy expression. When she left, I felt happy for her but I missed her a lot. A few months after she had returned to El Salvador, I got a letter from her in which she lamented not having had enough courage to fight for her future. She felt very guilty for having separated from her only son. She said in the letter that her life had lost all meaning.

Accepting the Verdict

Finally my day in court arrived. I got up early. My nerves were on edge. You never know what's going to happen. I just kept repeating to myself, "One more step towards freedom."

On the way to court I started praying and concentrating on my litany, "Let nothing disturb you. Let nothing frighten you. Whoever has God lacks nothing." I had to get a handle on this fear that had my stomach in knots and was making my heart race.

There were moments when my faith was truly shaken and I would forget that I had to be patient and not lose hope that God would act in His own time. I realized how fragile my faith was. I needed to work on strengthening my trust in God if I was ever going to overcome this fear.

Two people were going to be there from El Salvador – a lawyer who was working on my behalf on the case down there, and the moneylender who had submitted the fraud claim against me. Everything pointed to the fact that this session would be very significant and tense. The prosecutor for immigration had brought the moneylender as his ace in the hole to show the judge that we didn't deserve political asylum status because we were criminals.

My lawyer, on the other hand, would offer the findings of the lawyer who was pursuing the case in El Salvador showing that the accusations were false, that no fraud had been committed, and that in fact, this was a business debt that had been paid off at 60% annual interest!

The session lasted three hours. The moneylender lied when he said we'd never tried to negotiate paying off the debt, but I didn't care about that. The most important thing that came out, in my opinion, was that he declared in his own words that the debt had originated as an approved loan. It wasn't a case of fraud as he had claimed.

At the end of the session, the judge set the next date for within a month. It was already June, we'd been in detention for four months, and nothing concrete had happened yet in our case. The only thing we knew was that in our next court appearance we would be questioned in detail and that the judge would then make a decision on the request for political asylum based on the information he had.

* * * * *

June was a really tough month for me. My daughter Amy turned seventeen. She felt the most hopeless and upset by our absence. She felt very alone and called once to say she couldn't stand it anymore. Her relationship with her sister had gone from bad to worse and she wanted to leave but didn't know where to go. I was also worried about my son because he was the smallest and he never said anything. He just took it all in quietly.

I knew things weren't going well between the children. They came every Sunday to see us, but they'd argue about stupid stuff. I could see impatience and frustration in their interaction. The distance between them concerned me and I asked them to try their hardest to understand each other. I told them that if they loved me like they said they did, they had to prove it by behaving themselves. Whenever they decided to do something, they had to think about whether I'd be proud of them. I knew I was putting a lot of pressure on them. It was a kind of blackmail, but I had to do it. The love that we all had for each other was my only ally.

It turned out I had no idea what a hell they were actually living in. Diana's boyfriend had moved in under the pretext of helping out and then decided he'd take on the role of the head of the family. Amy and

Gilito were feeling like he'd usurped their father's place. In addition, it was slowly dawning on them that they were really alone and that their family had fallen apart. To make things worse, the boyfriend didn't like the fact that they spoke Spanish at home. He gave them a hard time about it and verbally abused them. He also didn't understand why Diana was so worried about her siblings since he thought they were old enough to take care of themselves. He was pressuring her to quit being so protective.

But I wasn't aware of all this, and since it distressed me so much to see them alienated from and resentful of each other, I told them it was really inconsiderate of them to be causing me these kinds of problems. I stressed that the suffering I was experiencing in jail was nothing as long as I could see that they were united and working well together.

* * * * *

Time went on. It was so hard to face each new day. There were so many detainees they didn't have room for them all in the sleeping area, so they gave them plastic beds and made them sleep along the walls of the dayroom. It was very noisy and, of course, there were lots of fights. I kept myself busy doing my handicrafts, cleaning, and coordinating a prayer group, but I was really tired of being locked up.

My hair started to fall out. I had a lot of dandruff and athlete's foot, and my skin was so dry, it was all scaly. I wanted to see a doctor and hoped there was something I could take to feel and look better. I asked to see the doctor and in three days they called me. The visit to the clinic was interesting and at the beginning I really enjoyed myself. The clinic was in the same building but at least I was out of the pod's atmosphere. It looked like any regular clinic with chairs to sit in and wait your turn. The officers who took us there were really nice and funny. They treated us super-nicely, and we were relieved to get away from our normal 24-hour routine.

I saw the doctor and explained my symptoms. He gave me some shampoo and a cream for the fungus infection. That seemed to be all but then I asked him what I should do for my skin. He looked me in the eyes and said, "This is a jail. We don't treat cosmetic complaints. Your skin is aging. You're 43 years old and you can't expect to have the skin of a 15 year old. You can go now. I can't keep wasting my time on this."

I was so upset. He hadn't just called me "old," he'd said he was wasting his time with me. But there was nothing I could do. I went out and waited for the others to finish. I wanted to cry so badly. I felt humiliated and usually when I get angry like that I want to cry. This time I just had to hold back.

My friend, Luci, was along too. She had a hard lump in her breast and she complained a lot about the pain. But they didn't treat her well like she had hoped either. The doctor gave her Tylenol, the magic-cure-all. It turns out that's what they always give you when you go to the doctor.

* * * * *

Day by day, I'm getting to understand the system a little better. Detainees are like inventory. Three times a day, the officers count us to make sure we're all there. They give us what we need to eat. They give us painkillers for our aches and pains. And they wash our clothes. But that's all. They don't invest an extra penny in us. They give us the bare minimum to avoid problems with Detention Watch Network, an organization that monitors and advocates for humane conditions in the immigration jails. So I guess I won't die of some disease here because if it's life threatening, they take you to the hospital. But they sure don't do anything as preventative medicine.

They make everything difficult for you here. You have use of a telephone but only to make collect calls. There isn't a phone directory, not even in the library. The only good things that happen are the visits by the religious volunteers. I really admire them. The guards don't treat them very well and sometimes leave them standing at the entrance for 15 minutes before they let them enter our Pod. We tell the volunteers all our complaints. They're the only ones we trust. We know they care about us from the bottom of their hearts and that they agonize because they can't help us even when they see so much pain and injustice.

I always wonder why they come since the guards make it so difficult for them. They treat them rudely and search them from head to toe. But they still come every week with radiant smiles and hearts filled with love – rain or shine, bitter cold or holiday – always.

*   *   *   *   *

Well, the month of June is over. Gil turned fifty on June 21. I was able to send him a birthday card through the children but it's hard to feel so far from each other when we are so close by physically. I've been locked up now for over three months. I'm past the adjustment and uncertainty phase. I understand the rules of the game. I don't have false expectations anymore that I'm going to get out anytime soon. Now I have to be patient and understand that I'm not in control of my children or my future. I can't expect anything concrete to change so there's no point in being worried about tomorrow. I need to live one day at a time.

Gil writes to me often but his letters really annoy me because he just quotes passages from the Bible. I think he simply chooses a Bible verse and copies it down. So in the letter I sent him this week, I told him that I don't need for him to write down Bible passages. . . I have my own Bible and I read it every day! I want him to write about what he's feeling, his worries, his thoughts about the children, anything and everything having to do with the family. But most of all, I want him to write about what's happening in his Pod. Is it dangerous? Does he feel safe? I just want to hear about so many things!

Fortunately, my dear husband didn't resent the "scolding" he got in my letter and the next one he sent me was completely different. He said that he was going to start working in the kitchen and get paid a dollar a day. He said that he'd get to spend more time outside because they ate on the patio, and that he'd have more time to write.

He also asked me to forgive him for what had happened. He felt responsible for our misfortune. I told him I didn't see things that way. I think there is a purpose to everything that happens and that the key is not to point fingers but rather to face reality, live as best we can, dwell in the positive and not the negative, and learn from it all. From the window of my Pod, I sometimes catch a glimpse of him when he goes out on the patio to eat or write. He always looks lost in thought and kind of off by himself. But I am happy to see him.

* * * * *

One Wednesday, a minister I'd never met came with a group of religious volunteers. He asked for me and told me his name was Ron. He said he usually visited the men and that Gil had asked him to visit me. We talked for a little while before several of us sat around a table to listen to his message.

I really liked the way he conducted the meeting. He talked a lot about forgiveness, especially of letting go of guilt and forgiving ourselves for any wrongs we may have done. He stressed how if God forgives our faults and errors, who are we to keep on blaming and punishing ourselves for our past offenses? He said we needed to try to find peace within ourselves; otherwise we'd never be happy, and therefore, we'd never be able to make our families happy.

And he was right to say so. It's a heavy load to carry to keep your feelings of guilt all bottled up inside. Those hidden feelings can keep you from successfully starting a new life in peace and from seeing the present and the future with hope. Many tears were shed but at the end of the meeting, there was a real sense of peace. Until that moment, I hadn't forgiven myself for causing my children so much hardship, or for all the suffering and anguish the whole family was feeling as they worked to get Gil and me out of this place, or for so many other things that came to mind in that moment of reflection.

What a privilege and blessing it is to be able to count on these volunteers! They come to give us strength and hope to persevere in this hell. It's incredible to see how when they come, there is actually more peace in the Pod; it's a different day. It does me so much good. I feel so alive when I see their smiles and I listen to their words so full of faith and love. I think it would be very difficult for me to live in this jail without them. I'm not the only one who feels this way; most of us do. I think God works through them. They always have just the right words to say for the particular moment.

* * * * *

This week of my final court date arrived. We expected the judge to hand down his judgment concerning our political asylum case. There were only two possibilities – he was either going to give it to us or he wasn't. I tried not to think about it since it made me tense. But one night I begged God to show me in my dreams what would become of us and what the results of the court appearance would be. And that's what happened. I dreamt I was on a plane with other people and that an immigration officer was guarding us. The plane made several stops but I never got off; I always stayed on the plane.

The next day I told my prayer group that I was going to lose my political asylum case and be deported. I said it didn't matter anymore because I knew I was in God's hands, and if that was God's will, I accepted it. That's exactly what happened in court. The judge denied our asylum and gave us 30 days to appeal the decision to a higher court. As I returned to the Pod, I was calm; I wasn't upset or worried about the verdict. I think I was prepared for it and so it didn't affect me as much.

But that night I talked with the kids and they were upset and down in the dumps. None of them wanted to go back to El Salvador. The three of them said they wanted to continue to go to school here. I couldn't accept the idea of leaving them behind. But at the same time, I thought that for better or worse they seemed settled here and the last thing I wanted to do was to create more instability. So I explained that we had a month to decide what to do. I needed to talk to Gil to find out what he was thinking.

* * * * *

I'm in a phase of resignation. I already went through the adaptation and uncertainty phase. The judge has made her decision and I have to accept it. I have to plant my feet firmly on the ground and confront this new stage in my life. I'm worried about my kids' attitude. They seem so convinced and set on the idea that this country is the best place for them. I don't understand how they can say that since anyone can see the troubles they're going through. But I can't do anything for the time being except to ask God to give me the strength to make the right decision.

The court verdict against me lowered moral among some in my prayer group. Faith seems to fall apart when we don't get the results we hope for or when we don't see the "fruits" of our fervent prayers. But the fact is we always end our petitions by saying, "Not my will, but Yours be done." And prayer and good works are no guarantee of a miracle. That's something my cellmates refuse to understand. The test by fire is accepting God's will.

So this was the theme of our prayer group: if we truly believe that our future is in God's hands, we don't need to worry even if things don't turn out the way we'd like because there isn't any place better for us than the one God chooses. At the core, I really want to trust. I know God is in control of my future and my family. I believe that what has happened has happened for a reason. God has other plans for me, plans I don't know yet but ones that will be good for me and my family.

Finally A Victory

I got a letter from Gil saying that our lawyer recommended we appeal to a higher court, arguing that the judge had given a mistaken verdict since we had shown clear proof of persecution. The lawyer can't guarantee we'll win the case but she thinks that it's worth a try. This means we will have to stay in detention for another six months to a year until the higher court hands down its verdict.

What a huge decision we have to make, and in this moment, I have no idea what to do. The only thing I'm sure of is that I don't want to be far from the kids. I can stand anything except leaving them alone here in the United States without supervision and without being able to see them.

* * * * *

This week, my cellmate, Luci from Peru, has had a lot of pain in her breast. She has an inflamed lump. We all hope it isn't a tumor. She went to the doctor again and he gave her more Tylenol. We're really concerned because she cries a lot. Her court date is coming up and she doesn't have a lawyer, or any money. In short, she's completely alone. And on top of all of that, she's seriously sick with no chance of seeing a good doctor. I offered to help and advised her to seek political asylum. We're just waiting to see whether the judge will listen to her case or not.

A tall, elegant, and very pretty American nun named Molly came to visit. She is from the Maryknoll order. She inspires confidence and shows she is interested in your situation. I loved the way she led the conversation group. She had us thinking about the happiest times in our lives and then giving thanks to God for all those times.

She helped us to see that this was a passing moment, that we wouldn't be prisoners our whole lives, and that we had family waiting for us to begin a new life. We received Holy Communion and closed with a prayer giving thanks to God. She brought a bag of rosaries and holy cards and everyone loved their little gifts. Before she left, we told her about Luci's problem and she said she'd see what she could do. She wrote down Luci's name and number and left.

* * * * *

The mail comes every day at three o'clock in the afternoon. I usually don't bother looking for my name because I don't get much mail. But this afternoon I got a letter. I couldn't imagine who would have written me so I rushed to be one of the first in line. To my great surprise it was a letter from Martha, my friend who'd renounced her chances to stay here with her son because she couldn't stand being locked up any longer. Well, she writes that she can't stand to be separated from her only son. She plans to return on foot and to pay a *coyote* in Tijuana to help her get across the border. She says she's really afraid since she has to cross the desert and go through many obstacles, but that she is sure that's what she must do. She asks that we pray for her to arrive safe and sound at her destination.

Her letter was like a sign to me. I understood her suffering at being separated from her son. I could see myself, like her, going through the desert, enduring hunger and thirst, ready to risk my life to be with my children whom I love so much. Now, I definitely want to appeal the decision of the judge. I don't know what kind of time frame that will mean for being in this hell, but I prefer it because at least I get to see my kids every week. Their visits only last a few minutes but they're enough to encourage me to keep on fighting for a better future.

* * * * *

Luci went to court and the judge gave her an application for political asylum. The judge said she could represent herself if she didn't have a lawyer so that same night we went right to work filling out the application. The key to gaining asylum was to prove that you've been persecuted in your own country. Luci is very insecure and she has suffered a lot but after several hours of just talking, I asked her to tell me her story. If her story exposed possible facts that would help her win her asylum case, we'd fill in the form with that information. Luci was terrified to think she might have to go back to Peru since she'd borrowed close to $8000 to come to the United States and if they deported her, it would be impossible to pay back that debt.

This is her story. She lived in a place called Human Settlement, a mostly indigenous town, in the Arequipa region of Peru. Luci spoke the Quechua dialect and managed to find work in a small food bank that distributed food to the indigenous people. The weak are often taken advantage of, and in this case, the indigenous people who received services there were made to sign that they had received a certain quantity of food although they had actually received less.

Luci explained to the people how much food they should be receiving and urged them to make sure that was the amount they were signing for. She made enemies because of this and began to have problems with the ones who had been exposed for having robbed the poor. It was so serious that one time she'd been followed by someone with a machete who planned to kill her. Luckily, she was helped by some neighbors but from that day on her life started to fall apart.

To make things worse, she couldn't count on any help from her husband. He was an alcoholic who often abused her to such an extent that once she had filed a claim against him at the police station. Nothing positive had come from that. On the contrary, her husband was even more arrogant and self-satisfied to see that she hadn't succeeded in getting him in trouble. After hearing her story, we decided to apply for asylum for ethnic and spousal abuse reasons. She wrote to her country and asked people there to send the necessary evidence, and she turned in her application. A court date was set for a month later.

* * * * *

One day they called me on the loudspeaker. They said I had a counseling session. I didn't know what they were talking about but got ready anyway. To my great surprise, Reverend Ron was waiting for me when I got to the room.

He had a big smile on his face and said, "I have a surprise for you. I've been able to arrange a session for you with your husband. All three of us will be together and you'll be able to talk. A guard will be watching at the door. We just need to wait for them to bring your husband."

Just then Gil arrived and we greeted each other without hugs or anything because it isn't allowed. He looked thinner and he'd grown a mustache and a beard. I didn't think he looked well. He'd lost so much weight and he looked unkempt and sickly. But I imagine he probably thought the same about me. I told him of my decision to appeal the case. I didn't care how much time I would have to wait. I would rather die trying than be left with any regrets and doubts that I had been too afraid to fight the good fight. Gil supported me and said he'd speak with the lawyer about getting right on the appeal.

It was a blessing to be able to talk together and agree on our future because it had been really frustrating to not be able to communicate at all. It was even more frustrating because Gil was in Pod 5, separated from me in Pod 6 by a single concrete wall. Reverend Ron asked us to renew our marriage vows and to forgive each other for all our past mistakes. We did that and we prayed. Then we had a three-way hug so we wouldn't raise suspicion.

It was a short session – about twenty minutes long. I felt so grateful towards this good man for all the compassion he'd shown us and for all the effort he'd made to get the officials in charge of the detention center to allow this meeting to take place. That night I felt very peaceful. It had been four months since I'd been able to speak to Gil personally, much less touch or hug him. The next day I told the children about the meeting and they were very happy.

* * * * *

It's July and there have been large numbers of detainees. Most of them have prior criminal records. A Bolivian woman named Jessica and a Chinese-Filipino woman named Chin-Chin caught my attention. I got along with them fantastically because they both like sports. We play ping-pong and the time flies. These games do me a lot of good. We laugh and play and I don't feel like I'm locked up. We also like to play basketball. We try and convince someone else to play so that we're a foursome and can play in teams.

But every day is just awful. It's like we're in a concentration camp. We don't all fit in the dormitory and some people have to eat sitting on the floor of the dayroom. There are lots of fights over the one TV even though there's a schedule for viewing programs in Spanish and English. There's always someone with a "jail mentality," who believes that only the strong get their way. But here things don't operate like that. We treat each other equally and try to show respect for others. Not everybody understands that, especially the gang members who want to make this tiny space their territory and do whatever they want. That's when things blow up and the officers have to use force to reestablish order.

* * * * *

This morning the cries of my cellmates woke me up. They were gathering up the little they had because they were going to be moved to some unknown place. Everything happened so fast. Everyone was crying and asking for more information about what was happening and where they were going to be taken. But it was like talking to a wall. There was no answer. The only thing you heard was a loud, demanding voice saying, "Move it! Hurry! Pack your things!"

The women were crying with anxiety. There were several officers in the dormitory and we knew we had to obey them as fast as we could. They didn't let anyone use the phone to tell their families they were being moved. It was terrible. I felt so much anguish over what was happening, everyone crying with fear.

I was afraid, too. The scene reminded me of something out of the movie, Schindler's List, when the Nazis are separating the Jews into groups to execute them. It was an indescribable anguish, and I begged God not to let my name be mentioned. They took away about 20 of our friends. There weren't as many mattresses on the floor after that, but the next morning we all breathed in an air of sadness.

* * * * *

It's incredible to me that you don't hear loud protests about these kinds of injustices. In El Salvador where I was born, and in many countries, there are US citizens struggling, protesting, and demanding respect for human rights. It has cost some of them their lives to fight for the marginalized, the unprotected, the people who don't have a voice or any rights, but. . . Where are they now? Is it possible they don't know what's happening in these jails? Or are they too afraid to denounce things in their own country? I hope some of them are in this struggle too.

It's ironic. The United States likes to present itself to the world as a country where injustice never occurs, but here I am living it every day! The government sends troops supposedly to take freedom to other countries, but the truth is that they are dying and spending their money to fix problems in other countries without paying any attention to their own.

* * * * *

This afternoon around 3 p.m., they called my name over the loudspeaker. I reported to the officer and she told me to get my things ready. I asked her where I was going to be sent and she said she didn't know. My heart started racing. I couldn't believe what was happening to me. All I could think of was my children. I wrote their number down on a piece of paper so that someone could call them and let them know I'd been moved somewhere and tell them they should contact my lawyer. All my friends were surprised. Luci, the Peruvian woman, cried because I'd been helping her get ready for her court date that was to take place in just a few days. It was chaos. My body seemed so heavy. I felt like I could hardly move; I felt paralyzed. I said good-bye to everyone and asked them to continue with their Bible study. We hugged each other and many of the women cried. I was very sad but I held back my tears.

They took me to the same room I'd been put in when I'd first arrived. I spent about 30 minutes in there without anyone coming to tell me anything when finally, an officer appeared with my passport and said I'd be leaving that night for El Salvador. I tried to explain that my case wasn't closed but she slammed the door in my face. I was terribly confused and full of anguish because I knew our case was before of a higher court and that Immigration didn't have the authority to decide something like that without an order from that court. But deep down, I knew that the people who run Immigration did whatever they wanted. They simply used their power.

I was especially distressed about what would happen to my children. I couldn't imagine them all alone in this country. Even though we were in jail and not with them physically, they always knew we were there to support them, to provide them with money for food, and most of all, to encourage and counsel them. This was too much to bear. I felt so insignificant, so defenseless, without weapons, voiceless, without any say in the situation. On top of it all, Diana's birthday was coming up the next week on August 19. That made me even sadder.

I started to pray and thank God for all I'd been able to accomplish with my children up to now and I asked Him to take care of them. I said if I had to leave like this, it was okay, but that He knew that deep in my heart, I was dying. I was in this depth of misery an hour. It was as silent as a tomb. Finally the same officer showed up and told me I'd be returning to the dormitory.

* * * * *

When I got back to the dormitory, my bed was already occupied by someone else. There was no way I was getting it back so I looked for an empty bed and started over. My friends were happy to see I'd returned, but it was all still a mystery to me. My whole body felt so heavy. I couldn't eat any dinner and I went straight to bed. I thanked God for letting me stay close to my children and prayed for my cellmates who'd been taken off at dawn.

The next day I called my lawyer and told her what had happened. She already knew. It turned out that the same thing had happened to Gil, and that he had called her immediately. Right away, our lawyer faxed the appeal papers and immediately Immigration suspended the operation. I was thrilled to know Gil had been so smart and quick to act. If he hadn't called the lawyer, I'm absolutely sure they would have deported us.

* * * * *

Luci has her court date in two days. She's feeling nervous, actually really, really nervous. We've gone over and over her story, but she really needs a lawyer, and so she found one to come to court. The only thing is, he hasn't called her to confirm that he will show up to represent her, so she's been pacing like a caged lion. We decided to take advantage of the fact that today was Wednesday, the day the volunteers come, and after Bible study, Luci gave one of them a piece of paper with the lawyer's name and number. She got down on her knees and begged, crying for them to please call the lawyer and remind him to show up at her final court appearance. The volunteer said she'd be happy to help but told Luci it wasn't necessary to get down on her knees.

At that moment, one of the nastiest officers called the volunteer and took her out into the hallway with the security supervisor. We could see that they were scolding her for something. They searched her Bible and her purse. They gave her a hard time and then left her.

* * * * *

That night we prayed earnestly in our prayer group that Luci might be able to get out of this place. Everything points to the fact that she has a tumor and she's in so much pain. They don't give you good medical attention here in jail, just Tylenol and more Tylenol. They never would do a mammogram. They're so indifferent to pain and suffering.

A few weeks ago, Sister Molly was so worried to see Luci crying when we were gathered in prayer that she asked an officer when Luci would be taken to the doctor. That question cost her! They brought it to her attention that she had permission to visit to help in religious matters, and not with medical concerns. And that's the sad truth about this place. If it wasn't for the work of the volunteers, I dare to say, they'd treat us like animals. But the volunteers don't let the guards intimidate them. They continue to visit us with love and dedication. They pray for us. They are our guardian angels.

* * * * *

Thank God! Luci won her asylum petition and the next day she left happily. The nightmare was over for her. We celebrated her victory because it was a victory for us too.

Out of Control

I've been here seven months now. Every day I have more worries about the children. The bank is going to take back the house. The kids have to move; the question is where? When they visit me I can see they're not getting along. They're always fighting and they don't want to move into an apartment, especially not with Diana's boyfriend.

It's very difficult for me but what can I do? I only see them 15 minutes a week. That's hardly enough time to find out how they're doing. The worst thing is they tell me half- truths and don't tell me what's really at the core of the problem. They are trying to spare me because they love me so much. Tonight I couldn't stand it any longer and I cried. I felt so helpless. I felt like my family was falling apart and I had lost all control. I couldn't guarantee that my family would stay together the way I wanted.

What I wanted didn't seem to matter. The circumstances the children were going through at their ages, in a strange country, were really agonizing. All I could do was to let things take their course. I had to accept things no matter how painful they might be.

* * * * *

The only thing we could do was to try to give the kids more money each week for their expenses, to take off some of the burden of having to support themselves. Gil and I agreed we would definitely have to make more money.

What I did was learn to make really nice decorations out of potato chip bags. The Chinese girls taught me this delicate art for which all you needed was time, a plastic playing card, a needle, thread, and a book to press the folded pieces with.

At first it was hard, but if I had anything in my life, it was time. Someone gave me a playing card, I found a good thick book, and I picked through the trash cans for the potato chip bags. It's not easy to find a needle in a jail so I decided to make a needle out of a staple. I went to the library, took a staple out of one of the magazines, hid it in my sock, and took it back to the dorm. For thread, I learned to remove some of the thread from my pants.

I started to work ten hours a day making them and my fingers were killing me. But it paid off, because that first week, I made $30 dollars. I made three heart-shaped decorations and the women bought them from me as fast as I made them. My poor husband just kept making bags that the men could keep their money in. He also sold part of his food. Between the two of us, we could give the kids a little more money.

* * * * *

The volunteers that come to visit are praying very hard for my children. I take heart from Alice and Donald and know they have their faith communities praying for the kids. Sister Molly and Father Robert are the same. That gives me a lot of assurance and makes me feel like I'm not alone in this place. They give me encouragement and hope when I feel weak. On the other front, my family in El Salvador and my sister-in-law, Tita, are always checking in to see what the children need.

But they don't know what's happening. The children are being very discreet about their problems and make it look like everything is going fine. But a mother can tell about problems just by the look in her children's eyes. Gil doesn't understand this and he tells me I worry just for the sake of worrying, but I know in my heart they're going through a family crisis.

* * * * *

It's already October. We heard on the news there was a terrible hurricane in Central America; many people are dead or homeless. Here in the jail it's total chaos. Lots of the women have children back in their countries and they don't know how they are. You can't make international calls from the telephones here. Everyone is hurting. Fear and pain are contagious and you can practically feel them in the air.

This week Sr. Molly offered to look into the whereabouts of prisoners' family members who lived in the most affected areas and asked for their names and the cities where they lived. Using her contacts with the Maryknoll nuns down there, she plans to try and trace these people and bring news back to their loved ones in the detention center. Today we prayed hard for all the victims of the hurricane.

* * * * *

Since I started doing the handicrafts, I've gotten a lot closer to the Chinese women. We can't communicate too well because of the language barrier, but I asked Chin Chin if she would think about forming a Bible study group with the Chinese speakers, and so she did. So now in our Bible study classes, we sing in Chinese, Spanish, and English. There are 25 of us in all. I love the fact that when you go to Bible study, you give all your troubles to Jesus and then you feel much better. You find meaning in the suffering and you feel at peace in your heart no matter how difficult it is to face your problems. It's a peace only God can give you. You know your future is in good hands.

* * * * *

Jessica, the Bolivian girl, went to court and they gave her an asylum application. She doesn't have any money to pay a lawyer. She came to this country alone, got into trouble, was put in jail, and then transferred to immigration detention. She asked for my help in presenting her case to the judge.

Hers is a story of a young girl full of life who lived with her mother, siblings, and stepfather. But as she grew up and became a young lady, her stepfather looked at her differently and began to harass her sexually. Her mother didn't support her and it ended with her running away from home. She went to live with her grandmother, but her stepfather stalked her there too and his obsession never left her in peace. She left her grandmother's home and, at the age of 15, went to Brazil to start a new life. Her immaturity and lack of guidance led her to make mistakes and she returned to Bolivia pregnant.

She lived at her grandmother's and gave birth to the baby. This time her stepfather's harassment was even worse. He didn't respect her at all and in a heated argument when he tried to force himself on her, Jessica took a gun and shot him in the leg. Her life had been torture since then. Her stepfather didn't bring charges against her but she decided to leave the country anyway. She left her daughter and she came to this country in search of a better future.

We filled out the asylum form. She wrote to her grandmother asking her to send the evidence she needed. When she went to court, the judge granted her bail so that she could be free while presenting her case. We were all really happy for her. She was barely 18 years old, very pretty, and had a great figure. She had suffered so much since she was little girl. But now came the hardest part. Bail was set at $3000. How could she get that much together? She said her mother had a business and some money. She wrote to her asking her help.

* * * * *

It's October and I'm still here. Things haven't changed much. Lots of people have come and gone but some of us are starting to feel like permanent inventory, like Mar and Laz (whose nickname is Cubita), who have no chance of release. They both have criminal records and Cuba doesn't want them back. They are both in very difficult circumstances. They came from prison where they'd been for many years, and here they have no chance to see freedom.

May, the Jamaican woman, has been in this place for four years. Her problem is complicated because she had a sex change and now she's a woman and there's no record of her in her country. It seems so unfair to me that she should be in this place for so long. She gets a lot of abuse because some of the women mistreat her and say offensive things. They say she should be in the men's prison, that she'll never be a real woman, and so on. They call her *culero, culo roto, marica* and other vulgar things. I've gotten a lot closer to her because she's a very wounded person and she's always on the defensive because she's been the victim of discrimination and rejection so often. But she is a beautiful person and I admire her for her courage. She is the man I was supposed to be careful of when I got here. But that was all wrong! She's really an excellent person.

There's also a Chinese woman who's been waiting a year to get her political asylum and an Ethiopian woman who's in the same boat. Whether or not you have a criminal record doesn't seem to matter, your wait is the same. That seems really strange and it depresses me. I've known people with serious criminal records who the judge lets out with a low bail, like $1500, or even lets them go on their own recognizance. But they want Jessica to pay $3000, and sometimes they set bail up to $5000 even if people don't have criminal records. What criteria the judge uses is a total mystery to me.

We heard on TV there won't be any deportations to Central America due to the crisis caused by Hurricane Mitch. Everyone's really glad and we hope that means some of us will be released.

*   *   *   *   *

We're planning a party for Halloween but we need permission so we can have sodas and potato chips or *nachos*. We'd have it from 7 to 10 p.m. We asked permission of the officer in charge in the afternoon and she said yes, but that she needed to speak to her supervisor. It's looking like we'll be able to have our little party.

The afternoon shift is special; they're strict but they treat you with respect, like you're human. When you have a problem, they try to help you in any way they can. They always have a smile for you. The atmosphere in the afternoon is a lot calmer. At night, the atmosphere is one of fear. Those guards yell and treat you like you're in a concentration camp. They won't help you solve a problem. The morning shift isn't too bad except for two of them who make your life miserable. They want complete silence and are always too busy to help you.

* * * * *

The problem of overcrowding is getting worse and worse. Lots of people have been detained and, with deportations to Central America suspended, everyone is really squeezed for space and unhappy about it. A hunger strike is being organized.

The cause seems just to me. They want the Central American women whose cases have already been decided and who have deportation orders against them to be deported. Why continue to hold them? They want to go back to their countries to be with their families at this time after the hurricane. It would be better to send them back because the anguish they're feeling not knowing about their families makes them very temperamental and they blow up over nothing. I understand the men are organizing a hunger strike too. Someone's calling from the outside giving us instructions.

They've asked me to be part of the group but I don't want to be because the organizers are troublemakers and I'm afraid there will be violence. Besides, I lose weight easily and I'm already too thin so I can't afford to lose another pound. But I said I could be part of an advisory team. They don't agree on who should be the leader. Everyone's afraid to step forward, but finally they pick a Mexican woman.

Almost everyone in the dormitory has signed up to participate. Lots of the women come to ask my advice and ask whether I'm going to participate. I just tell them that if they're going to be part of the strike, they need to be responsible and really commit to not eating in order to strengthen the whole group. Of course, it seems like there's an informant in the group because the guards know all about the plans. The strike is going to begin in two days. The organizers are preparing statements to the INS authorities, addressed to G.K., the officer in charge of this detention center.

* * * * *

The hunger strike started this morning. Thirty people didn't get up to go to breakfast. The guards went to wake them and ask them to get up but they received no answer. At lunch, it was 20, and the same at dinner. A press release explaining the hunger strike was sent to the newspaper, *La Opinión*, and I think somebody called the TV Channel KMX.

On the second day of the strike, the guards said that if they didn't eat, they'd be taken to the hospital and be put on IV. They took down the strikers names. That made some of the women quit the strike because they feared INS would retaliate. At noon, it was down to about 15, and around 3 o'clock some immigration officers arrived asking who the leader was. There was total silence. The appointed leader was too afraid to make the demands. Finally, the officer said that the strikers had half an hour to let them know who would represent the group in a meeting with G.K.

They chose a Panamanian named Eloy. She was 56 years old. She liked for people to think she was a major drug dealer. She was street smart and expressed herself well. She wasn't feeling very well because she suffered from asthma and the chemicals used to clean the floor irritated her lungs. But she had the qualities of a leader. She went to the meeting with G.K. and came back an hour later. She had turned in the sheet of paper with the list of demands which were:

1. Immediate deportation for the Central American women with deportation orders.
2. An accelerated process for the rest of the women with deportation orders.
3. Better food.
4. Less waiting time for court appearances in front of a judge.
5. Improved medical attention.

When Eloy got back from her meeting, she said that Mrs. G.K. had been very nice and had promised to study the list of demands.

The strike continued but with fewer women participating. At about 5 p.m., the dietician in charge of the food at the center came and asked what we'd like to eat. That caused quite a stir. No one had ever come to ask us about what we'd like to eat! The next day Eloy met again with the authorities and came back with a warning that if the strike continued, they would suspend the deportation of the group that was targeted to leave that week. So the strike ended. It had lasted only two days. The next week, two of our friends left, one from Guatemala and one from El Salvador. There was great disappointment. It wasn't what we'd expected. There were 15 women with deportation orders who wanted to go back to their countries and all of them thought they'd be given the chance.

A month after the two left, we received a letter in which they told us they'd been put on a military plane, handcuffed to the seats together with several men, and guarded by police who told them not to move. They were taken to a jail in El Paso, Texas where they were given neither good food nor clean clothing. They were kept there for two weeks before they were sent back to their own countries.

* * * * *

One day, Jessica went to the library where she met a young, male officer who was on duty there. They started exchanging notes and Jessica came back all excited. She kept going back to continue with her flirting. Her mother hadn't sent the money for her bail and she was afraid she'd lose the chance to get it. So without thinking twice, she asked the officer to help her. She was very discreet about it because it's not allowed. But nothing's impossible for love, as the saying goes! At night, the nurse who brought people their medicine slipped Jessica his letters and the guard on duty never knew anything about it.

Some of the women were jealous and, of course, they didn't miss a chance to gossip about it. That made it more difficult to communicate with him, but eventually she got what she wanted and he promised to get her out of this place by paying her bail. That's exactly what he did, and some months later, the two were married.

* * * * *

Time goes on. It's already November and more and more people are arriving. There are people sleeping in the dayroom on mattresses on the floor between the bunk beds. I've counted 125 people though there is only capacity for 70. Immigration is conducting raids on workplaces and lots of people say they were picked up at their jobs.

Another group has arrived from prison. They are gang members – Central Americans unfortunately – young people with a future who have chosen the wrong path. Yesterday they attacked a rival because she looked at them wrong. They kicked her when she was lying down without giving her a chance to defend herself. I don't understand their mentality. I think the overcrowding contributes to it. The atmosphere is unbearable.

Everyone who comes from jail or prison says that this place is the worst. At the other places, they are allowed to wear their own clothes and use make-up. They have programs to keep them occupied, even outdoor sports in the fresh air. When they have visitors, they can hug them and the visit lasts for hours. They can take a class to learn something. But here, we're locked inside four walls with no room to move in, no privacy, lots of restrictions, and visits that last only 15 minutes.

* * * * *

A Colombian woman with a group that arrived yesterday snuck in some make-up; just an eyebrow pencil and a lipstick, really. The officers figured it out when they saw some of the women wearing make-up. They made all of us go into the dayroom. They started to search our beds looking for the darn things and when they didn't find anything, they told us they were going to make us undress unless it appeared.

There was some resentment and anger towards those who were wearing make-up since it's not fair that we should all have to pay for a troublesome few. All this took about an hour. Finally they took away the ones with make-up on to search them. Several people had an exchange of words over this situation.

I still don't understand why it's a problem to wear make-up. I think they want to make us feel like we don't have a right to anything. It's depressing to see your face in that thing that passes for a mirror. You want to look a little better so you can feel better. I understand that. Personally, I avoid looking in the mirror because it depresses me to see myself looking so much older in just a few months – so haggard, with pronounced dark circles under my eyes, and such dry skin. It's just really unpleasant.

When the group came back after the search, the Columbian woman, whose pencil and lipstick it was, said she was going to file a claim. She said they had stripped them and lined them up, and that an INS officer had put on a glove and searched each one's vagina and anus, but that she had never changed her glove! There was an uproar. She sued them and reported it to Washington. Everybody was criticizing the police because it was a violation of their rights, a humiliating act, and a threat to their health. I agree. But we know the rules of the game here, so sometimes I wonder why we break them. We know very well we'll have to face some kind of consequence and that the guards here don't think twice about getting abusive.

* * * * *

Thanksgiving Day arrived. At noon they served us an excellent meal: quail, mashed potatoes, lots of salad – a real banquet. As I prayed before eating, I couldn't stop the tears. I was about to enjoy a wonderful meal and who knows how my children were spending Thanksgiving? Probably not too well. And here I was with my friends laughing and remembering better times, but. . . them? Were they filled with anxiety over looking for a place to live? They'd be alone, without turkey to eat, but even more importantly, without the loving presence of their family.

I felt sad the rest of the day. In spite of it all, I gave thanks to God for all that He's given me, especially for His love and the courage not to give up and to go forward trusting that I would soon be reunited with my children. We would be a family again, and I would take care of them, and give them guidance like I'd always done before to bring back their happiness.

Christmas in Pod Six

More than at any other time, today I feel like I'm sinking into the mud and my life is miserable. I've been uncomfortable with the presence of lesbians here, and the problem has gotten worse. I can't stand to see them kissing or on top of each other at night. Each person is free to live their life as they see fit, but this isn't the place for such behavior. My friends from Sri Lanka, India and China are the most affected. Their culture doesn't permit it, and they could be killed for that kind thing.

I have friends here who are lesbians, and because I trust and care for them, I explained that they have to respect the rest of us. I told them they can do their things discreetly when everyone's asleep but not to do it so openly. No matter what though, they get into trouble because someone always tells the guards and they penalize them.

Thank God, I talked with Fr. Robert and told him everything that was happening and how I felt about it. With his words of wisdom and with great peace, he asked me to remember that these women were daughters of God too, and to pray hard for them so that they could find the way. His words helped me a lot to not feel such anger and repulsion.

I'm also greatly affected by the belligerent atmosphere you breathe in around here. All you hear are people exchanging obscenities and threats, and every little while, a new quarrel breaks out. And since there's nothing to do here and the space is so small, people actually get excited about seeing a fight. They seem to enjoy the violence. It's so difficult not to get caught up in it.

I'm much more vulnerable to anger and to seeing only the negative in this place. But I'm aware that if I continue this way, I'll become just like the group that I detest. They rob you of any peace of mind. I'm not going to let that happen to me. That would be the worst! I have to work hard every minute to persevere and remember the principles my mother worked so hard to instill in me.

* * * * *

It's the beginning of December. I'll be spending Christmas here so I decided to organize a short play about the birth of Jesus. The first thing was to write the script. I consulted with Chin Chin and we agreed that she should write it and that we would both make corrections to it. I planned the program, including songs and a time for testimonies, so that everyone could participate.

It was hard to get actors. In the circumstances we live in, everyone is apathetic. They don't understand that we can celebrate Christmas – that there's a place in our hearts to live, laugh, and remember wonderful moments like the birth of Jesus. Despite the negativism, we were able to get 15 people. The Chinese girls were the angels because they don't speak English. The Hispanic women were the shepherds since they're too shy to say a word. And of course, we had to have the Three Kings, and Mary and Joseph.

We rehearsed everyday with lots of enthusiasm, and, as an extra blessing, the Sisters of Mother Teresa's congregation visited us and showed their support by loaning us clothing for a wardrobe. They also brought colored pencils and Christmas pictures so we could decorate the dayroom wall and give the place a Christmas atmosphere. The sisters left and we devised a way to stick things to the wall using toothpaste and the dayroom ended up decorated very nicely. We felt like we were in a different place. But just as we finished decorating, the officer came and told us to take it all down because we weren't allowed to do that.

All of us were in a horrible mood. Why should such a little thing bother them? But, of course, the point to a place like this is to make life impossible any way they can. So what could we do? We had to take all the decorations down. But we decided to put them up again around our beds because we wanted to have a Christmas.

This month is very tense. There are lots of tears and quarrels. Most of the Central Americans who've already received deportation orders are still here. It's very hard.

* * * * *

Father Robert comes to visit us, as always. Another priest is coming also, a Father Peter. He speaks perfect Spanish and his masses are just like the ones in our little towns in El Salvador. He uses simple words and we all like how he says the mass because he explains the meaning of all the parts of the mass. He often talks about how Christians used to go to church just to receive, but that it's now time to give. We have to collaborate with the Church. There is a lot of need and we cannot be indifferent to the needs of others. Even in this place we can do good works, he says.

Unfortunately not everyone likes the idea and there are those who insist on charging for any small amount of help they give. Some people ask for rosaries and then sell them later for a dollar. They sell everything they can, including medicines.

* * * * *

This week, the volunteers brought us Christmas cards so we can send them to our families and friends. On the average they gave each of us six. Since the Chinese girls are Buddhists, they don't really care about cards because they don't celebrate Christmas. So my dear Cubans took possession of almost all the cards and started to sell them.

I was really angry so I started to give my cards away, and that motivated others to give theirs away when someone needed one. This didn't make the businesswomen any too happy so when I wasn't paying attention, they stole my cards so I couldn't give them away anymore. This incident caused a quarrel in the dormitory and somebody told the officers what had happened. When we went out for recreation, they did a thorough search and confiscated all the Christmas cards so we'd learn our lesson.

* * * * *

On December 17, I'll have been married 23 years. I can't believe it. It feels like a long time but when I look back, I see that the time has flown. It's gone by so fast. I've shared so much with Gil – triumphs, failures, happiness, sadness, and disillusions. . . In the end, I think we've had a true marriage, full of every kind of thing, and in spite of the boring and bad times, we're together. We've managed to stay together as long as God has permitted. In my case, I believe our marriage has survived because we've both accepted that we're not perfect. We recognize our faults and we know that living together means accepting the good and the bad in your partner, even as you try to improve.

One afternoon, an officer told me to prepare for confession. At that moment, I thought, "Confession? I didn't sign up for Confession. But that's okay because I'll get to see Fr. Robert and get a chance to talk to him for awhile." I got ready and soon they called me. When I got to the small room, I saw Father Robert and Gil waiting for me.

Father explained that he'd asked immigration if he could have some time to do marriage counseling with us. He asked us to renew the vows we'd taken at the altar on our wedding day. It was a very emotional time for both of us. I felt the time was too short but it was wonderful, that despite all the suffering, we shared an unbreakable spirit to persevere as family.

I can imagine how difficult it must have been for Father Robert to arrange this time for us to be together. He had to prove we were legally married, and I don't know how many other hoops he had to jump through or signatures he had to get. It was so valuable for us . . . we healed many wounds, and most of all, we forgave each other.

* * * * *

The play is ready. We're going to present it three times. During Christmas week on Wednesday, we're going to do it for the Protestant missionaries who visit us, Reverend Ron, Alice and Donald. On Saturday, we'll do it for the Chinese Protestant missionaries who always come, especially for Albert. Albert never misses a Saturday with his guitar. He delights us with his music, and we have a wonderful religious service of praise with him. The presentation on Sunday will be for the Catholics, starting with Father Robert, Sister Molly, Father Peter, Father John, Vicente and Josefina, Kent, and the sisters of Mother Teresa's congregation. That day we'll have a visit from someone important like Bishop Torres who will say mass for us.

We were feeling very emotional. We didn't have anything to give these wonderful people for Christmas and they'd all been so splendid to us, so caring and understanding, always giving us encouragement and advice, always bringing us happiness and hope in this place. They had been the only good thing in our lives in here. We wanted to tell them how much we appreciated their work.

* * * * *

Everything turned out wonderfully. It made us happy, very happy, to see our dear friends sitting there – listening, laughing, singing, enjoying themselves, and feeling loved by us. Some of them had tears in their eyes, especially the most emotional ones like Reverend Ron and Alice. They knew we'd put it together with a lot of love.

All of us who participated agreed that it was like when we were in school and we had put on little plays in honor of our mothers or fathers. For a little while it didn't feel like we were in jail. Of course, some of the women had never gone to school and this was their first experience doing something like this. But, they felt just as happy as we did. I personally felt very moved that we had finally gotten all the different races together, without rivalries, resentments, or prejudice.

We all had only one goal – to pay our respects to those who deserved it and show in some small way our gratitude for their work and the way they give themselves to the immigrants, accompanying us in this Calvary. Here, we live the Passion of Christ, and they play the part of Veronica and the man of Cyrene, trying to lessen our suffering. The play was something extraordinary for some of the Chinese girls, since they had been raised as Buddhists, and had converted to Christianity in here. They were celebrating Jesus' birth for the first time in their lives. When one of them, Hong Chi Chi, gave her testimony, she spoke with tears in her eyes and said even if she was deported, she'd always be grateful to this country because it was here that she met Jesus Christ.

* * * * *

Christmas Eve arrived. We organized a gift exchange but almost no one took part. Many of the women didn't stay up past midnight to give each other a hug; most stayed in bed thinking about their families and crying. My children had come to see me earlier that day. It was a short visit. I asked them if they had anything planned, but they said no. There wasn't a lot to talk about and, on this occasion, we were all sad.

That's how it was during the last week of the year. The days seemed longer than normal. There were no court dates because the judges were all on vacation. A lot of people were detained but no one was released and so the overcrowding was unbearable. There are still about 125 people in this tiny space. It's very noisy and the television is on 24 hours a day. It's harder to feel peaceful, but there isn't any thing to do but persevere, show lots of patience, and most of all tolerance.

Beginning Y2K

The new year has begun. By my calculation, it should take six months to get the court's decision on our appeal. So I'm thinking there's only two months left before I get out of here. It helps me to bear the atmosphere in here to think how little time is left.

One night, at about 2 a.m., there was smoke in the dormitory. "Fire! Fire!" people screamed. I got up and followed the rest who ran panic-stricken to the dayroom. I didn't understand what had happened. I was very cold and half asleep. I sleep very soundly, thank God. At that moment, INS and security officers arrived. The officer wanted to know who had set fire to some magazine covers that had been put up on the wall. She asked if we didn't know that the building could catch on fire and we'd burn to death because the door wasn't going to be opened.

Most of us had no idea what she was talking about because we had been sound asleep at that hour. But there are always some night owls. They had to know. Twenty minutes went by. I was cold and sleepy and just wanted to go back to bed. The officer was screaming at everyone trying to find out who did it.

Finally, they took Zad, an Ethiopian girl, a troublemaker, one of the ones who was always in fights. She has mental problems and they're always giving her medicine to calm her down. It affected all of us to just imagine the tragedy that might have happened. It was almost 4 a.m. when they let us go back to bed.

The next day we found out the whole story. Zad had gone to the doctor and had stolen a lighter. She brought it back to the dormitory without any of the guards noticing. She stayed up very late. It seems she didn't take her medicine to help her sleep, and through some carelessness, she set fire to some magazines that were next to a pillar in the dormitory. Fortunately, somebody realized the magazines were on fire and sounded the alarm. After this incident, they wouldn't let us have magazines in the dormitory, or even the newspaper, *Vida Nueva,* with news about the Church. They conducted a search the next day and confiscated all the books and magazines we had, except our Bibles. We had quite a scare.

Talking with Zad, she told me she was upset at INS because she'd spent six months in a detention jail in Phoenix, Arizona and she'd already spent another eight months here. They don't deport her and they don't tell her anything about her situation. They want to deport her without her daughter, and she wants to take her with her. Unfortunately, Zad isn't mentally capable of taking care of her, and she doesn't want to accept that.

* * * * *

Every day that goes by I feel I'm growing weaker. I feel a great burden. On the one hand, there's the problem of my children. They are definitely going to separate. Diana got a job in a valet parking and an apartment with her boyfriend. The two younger kids aren't going to go with her. A woman has offered them food and lodging if they do child care for her two children, a little girl 7 years old, and a boy 5 years old. The woman lives three blocks from the school my children go to. She's a single mother who one of Amy's best friends knows, so I supported the idea since I didn't have any other alternative. But inside it pained me so to see this split between them. The only condition I imposed on them was that they be in contact with each other and that Diana continue to bring them to visit. And of course, I emphasized they needed to support each other.

Being a leader, I had to give the example of strength, faith, patience, hope, and all the other things I told my companions about when I'd see them struggling with problems like mine. I had to preach by example; that took double effort. Sometimes I pretended that everything was fine when, in reality, I felt like I was breaking in pieces.

Thank God, I always got books, prayers, and precious letters from my family in El Salvador (sisters and brothers-in-law) that brought tears to my eyes because they made me feel so loved. I felt like I had all of them behind me, giving me encouragement, working hard for us, knocking on doors, and doing everything possible to get all the evidence needed to get us out of here.

Still, I felt myself getting more troubled and upset in these surroundings. I was tired and fed up with seeing so much injustice, so much pain, so much wickedness, so much degenerate behavior and violence. I felt very conflicted inside. Ten months had gone by and I'd used all the "tools in my toolbox" to try to see some good in this place. I had found meaning in my time in jail by helping the most vulnerable. I'd acted as counselor, confidant, lawyer, and minister. But I now felt like I was swimming upstream and didn't have the strength to go on.

I started to play cards. I learned how to play Spades and loved it. I spent hours playing with Chin Chin, Blondie, and May. We were the veterans in this place. We had a good time playing and felt disconnected from our surroundings. We imagined ourselves playing in a casino in Las Vegas, betting, and having a grand old time!

This new routine in my daily business had people talking. How awful! Mother Teresa playing cards! I didn't see anything wrong with what I was doing, but not everybody agreed. Still, after a few days, my friends realized that I was still the same person and that when they needed me, I would stop playing to be with them. And of course, we always had our Bible study.

* * * * *

It's February and I haven't been able to get an appointment with the dentist. My gums are bleeding a lot since they don't let us use dental floss. My molar hurts, and I don't know if I have a cavity or what. My cellmates say that when they take you to the dentist, the officers are very considerate, and even give you a cigarette. I was dying to go and finally got permission.

I hoped that when it was my turn, one of the Cubans would go to because they're lots of fun, and they talk to the officers informally as if they were old buddies. That's exactly what happened. I went with Cubita (we called her that affectionately because she was the shortest) and Pachi. They took us in a minibus. Cubita asked the officers for a cigarette and they gave one to each of us. I smoked it slowly while we talked and laughed on the bus.

It was the first time I had seen the outside world in ten months and everything looked so beautiful. I enjoyed seeing the flowers and trees and the beautiful view. It was fairly early, around 8:30 a.m., and I loved seeing the people walking to their jobs. I'd never taken so much pleasure in all the beauty. We drove by a fast food restaurant and Oh! the aroma! How I longed to live in freedom!

We arrived at the dentist's office and they saw us right away. They took an x-ray of my mouth and got ready to pull my molar. When I saw this, I told the doctor I wouldn't allow them to pull my tooth because the x-ray didn't show any decay. So begrudgingly, they cleaned my tooth. They also gave me a note that said I needed a complete dental cleaning. My two friends each had a tooth pulled.

Cubita was still joking and in her characteristic good humor on the way back, but Pachi was crying. She'd never had a tooth pulled and she was barely 28 years old. I asked her why she hadn't asked them to put in a filling, and she told me there isn't any money for fillings; the only thing they do is pull teeth because that's the cheapest thing to do. Most of the time, the pain is so awful that you prefer to lose the tooth, even though a simple filling would take care of the problem.

On the way back, I think the officers took a different route because we got to see the ocean and breathe the ocean air. It was a wonderful trip. When we got back, they searched us thoroughly to make sure we didn't bring in any dangerous items like Zad had.

* * * * *

But going to the doctor is not always a good experience. I remember one woman we called Jamaica (because that's where she was from.) She was really happy because they'd given her permission to buy glasses. She'd been in detention for a year and hadn't ever had an eye exam even though she had trouble reading because of her vision. After she asked and asked, they finally authorized a visit to the optometrist.

The day of her appointment she fixed herself up the best she could. She paid another woman $5.00 to braid her kinky hair, and she put some vaseline on her lips to look a little nicer. She was dying to smoke a cigarette. But to her surprise, they put her in a minivan with chains on her feet and hands and around her waist. She was escorted by two INS officials. That's the way she had to walk to the doctor's office, which was located in the middle of a shopping center. She said that everyone was looking at her in horror, and that she felt so bad that she just looked at the floor the whole way. It was a terrible humiliation, and when she got back, she just cried her eyes out, complaining, and cursing the men from the *migra* who had taken her there.

* * * * *

I asked to see the doctor again. I told him I needed to go back to the dentist, and I also said I wanted an appointment with a gynecologist since it had been a year since I'd had a pap smear. The doctor wasn't too happy about all this and said to me, "Why don't you ask to be deported so INS won't have to keep spending money on you?" I had to bite my tongue to not answer back. I just reminded him I had a right to preventative medicine and asked him to do his job and authorize both appointments.

I took advantage of the opportunity to write to Gil and ask him that he also ask for a medical exam. He looked so thin and run down. But Gil had no interest in doing that. He told me he'd also gone to the dentist and that they'd pulled two of his molars. He'd broken a crown, and when he knew for sure they wouldn't replace it, he chose to have them pull the teeth rather than put up with the horrible pain.

* * * * *

Twelve months have passed and I'm still in this place. Hundreds of women have gone through here and very few have stayed in this country. The majority have been deported. I'm feeling like I can't stand it anymore. Besides the frustration and the pain of being in this place, there are disputes between the gang members. This atmosphere is making me sick. I'm fed up with all the fighting and I've decided to intervene in the next fight.

It's always the same people – Mina and Rosa, two young Salvadoran girls, gang members who were best friends at first, but have become mortal enemies in the last few months. The other day they exchanged threats. The atmosphere is very tense. These girls don't leave us in peace. They make a lot of noise while we're having Bible study, and make fun of us for studying the Bible. They are causing lots of problems. It's so bad that I've asked to be taken to solitary confinement. I wouldn't care as long as I could listen to silence for a little while. I'm so sick and tired of the atmosphere. I feel like I can't do it anymore.

Chin Chin feels the same and has also asked to be taken to solitary confinement. We've brought it up to several of the officers but they just find it funny. Finally, Officer Willy called a captain in INS and he agreed to talk to us. The truth is that both of us are leaders, Chin Chin is a leader of the Chinese women who make up 30% of the prisoners, and I'm a leader of the Hispanic women who comprise 50%. So we were brought to a meeting with the big boss. He acted very nice but, in few words, he told us he would not put us in solitary confinement. He said the place was horrible and that it's where the most troublesome and violent criminals are, and the mentally ill. All day long, you hear lots of yelling, bad words, cursing at Immigration, and people crying. He thought that it would be more damaging to us.

I asked the director why they didn't do something about the prisoners they knew were the troublemakers. I told him that the atmosphere in our pod was getting tenser every day, and that we all paid for the actions of a small group of troublemakers. If they didn't do something to improve the situation in the women's dormitory, the same thing was going to happen that had happened in the men's dormitory where a man had died after being attacked by another prisoner. The officers there had been aware of a serious problem of hatred between the men, but they had done nothing to prevent the death. The director didn't answer us. He just left and we were taken back to the dormitory.

* * * * *

Things didn't change. I was really afraid there might be another fight, and that's what happened. Mina attacked Rosa when she was resting in bed. Immediately, the other women formed a circle around them. They were enjoying watching the two women going at it on the floor. Without even thinking, I ran and grabbed Mina by the hair and hauled her off with all my strength as if she was a sack of potatoes. I don't know who took care of Rosa but we separated them. The officers came running quickly and took them away. Mina's face was bleeding where Rosa had succeeded in sinking her nails into it. I felt great. I had released all my frustration and anger by dragging Mina away by her hair. But a moment later, a Philippine woman said to me, "Shame on you, Mother Teresa. How could you? It should have been anyone else but you!" "This has got to stop," I answered. "I can't take it anymore. This place used to be somewhat peaceful but it's turned into a living hell. I can't do it anymore. I won't let this go on."

I went and lay down on my bed and cried. I felt bad for having let my impulses get the better of me, but what was done was done. The fighters spent three days in solitary confinement. Rosa was then transferred to another jail to see if that would help to improve things.

When Mina returned, she started asking who had pulled her off by the hair, and they told her it was me. So the second day after her return, while I was in the dayroom making my handicrafts surrounded by others who wanted to learn or who just wanted to chat, she sat down at the table directly in front of me and said, "Who was the idiot who pulled me by my hair?" I immediately answered her, "It was me, and I'll do it again if you fight again." She got up with a threatening stance, and immediately there were about eight people around me, protecting me. Oh, my God! What a scare! The officer on duty got Mina out immediately, called a supervisor, and they took her away. We never saw her again. She was moved to another jail to avoid more problems in the future. The atmosphere in the pod changed immediately, and everything returned to normal.

* * * * *

The religious volunteers always come so faithfully. We are treated like kings. What great love, dear God! We'll never be able to repay everything that they do for us. I don't think they realize how important their work is, but they are the light in the darkness. If they asked me to describe them, what comes to mind is the song, *They Come Filled With Happiness:*

They come filled with happiness, Lord.
Singing, they come with happiness, Lord.
Those who go through life, dear Lord
Sowing Your peace and love.

They come bringing hope
To a world laden with anxiety.
To a world that suffers and never achieves
Your paths of love and peace.

They come bringing in their hands
The efforts of sisters and brothers in faith
The wishes for a more human world
Born of goodness and justice.

They've changed the lives of a lot of people who've been in this place. They help us see that this time is important and valuable if we use it to reflect on our own lives. In general, when we're free, the daily grind doesn't let us look at our mistakes. Instead, in here, there's lots of time to think, recognize the error of our ways, correct them, and plan our future. It's really important to take advantage of this time.

Father Robert focuses on having us think positively. Every time he comes, he says, "It's a pleasure to come visit all of you in the San Pedro Hotel. Look out the window and see how beautiful the ocean is, and think about all the people who pay thousands of dollars to have an apartment with this view. Remember, your body is in this jail, but your spirit is free."

* * * * *

We heard on the news that they've approved a law that says that it's unjust and inhumane to detain a person indefinitely for immigration problems. We are all elated to hear this. There are Cubans and Vietnamese here who cannot be deported because their governments won't take them back. Immigration doesn't know what to do with them, and in the meantime, they're rotting in immigration jails.

Cubita and Mar will benefit from this law, thank God, since Mar is getting sicker and sicker. She coughs a lot and she almost stops breathing when she sleeps because she has so much phlegm. We can hardly get any sleep. She doesn't get sufficient medical attention for someone with HIV. She's losing weight. In the clinic, they don't pay attention to her symptoms because they say they're normal. The last time she went to the doctor, she told him she was bleeding from one of her breasts, and the doctor told her not to forget that she had AIDS. She came back really down and crying.

A Mother's Sorrow

My children are "fine." They never miss a visiting day. Amy will graduate in June. It hurts me to think I can't be with her, much less help her with all the preparations and enjoy all the excitement of her accomplishments. She is graduating with honors! The two youngest are still living with the lady with the two kids in exchange for taking care of them. It hurts me that they have to go through such a rough time.

My sister-in-law, Tita, wants me to send them to Miami where she could take care of them. They'd go to school and have a family. But in reality, I don't think it's advantageous for them because they are doing very well in school here. It's true they're having to go through lots of difficulties and constraints, but they have their parents close by and the bonds of love between us are so strong that the simple the act of seeing each other gives us the encouragement to go forward.

Plus, I've always told them that when the ship is sinking, the rats are the first ones to jump, and that love is tested in times like these. Of course, if I saw them in any danger, I wouldn't hesitate to send them to their aunt but for the moment they were all right.

* * * * *

It's the month of May and Mother's Day. It's a sad month. For the second year in a row, I'll spend it separated from the ones I love most in the world. I'm very lucky because I have my children. Some of my friends are suffering terribly because they're about to lose their kids for good or they already have lost them. The most painful cases are the ones where the judge orders the mother deported and the children have to face one of several different situations:

1. They stay with their father. In the majority of those cases, the father has to work and the children aren't well taken care of and don't get adequate nutrition. Their father can barely handle the situation.
2. They stay with a family member. This is the best option, but there's always pain and anguish about whether the kids will be treated well and whether the family is on a solid enough economic ground to keep and take care of them. Often they often have to ask for government assistance.
3. The children get put in a foster home. The jailed mother can't be present at the hearing in juvenile court to fight for custody of her children because immigration won't let her attend. When the woman fails to appear, she loses her rights as a mother.

This last case is the most painful since lots of times the children are put up for adoption. If a mother fails to appear in court for her children, she can't prove she can take care of them. The suffering and frustration having to do with children surpasses all boundaries. It's frightening! Horrible!

I witnessed the suffering of a Philippine woman who was given a lifetime deportation order back to her home country. She had two children: one six-year-old boy, and a three-year-old girl. She knew she was never going to see them again in her life. She got a letter saying they were being given up for adoption because she was a single mother. It was a huge blow to her. There was nothing we could say to console her.

Dor, my friend from Guatemala who saved me from being the butt of the Cuban women's joke when I first arrived, had better luck. She'd been ordered deported but her four-year-old son who under her husband's care. He was a taxi driver and took the kid with him while he worked because he didn't have anyone to watch him. Dor asked her husband to bring the little boy to see her for the last time, since up to then they'd only been in contact by phone.

They came to visit her and when she came back to the dormitory, she was in a sea of tears. She said her little boy was very thin, and looked pale and unkempt. She couldn't really blame her husband since he was doing everything possible to take care of the boy.

Dor's deportation day arrived. She left the jail with $400 on her to start a new life in Guatemala. But to our surprise, the next day they brought her back. She told us she refused to get on the plane knowing that she was leaving her son behind. She started screaming and crying hysterically, begging the immigration officer to have pity on her. She wanted them to let her take her son with her. Under those circumstances, the airline wouldn't let her board and so she was brought back. Dor succeeded in taking her son with her, but she had to pay for his ticket, so she went back to Guatemala without a penny to her name.

And there were many more like Dor. Mima had to leave her 13-year-old daughter with a woman she didn't even know. The daughter did chores around the house in exchange for some food and a piece of a mattress to sleep on.

* * * * *

It's incredible that these children – United States citizens – have to suffer all this. At the root of this is the Illegal Immigration Reform and Immigrant Responsibility Act of 1996 (IIRIRA), a law that made it much harder for undocumented people and non-citizens to avoid deportation, especially if they have ever had any run-in with the law. Even if the infraction or crime was committed years ago, they can be deported. That's the reason why people keep filling this place and why so many people – even American citizens – are seeing their families torn apart. It's horrible and cruel.

It breaks my heart as a woman and a mother to see these situations. I can just imagine the huge number of children without their mothers, some with family members, others with adopted families or foster family situations living off the "generosity" of the state. They make sure their material needs are met. But what about the emotional and psychological needs of these kids? How is this going to affect their development? Will they be angry, resentful adults because their family was broken apart? So many questions, so few answers, and so many people asking . . .

Victoria comes to mind. She was born in Perú. Her parents, American citizens, returned to the United States when she was just two months old. Now, at 38 and because of drug addiction problems, she was detained by immigration. She just found out that she is not an American citizen and will be deported to Perú, which is laughable because she's blond, blue-eyed, and doesn't speak a word of Spanish. There's not a thing Peruvian about her. She doesn't know the culture or have any family member in that country. If they order her deported, her parents will have to claim legal responsibility for her or turn her over to the state since they're old. And there are hundreds of other cases like these. They seem like they're straight out of Hollywood sometimes.

Mar, the Cuban with HIV, was released under supervision. Cubita was very sad because she expected they'd get out together. But after a week, they let her out, too, under supervision. I shared 13 months in this frightful place with them. But I'm happy knowing that Cubita has decided to change her life and fight for a better future. I'm going to miss them, especially since it's only Chin Chin, Blondie and I who are left from the original group, and some of the new people coming in seem a little strange.

* * * * *

This week they sent me to the doctor. It seemed odd since I hadn't asked for a visit recently. They did a physical and tested me for tuberculosis. They also told me that the following week, I'd finally get to go to the gynecologist. Everything seemed fine until the following day when I saw a red spot where they'd done the TB test. Oh God! This was like being shot in the back. The test was positive.

I felt so angry right away. How did this happen? I'm 45 and I've never been in contact with the disease. They took an x-ray to see if the TB was active or if I just had the bacillus in my lungs. Fortunately, it hadn't developed into the disease.

I asked if there was treatment for it and was told yes, but that because of my age, they couldn't give it to me because it causes severe liver damage. That was it. Period. I felt so helpless, so powerless to change the situation.

I remembered back to a few months ago when they had brought in a young Chinese girl wearing a mask. We always wondered why she wore it. Most of the time she took it off but when she went to the doctor, they made her put it on. Then I looked around and noticed lots of the women coughing, looking pale and sick. But since they only give you Tylenol in here, you get used to living in these conditions. I was so hurt, so wounded.

How many times had I seen other cellmates with that horrible red mark on their arm, and it never crossed my mind that they could be infected? I never saw them get any treatment.

The lack of medical attention is a huge problem. A few months back, a Mexican woman came who'd been operated on for stomach cancer. For some reason I don't understand, a hole had appeared at the site of her wound that oozed pus. She just lay there in pain. The doctor said it was nothing, told her to take some Tylenol, and wait for her court date because she was going to be deported.

One night they told me she was crying, and without hesitation, I went to her to see if I could help. She explained she was afraid she'd die far away from her children if they deported her. Her court date was the next day. She didn't have a lawyer, she came from prison, and her deportation was imminent.

I felt helpless. What message of hope could I possibly give her? We prayed, cried, and in the end, I suggested she write the judge and ask for an opportunity. She did it, figuring she had nothing to lose. She asked me to write the letter because she didn't speak English. I wrote a short letter only four lines long asking the judge for the opportunity to let her live her last days along side of her children. The next day, she went to court and the judge set her free. It was a miracle!

* * * * *

Eternal Father, how can there be so much cruelty in these people, so much wickedness? How is it possible that they can do so much physical and spiritual harm to a person? They treat us as if we were undesirable, miserable beings. We feel abandoned and forgotten. A criminal in prison gets better attention than we do. What's our crime? Is it to be undocumented or to be a legal resident that already served time for some previous mistake?

I ask myself if the American public knows what's going on in these jails? Do they know that families are being torn apart and that a new generation of American citizens are being left without a father or mother? Those kids are potential candidates for delinquency because they feel no gratitude to their country or government. That's the way the guerilla war began in El Salvador, when people saw the government's unjust actions and disrespect for human rights.

* * * * *

I talked with my lawyer to let her know what was happening with my TB test. Sadly, she couldn't do anything since the disease hadn't developed. I had to resign myself again to being here and keep on going. My kids were worried about my health. They learned everything they could about the disease.

I wrote to Gil telling him what had happened to me and asking him what the result of his test was. He said they hadn't done a physical on him. I asked him to please request one, and to ask for his medical records since it's impossible to know with these people what the truth is. I requested my records to see the written report of my x-ray, in order to assure myself that I really didn't have tuberculosis.

Finally, they took me to see the gynecologist. Everything was fine but he recommended a mammogram. I asked him when they might do it. He just smiled and said, "The best thing to do is request a deportation so you can go see your own doctor." That was all I needed to hear to know that they'd never do a mammogram on me.

A Painful Victory

It's already June. I feel a need to train someone else to be able to take over the Bible study. My children tell me one of my brothers-in-law is coming from El Salvador to bring some documents to present to INS and try to get them to let us out on bond so that we can wait for the appeal results in freedom. They also tell me that Diana has finally separated from her boyfriend. The three kids are living together again now in Diana's apartment. That's good news.

Life in prison just keeps getting harder, though. Deep down, I feel I can't take it anymore. Chin Chin, my closest friend, has a girlfriend! I'm so disillusioned to see how the atmosphere in here seduces you. If you don't cling to God it is really difficult to keep going. You're tempted to do crazy stuff and throw away your moral principles because you need an escape from so much pain and uncertainty. Luckily, Chin Chin has her final court date next week. I hope that she'll be able to go home to her husband and baby.

I also got a letter from Gil. He says his TB test came out positive. They've done three x-rays on him because the x-rays don't come out right. He asked the doctor what's going on. The doctor said, "No news is good news. Don't worry."

Gil said he has everything arranged and that we're going to get out of here in a week. The news made me very happy, but after 16 months and all I've been through, I don't want to have any illusions about the date. It will just make each day seem like an eternity. I ask God to give me strength – today – more than ever, to keep on going.

* * * * *

Bible study continues but I'm not the one directing it; Ani is. In this way, I want to leave them prepared to struggle for their faith, to remember they are not alone, and that God is with them in this Calvary. We need God to give our children and family the faith and strength that we often lack.

Chin Chin was successful in getting them to set bond, so she's going in three days, thank God. I'm happy but now I really am completely alone. All my friends have now gone. Yet, every day, this place gets more and more filled up.

* * * * *

On July 26, 1999, at 5 p.m., the officer called me and told me to get ready – that I was going to get out. I felt both happy and sad. I felt a lot of pain to see that ocean of people in such desperation and frustration. Part of me would be left behind in Pod 6. In this place, I experienced God's love for me in abundance and I'm no longer the same person. My priorities have changed.

With my cellmates, my friends, I shared sorrows, joys, frustration, and strength to keep on going. But most of all, we shared love. What would have happened to me without love? I don't want to even think about it. It would have been worse than hell.

Love played a very important role in these 16 months. Out of love – my children struggled by themselves to keep on going. They showed their father and me that they loved us by getting excellent grades in school and behaving themselves the way we'd taught them to do.

Out of love, the volunteers come to visit us, and give us strength necessary to struggle for our families, for our future, for our faith. They come to show us that God loves us, by sending them as messengers of His peace, love and hope. The volunteers are the heroes of my story. They were my inspiration, the model I want to follow.

Out of love, our family in El Salvador, Guatemala, and Miami were by our side helping us, giving economic support, being in spiritual solidarity with our suffering, and sending us their love in letters and books on spiritual growth.

Because of love, I was able to survive this hell. I survived because of the love I had for God, for my husband, my children, my family and my cellmates. In the most difficult moments, they, like me, let themselves be loved, consoled, and counseled. They gave meaning to my suffering.

* * * * *

After 16 months, I was able to take Gil's hand and walk with him toward the exit. There were no embraces and no words. An officer was with us and warned us she didn't want any hugging or kissing or anything. But I could feel his hand squeezing mine. When we got to the hall door, I saw Amy run towards us just like she used to do when she was little, saying "Papi! . . . Mami!"

I hugged her so hard. Still, I turned my face toward the detention center. Part of me stayed there. I felt both happy and sad.

When we arrived home to the children's apartment, Diana and Gilito were waiting for us. They'd prepared a delicious dinner. Finally, we were together again as family. What incredible happiness it was to be able to be together again.

* * * * *

Then the final blow. Six months after being freed, Gil's health got much worse. He had a tumor in his left lung and was diagnosed with cancer. What a cruel disappointment! That was the reason they did so many x-rays in immigration, but they never told him he might have cancer. And, of course, when it comes to cancer, time wasted without medical treatment is the difference between life and death. We lost six months of treatment. . . six months of life.

Gil lost his battle to cancer on June 20, 2001. As he lay dying, he told his children, very clearly, that he didn't want them to return to El Salvador. Their future was in this country. He didn't want his sacrifice to have been in vain.

He had fulfilled his dream to bring his family to the country he believed was the land of opportunity for education and progress. But he didn't find the American dream. He wasn't given the chance to live it. With a simple letter telling him about his medical condition, it would have been different.

* * * * *

But that's the hard reality of the immigrant. For the system in the United States, your life has no importance. You are of no value. If they did value our lives, they would do something to prevent the deaths of thousands of immigrants who die in the desert trying to reach this country, wouldn't they?

My fervent prayer is that someday, North Americans will realize what's really going on in their own house and dedicate themselves to rebuilding it instead of always trying to fix their neighbor's house.

About the Author

Born in San Salvador, El Salvador in 1955, Ana Amalia Guzmán Molina received her degree in Public Accounting from the Central American University, UCA. Subsequently, she received a Master's Degree in Finances from the Technological University.

Currently she is a Catholic volunteer for the Department of Detention in Los Angeles and collaborates with the Jesuit Refugee Service, visiting immigrant children imprisoned by the INS and offering them support and pastoral orientation. She has been invited to speak in favor of immigrants who have been jailed by the INS, based on her own experience, by different organizations in the United States.

Amalia lives in California with her three children, two adopted children, "Chiqui" and "Lucy" Molina, and her dog and cat.

El Poder del Amor

Mi historia en una cárcel de inmigración

por Ana Amalia Guzmán Molina

Traducción al inglés
Marilu MacCarthy

Presentación
Rev. Robert McChesney, S.J.

EPICA
Washington DC

El Poder del Amor: mi historia en una cárcel de inmigración

Programa Ecuménico sobre Centroamérica y el Caribe (EPICA)
1470 Irving St. NW, Washington, D.C. 20010
(202) 332-0292; fax (202) 332-1184
correo electrónico: epicabooks@epica.org
sitio web: www.epica.org

Traducción: Marilu MacCarthy
Arte de portada: Rosa Lozano y Zoila Elias
Redacción y coordinación: Kathy Ogle
Traducción de la introducción: Alex Taylor
Corrección de estilo, español: Mario Bencastro
Corrección de estilo, inglés: Siobhán Dugan
Diagramación: Scott Wright

Library of Congress Cataloging-in-Publication Data

Library of Congress Cataloging-in-Publication Data
Guzmán Molina, Ana Amalia, 1955-
The power of love: my experience in a U.S. immigration jail / by Ana Amalia Guzmán Molina; translation to English, Marilu MacCarthy; foreword, Robert McChesney.
p. cm.
In English and Spanish.
ISBN 0-918346-33-9
1. Guzmán Molina, Ana Amalia, 1955- 2. Immigrants--California--Los Angeles--Biography. 3. Immigrants--Government policy--United States. 4. Alien detention centers--California--Los Angeles. 5. United States-Emigration and immigration--Government policy. I. Ecumenical Program on Central America and the Caribbean. II. Title.
JV6926.S26G894 2003
365'.4--dc22

Indice

Este libro está dedicado con el amor y afecto más profundo a mis hijos, Diana Amy y Gilito. Su amor, su valentía y fortaleza ante las circunstancias que tuvieron que vivir a su corta edad, fue mi aliciente para seguir adelante. Ellos sufrieron durante 16 meses la ausencia de sus padres, la escasez de dinero, y la angustia de no tener un lugar estable donde vivir. Tuvieron que fingir que llevaban una vida normal para evitar que fueran reportados como menores de edad viviendo sin supervisión de un adulto y fueran llevados ante un juez de menores. Ellos son mi inspiración.

Agradecimientos

Agradezco a Dios por acompañarme durante estos 16 meses y darme la fortaleza y amor para ayudar a mis compañeras.

Agradezco a mis hijos por ser mis compañeros de sufrimiento sin jámas escuchar de ellos un reproche.

Agradezco a Gil, mi esposo – que en paz descanse – pues durante nuestros 24 1/2 años de casados me enseñó el valor de la familia y la importancia de luchar por un futuro mejor.

Agradezco a mi familia Molina y Guzmán por poner todo su esfuerzo y apoyo económico y moral, especialmente a mis cuñadas que estuvieron al frente luchando en nuestra ausencia.

Agradezco a todos los voluntarios religiosos que visitan el Centro de Detención en San Pedro quienes fueron como un rayo de luz en las tinieblas:

Fr. Robert McChesney, S.J., Fr. Pete Neeley, S.J., Fr. John Galvan, S.J., Sr. Molly Mertens, Pastor Ron Bayer, Sra. Alice Amaro, Congregación de las Hermanas de Madre Teresa de Calcuta, Albert (el hombre de la guitarra), Sr. Ken Auyeng, Sr. Vicente y Sra. Josefina Zepeda, Donald Frederick, y muchos más que se escapan a mi memoria. Todos han hecho una diferencia en mi vida al mostrarme su amor y compasión en los momentos más difíciles.

Agradezco a todas mis compañeras detenidas que abrieron su corazón para compartir su historia, por permitirme compartir sus alegrías y tristezas, sus derrotas y fracasos.

Le doy las gracias también a los guardias de buen corazón, los que hacen su trabajo con profesionalismo, siguiendo las reglas, los que mantienen la disciplina sin humillar, despreciar, o maltratar a los detenidos, especialmente a Mrs. Davis, Harper, Willeby, Jackson, McCaughin, y Mrs. Franks.

Agradezco a Ms. Alice Linsmeier que desde el momento que leyó mi historia se encargó de tocar puertas para que esta publicación fuera posible.

Agradezco a todo el equipo de EPICA por su profesionalismo y apoyo para hacer realidad este libro

Presentación

por Rev. Robert McChesney, S.J.

«Me pregunto si el público estadounidense sabe lo que está sucediendo en estas cárceles.» En este importante libro Amalia Guzmán Molina presenta una narrativa conmovedora de los 16 meses que pasó detrás de las paredes del centro de detención federal de inmigración cerca de Los Ángeles. De esta forma ella abre el telón para asegurarse que el público estadounidense logre enterarse verdaderamente de lo que allí sucede.

El Poder del Amor logra su objetivo en varios niveles. Desde 1996 es la mejor narrativa testimonial que ha salido de la población detenida no ciudadana, la cuál ha crecido tremendamente en Estados Unidos. El impacto nocivo de la legislación reciente en la unidad y estabilidad familiares es solamente un aspecto de la historia más amplia que es muy bien narrada aquí.

Después de la puesta en libertad de la Señora Molina, los trágicos acontecimientos del 11 de septiembre del 2001 resultaron en maltratos aún más arbitrarios e inhumanos contra los no-ciudadanos. A la vez que la guerra contra el terrorismo se intensifica los inmigrantes y los que buscan asilo, predecible pero tristemente, están siendo usados como chivos expiatorios. La publicación de *El Poder del Amor* coincide con la intensificación de los debates sobre los procedimientos y lineamientos federales de detención.

La narrativa que aquí se presenta logra reflejar – en una forma dura, impredecible e imposible de dejar por un lado – la historia de la supervivencia humana. En este aspecto, este libro es una tremenda contribución al género de la Literatura de Prisión. Los estudiantes de los temas étnicos y los movimientos migratorios serán conmovidos y fascinados por los dramas humanos de más de 100 mujeres de más de 40 países, las que son confinadas por 23 horas al día en un área más pequeña que la mitad (en pies cuadrados) de un campo de fútbol. Ésta es una interpretación muy refrescante, pero al mismo tiempo muy amarga, del «sueño americano.»

Finalmente, la historia de Amalia es un testamento de su sólida fe religiosa y un lamento épico del siglo XXI. Ella es Job, puesta a prueba misteriosamente por Dios en los límites más grandes del sufrimiento solamente para emerger como una testigo profética del poder del amor. Su esposo Gil, detenido en un sector que está al otro lado de la pared donde está Amalia, es Abraham. Después de que su padre sufriera un violento ataque en El Salvador Gil escuchó el llamado de Dios, el cuál en el Libro de Génesis le ordena a «dejar tu país, tu familia y la casa de tu padre para ir a la tierra que te mostraré.»

Las dificultades de ser atrapado en un ambiente tan duro y bajo circunstancias tan difíciles son algunas veces intensificadas por los conflictos entre las denominaciones religiosas y los voluntarios. Fundamentalistas intolerantes y farisaicos – cristianos y musulmanes – ocasionalmente se abalanzaban sobre este grupo vulnerable de prisioneros. Una de las contribuciones notables de Amalia fue la de guiar a las otras personas en su unidad a través de este campo de minas ecuménicas e interreligiosas, siempre fiel a sus propia creencia religiosa pero también respetuosa de las otras.

Amalia y yo llegamos al mismo tiempo al Centro Federal para los Servicios de Procesamiento, como entonces el Servicio de Inmigración y Naturalización (INS) llamaba al centro de detención para los no-ciudadanos. El Centro está ubicado en la Isla Terminal de la Bahía de Los Ángeles, a la par de un canal de aguas profundas por donde regularmente podíamos observar los barcos de la compañía Crucero Carnaval salir hacia los centros turísticos ubicados a lo largo de la costa del Pacífico mexicano.

Durante los 1920s y 1930s la Isla Terminal sirvió de hogar para una colonia muy activa de pescadores japoneses, entre los cuáles había muchos que eran ciudadanos estadounidenses. Después de Pearl Harbor el gobierno federal les confiscó sus tierras, para luego removerlos forzosamente y detener a la mayoría. Muchos años después el gobierno federal se disculpó formalmente por esas injusticias y les dio resarcimiento a algunos. Recientemente a los isleños «terminaleños» de origen japonés sus descendientes les erigieron un monumento para honrarles su patriotismo, dedicación y sacrificios. El mismo está ubicado en el parqueo que está afuera de la puerta de seguridad del actual centro de detención.

En 1997 la oficina nacional del Servicio Jesuita para Refugiados (JRS) de Washington DC me pidió que estableciera un programa en las instalaciones de San Pedro y otras ubicadas en el Condado de Los Ángeles. Con esas responsabilidades, y como capellán voluntario, en 1998 comencé a visitar regularmente San Pedro. Fue entonces que llegué a conocer muy bien a Amalia, Gil y sus tres hijos tan adorables.

El Poder del Amor es una historia descrita por una mujer poco usual sobre un mundo envuelto en las sombras, un infierno al que ella decidió «redecorar» – como lo expresa en su lenguaje tan colorido – para evitar volverse víctima de su maldad. Gil, en esa misma forma, encontró una manera no solamente para sobrevivir sino también para cuidar a sus hijos y guiar a los otros detenidos.

Aunque durante los cinco años de mis experiencias esta pareja sobresale, recuerdo a otros que tenían historias inolvidables que contar y que similarmente encontraron los recursos no solamente para sobrevivir sino también significado y propósito en la solidaridad. La detención de los no-ciudadanos, tristemente, brutaliza a demasiadas personas y familias; pero aún así hay otros que logran sobreponerse y aprender de dichas experiencias. *El Poder del Amor* tiene un gran valor para pintar una imagen muy viva de una experiencia muy compleja que ha permanecido escondida por mucho tiempo, y que demuestra las contribuciones que una nueva generación de inmigrantes y buscadores de asilo traen a los Estados Unidos.

¿Quiénes son los que están en detención para no-ciudadanos?

En cualquier día en el Hotel San Pedro, como me gustaba llamarlo, uno encuentra aproximadamente 500 no-ciudadanos de más de cincuenta países diferentes. Entre estas personas hay hombres y mujeres de dieciocho años para arriba. Los menores de dieciocho años son detenidos separadamente. La mayoría son de México y Centro América, pero también hay un gran número de gente de la China. Cuando yo llegué por primera vez, trabajé en las siete distintas unidades, o Pods, pero ya cuando el programa iba progresando estuve acompañando exclusivamente a las mujeres.

Algunos son refugiados tradicionales que han sido capturados en el Aeropuerto Internacional de Los Ángeles cuando trataban de ingresar a Estados Unidos con documentos de identidad falsos que consiguieron para escaparse de regimenes dictatoriales. Me recuerdo de un pequeño comerciante nigeriano que había estado activo en el movimiento pro democracia durante la década de los 1990s, cuando la represión era común en su país. Después de pasar un año en una prisión nigeriana bajo condiciones muy brutales logró escaparse de ese lugar, ocultar su verdadera identidad con un pasaporte falso, y dejar su país. Este decente caballero pasó más de un año en dos centros de detención de Los Ángeles antes de ganar asilo político en un proceso de apelación.

Las personas en un segundo grupo muy grande de detenidos estaban, en efecto, legalmente en Estados Unidos, lo que sorprende a la mayoría de estadounidenses que se enteran de esto. El INS (el cuál ha sido dividido y parcialmente reorganizado dentro del Departamento de Seguridad Interna como el Buró para el Aplicación de las Leyes de Inmigración y Aduanas,) califica a dicho grupo como «extranjeros criminales,» con lo que quieren sugerir que los detenidos son no-ciudadanos con pasados criminales. Sin embargo, los así llamados «extranjeros criminales» no son ni extranjeros ni criminales, al menos desde la perspectiva de las personas ordinarias.

La referencia a lo «criminal» indica correctamente que estas personas han sido declaradas culpables de cometer delitos en Estados Unidos, los que típicamente son actos no violentos. Sin embargo, posteriormente han completado sus condenas en prisiones estatales, pagado sus deudas a la sociedad, y subsecuentemente liberados.

Pero como lo sugiere la etiqueta de «extranjero,» en sus casos existía un tema adicional: estas personas no eran ciudadanos pero residentes permanentes legales de Estados Unidos y poseedores de la «tarjeta verde.» Muchos, en efecto, estaban casados con ciudadanos estadounidenses, tenían hijos ciudadanos de este país y vínculos comunitarios muy estrechos en Los Ángeles o en otras comunidades en el país. Muchos habían estado viviendo en Estados Unidos por varios años. Las leyes que fueron aprobadas en 1996 estipularon que los miembros de la población que había entrado legalmente a Estados Unidos tenían que ser detenidos por el INS después de completar sus condenas en prisión, procesados por un juez de inmigración y subsecuentemente, en la mayoría de los casos, deportados.

Si estas personas hubieran decidido hacerse ciudadanos hubieran pudieron haber tenido la libertad de regresar a sus familias y a sus empleos. Una de las lecciones más importantes que aprendimos los que acompañamos a los detenidos fue que los residentes legales permanentes son tremendamente vulnerables a dichas leyes. Los cambios legislativos muy significativos que se han desarrollado desde 1996 y la tragedia del 9/11 han empeorado dicha situación. Es imperativo hacer que se conozca ampliamente esta información.

En mi opinión, para los religiosos voluntarios el aspecto más difícil del ministerio fue acompañar a las mujeres que eran residentes legales permanentes cuando se preparaban a ser separadas, por la deportación, de sus hijos (algo que el INS llama «remoción»). Las celebraciones del Día de la Madre en el Hotel San Pedro, como lo muestra *El Poder del Amor* podía algunas veces ser una experiencia dolorosa.

Un subgrupo de la población denominada «extranjera criminal» incluía a gente nacida en Cuba, Vietnam y Camboya. Generalmente estas eran personas que poseían la tarjeta verde que también habían violado las leyes de Estados Unidos y cumplido sus condenas, frecuentemente por posesión de drogas u otras infracciones causadas por el consumo de alcohol y manejo de autos. Entre ellas habían «gentes de los botes» (boatpeople) que llegaron en los 1980s a Estados Unidos cuando eran bebés o infantes. Dichas personas recibieron la tarjeta verde pero cometieron el error de nunca hacerse ciudadanos de este país.

Por razones políticas que tienen un largo historial, los gobiernos de esos países se han rehusado a aceptar el regreso se sus «nacionales,» argumentando que eso es la responsabilidad de Estados Unidos ya que recibieron la residencia permanente en este país. Trágicamente esto ha resultado en que dichas personas se conviertan en algo equivalente a seres olvidados que no tienen estado. Debido a esa situación dichas personas muchas veces pasan años en los centros de detención para no-ciudadanos. A pesar de que la Corte Suprema (CS) dictaminó que el INS no puede mantener a las personas en detención indefinida, el Fiscal General John Ashcroft ha puesto en práctica una interpretación bastante limitada de la decisión de la CS. Por esa razón, muchas personas en dicho grupo viven en un limbo detrás de esas paredes.

Otra población bastante grande dentro del Hotel San Pedro era la de los inmigrantes económicos, frecuentemente latinoamericanos. Estas personas y sus familias habían sido forzadas por difíciles situaciones económicas a buscar trabajo en Estados Unidos. Es casi imposible para los pobres conseguir documentación legal para hacerlo y por eso la mayoría llega sin documentación y no tienen autorización legal para trabajar.

Además de tener sus propias necesidades, los inmigrantes económicos son el resultado de las necesidades de muchos sectores e industrias de la economía estadounidense que buscan buenos trabajadores pero a bajo costo. Sin embargo esta situación es precaria. Por un lado dichas personas algunas veces trabajan en condiciones inhumanas a cambio de salarios muy bajos, y por el otro, muchas veces son capturados en los lugares de trabajo por redadas del INS para luego ser detenidos como no-ciudadanos y deportados.

Históricamente Estados Unidos ha mostrado ambivalencia hacia los inmigrantes, denigrándolos políticamente pero a la misma vez dependiendo de ellos económicamente, por ejemplo para mantener bajos los costos de alimentos, hoteles y restaurantes y resolver la escasez de empleados. Una de las «bajas» de los ataques del 9/11 fue la conversación calurosa entre el Presidente George W. Bush y el Presidente Vicente Fox de México, la cuál estaba programada para tratar con el tema de la normalización del estatus laboral y también migratorio de muchos de estos trabajadores, pero que fue suspendida.

La historia de Amalia Guzmán Molina, como otras que escuché en San Pedro, no puede ser catalogada. Su suegro fue víctima de la violencia durante la guerra. Ella y Gil estuvieron buscando un nuevo comienzo económico. Y, como su historia lo narra tragicómicamente, a Amalia y su esposo los marcaron uniformemente como criminales. Cuando los detenidos me preguntaban porqué esto o aquello había sucedido en San Pedro yo a veces les respondía «porque había luna llena,» tratando de sugerir cómicamente que el proceso no tenía ningún sentido. El caso de Amalia sirve para demostrar que el sistema de detención para no-ciudadanos solamente puede funcionar bien al determinarse individualmente la situación legal de cada detenido, con defensoría justa ante un juez de inmigración.

Amalia y Gil eran poco comunes debido a su educación relativamente avanzada: Amalia se graduó de economista contadora en la Universidad Jesuita de Centro América en El Salvador y operaba exitosamente pequeños negocios allí. Gil se había graduado en la Universidad Estatal de Louisiana y también había tenido éxito en los negocios en El Salvador. Los Molinas eran parte de un pequeño porcentaje de graduados de universidades que se encontraban en San Pedro, y quiénes también podían ser reconocidos por sus conocimientos modestos de inglés. Ellos percibían sus dotes como regalos para la solidaridad y para beneficiar a sus hermanos y hermanas que los necesitaban.

Algunas estadísticas sobre la detención de no-ciudadanos

Los no-ciudadanos detenidos por el INS han sido el sector que ha crecido más rápido entre la población encarcelada de Estados Unidos, habiéndose cuadruplicado entre 1996 y el 2003. De acuerdo a estadísticas federales, en febrero de 2003 había 22,716 adultos detenidos por el INS. Este número pone en relieve la cruda realidad de que la mayoría de esos detenidos son rápidamente expulsados hacia sus países de origen.

La detención de no-ciudadanos es una puerta en constante movimiento de la cuál únicamente se sale hacia la deportación. Estadísticas federales revelan que aproximadamente 150,000 no-ciudadanos fueron removidos del país en el Año Fiscal (AF) 2002, y es bastante posible que ese número se incrementará grandemente durante el AF 2003. Estos números se tienen que agregar al casi un millón de aquellos que eligieron el «retorno voluntario» a sus países en el AF 2002, y la cuál es una cifra que no incluye a los que fueron enviados de vuelta en puertos de entrada tales como las fronteras.

Hacia el 30 de septiembre del año 2002 el INS (conjuntamente con el Servicio de Alguaciles de Estados Unidos) tenía detenidos en 1,072 instalaciones nacionales. De estas, 123 eran instalaciones federales; 915 locales o estatales; 22 privadas; y las otras 22 eran instalaciones tales como hospitales y lugares de mínima seguridad. En la actualidad hay una tendencia hacia la privatización.

El número de menores de edad no acompañados que están detenidos en Estados Unidos se ha más que duplicado en los últimos seis años, aumentando de 2,375 en 1997 a 5,385 en el año 2001, de acuerdo a un informe reciente de Amnistía Internacional. En un día cualquiera se estima que hay 500 niños detenidos por Estados Unidos. Muchos de ellos han viajado solos desde Centro América o México, viajando al norte para reunirse con uno o ambos padres. Muchos son víctimas de abusos domésticos y escapan tratando de buscar, además de la reunificación familiar, una vida más humana.

¿Qué se puede hacer?

Amalia menciona el impacto positivo de la Red para el Monitoreo de la Detención (Detention Watch Network – DWN) en las vidas de los detenidos. La DWN es una red nacional de agencias y organizaciones religiosas, legales, de derechos humanos, comunitarias y populares que ofrecen un foro y mecanismos para organizarse a cualquiera que quiere aprender más y mejorar la situación actual de la detención para no-ciudadanos. Los miembros de la DWN también tratan otros temas relacionados con el refugio, el asilo y la inmigración.

Una de las organizaciones fundadoras de la DWN es el Servicio Luterano de Inmigración y Refugiados (Lutheran Inmigration and Refugee Service – LIRS). En su sitio de Internet (www.LIRS.org) se puede consultar una variedad de enlaces útiles. El enlace de la DWN, por ejemplo, incluye «Materiales de Auto-ayuda Legal» muy útiles, en inglés y en español, los cuáles pueden interesarles a los no-ciudadanos detenidos y a sus seres queridos.

El sitio de Internet del LIRS también publica información al día sobre el reasentamiento para refugiados, las protecciones de asilo, y las leyes de inmigración. El espectro del 9/11 aún está presente, aquí en todos lados, en lo que respecta a las políticas estadounidenses para la inmigración.

Durante los primeros nueve meses del año 2003, el LIRS informa en un reciente «Washington Update,» la crisis en el Programa de EE.UU. para el Reasentamiento de Refugiados ha continuado. Este año, menos de 18,000 han encontrado nuevas esperanzas en Estados Unidos – apenas un 25% de los 70,000 que la Casa Blanca había indicado que reasentaría. El número de admitidos en el AF 2002 fue el más bajo en los últimos 25 años. Sería trágico si el gobierno federal permitiera que el miedo del terrorismo dañara este programa tan importante, ya que éste es un camino muy poco lógico para que un terrorista trate de llegar a las costas estadounidenses.

En un Noticiero Legal reciente, el LIRS informa sobre los constantes ataques contra los estándares tradicionales para las protecciones de asilo. Uno de los informes tiene que ver con el uso de documentos falsos para escapar de la represión en los lugares de origen y buscar asilo en EE.UU., lo que tradicionalmente ha sido visto como algo legítimo por las leyes de inmigración. Sin embargo, desde el 9/11, los nuevos mecanismos para implementar las leyes han debilitado está tradición.

Para mencionar solamente un ejemplo: los fiscales federales en la Florida han comenzado a acusar a los que buscan asilo usando documentos falsos con «uso de documentos fraudulento.» Los que han sido condenados pueden aún aplicar para el asilo después de salir de la prisión, pero sus posibilidades de tener éxito se reducen grandemente debido a sus pasados criminales.

Otra agencia que es miembro fundadora de la DWN es la Red Católica de Ayuda Legal (Catholic Legal Immigration Network Incorporated – CLINIC), la que es subsidiaria de la Conferencia de Obispos Católicos de EE.UU. (U.S. Conference of Catholic Bishops). Con oficinas nacionales en Washingon, DC., CLINIC (www.cliniclegal.org) mantiene sedes en varias diócesis a lo largo y ancho del país, y además es el mayor proveedor de servicios legales pro-bono para los no-ciudadanos que se encuentran detenidos.

Los miembros de CLINIC están presentes en la vanguardia de la lucha, pero también juegan papeles importantes dentro de la red de organizaciones en Washington que promueven políticas más humanas en la inmigración, el asilo y la detención. CLINIC también consulta regularmente con la Conferencia de Obispos Católicos de EE.UU.

CLINIC es una de varias agencias y organizaciones no gubernamentales importantes que continúan presionando al gobierno federal para que diferencie entre los inmigrantes, los que buscan asilo y los refugiados, por un lado; y los terroristas, por el otro. Como lo señaló su Director Ejecutivo Donald Kerwin en un artículo reciente: «El gobierno ha justificado sus medidas de control para la inmigración basándose en teorías dudosas sobre la seguridad nacional: Pocos aceptan la presencia (o el tratamiento) de los varios millones de personas indocumentadas en Estados Unidos, y sin embargo los indocumentados no representan una amenaza mayor contra la seguridad. Casi el 80% vienen de México y América Latina, no de naciones donde existe fuerte presencia de Al Queda.» Los investigadores han llegado a la conclusión que los operativos de Al Queda implicados en los ataques del 9/11 entraron, en su mayoría, legalmente a Estados Unidos.

En la lucha tan importante contra el terrorismo, el gobierno federal necesita ser más duro pero también más inteligente. Las políticas de inmigración no deberían ser usadas para suplantar la obtención de buena inteligencia o la implementación tradicional de las leyes, las que son aún los mecanismos investigativos más efectivos para encontrar a los que tienen asociaciones con el terrorismo. ¿Están siendo usados los inmigrantes, incluyendo a los económicos, como chivos expiatorios para explicar los fracasos tan colosales de la Agencia Central de Inteligencia (CIA) y el Buró Federal de Investigaciones (FBI)? Como lo demuestra la experiencia de los japoneses de la Isla Terminal, la historia de EE.UU. enseña que los inmigrantes se convierten en blancos muy tentadores cuando el gobierno decide irse a la guerra.

¿Qué se necesita hacer concretamente en el tema de la detención de no-ciudadanos para resolver los problemas que *El Poder del Amor* saca a la luz? Amalia nombra a los voluntarios religiosos como los verdaderos héroes de su historia. Mi propia experiencia confirma lo importante que es este grupo tan poco común, y el cuál es el único capaz de recibir aprobación oficial para servir directamente a los que están detenidos detrás de esas paredes. Este es un ministerio de presencia y acompañamiento. El principal propósito es estar presente, no para hacer proselitismo sino para darle dignidad a dicha experiencia, apoyar solidariamente a todos los que desean una sonrisa en simpatía, o simplemente un pequeño acto de bondad. Dentro de este contexto, por supuesto, los voluntarios alaban y oran con los detenidos de acuerdo con lo que estos últimos consideran útil.

Desafortunadamente el gobierno federal ha sido muy lento en responder a las recomendaciones hechas por el Servicio Jesuita para Refugiados, sus aliados, y otras agencias basadas en la fe. Se debe proveer fondos para contratar a más capellanes en todos los Centros Federales para el Servicio de Procesamiento similares a San Pedro, y también en instalaciones tales como Mira Loma en el Condado de Los Ángeles, el cuál es administrado por el alguacil local de acuerdo a un contrato con el gobierno federal.

Ya es hora para que el gobierno dé financiamiento total e institucionalice el papel de los capellanes en los centros de detención para los no-ciudadanos. Bajo lineamientos federales existentes, los cuáles son excelentes, ellos trabajarían monitoreando fanatismos religiosos dañinos y asegurando que los detenidos, sin importar su fe religiosa o creencia, tengan acceso a sus líderes religiosos, a los voluntarios y a lo que necesitan para ejercitar esos derechos.

Como lo documenta *El Poder del Amor,* los no-ciudadanos en detención no desearían perder la salud. El gobierno a través de un dialogo con grupos no gubernamentales de derechos humanos, salud, y médicos necesita establecer estándares mínimos de humanidad y profesionalismo. Lineamientos decentes para el cuidado médico han sido establecidos pero no tienen la fuerza de la ley, ya que sin mejores mecanismos de monitoreo no hay duda que no pueden ser implementados.

Otra área de preocupación es el arreglo predatorio de costos que les exprime a los detenidos sus escarzos fondos económicos. Desde que la población de no-ciudadanos en detención comenzó a crecer explosivamente en 1996 una red de gobiernos locales, prisiones con fines de lucro y contratistas de prisiones hizo su aparición para promover propios intereses financieros en el sistema de detención. Las municipalidades y prisiones de lucro se benefician tremendamente de los contratos para servicios telefónicos, por ejemplo, y cobran tarifas exorbitantes a los detenidos y los que reciben llamadas por cobrar desde los centros de detención. Esto causa un sufrimiento inimaginable para familias tales como los Molinas.

Aún bajo la ley actual, CLINIC señala que miles de no-ciudadanos detenidos podrían ser puestos en libertad. Aún así, históricamente el INS se ha rehusado a adoptar programas efectivos de libertad supervisada. Aunque por varios años se ha demostrado el éxito de los modelos para programas alternativos el gobierno federal aún no ha institucionalizado alternativas para la detención de personas como Amalia y Gil, quienes no representan amenazas para la comunidad, ni son el tipo de personas que escaparían si son puestas en libertad.

CLINIC y sus contrapartes hacen otras dos recomendaciones claves en áreas de preocupación de se remontan al periodo anterior al 9/11, pero que ahora salen a la luz a través de una importante investigación interna reciente hecha por el Departamento de Justicia sobre el tratamiento dado a los que han sido detenidos por razones migratorias y que están relacionadas con las investigaciones sobre los ataques del 9/11.

1. Cada no-ciudadano detenido debería recibir una audiencia ante un juez de inmigración para establecer fianzas. Dichos individuos deberían recibir fianzas razonables a menos que se sospeche que pueden escapar o que son peligrosos para la comunidad.

2. Una vez que se encuentran detenidos, los no-ciudadanos encaran muchas barrieras para obtener «derecho a la representación legal.» Por ejemplo, a muchos de los detenidos en relación al 9/11 se les prohibió el acceso a la información, y también información sobre sus paraderos, por lo que esencialmente «desaparecieron» de sus familias. Es escalofriante saber que en el Centro de Detención Metropolitano de Nueva York la primera llamada legal de un detenido en relación al 9/11 no fue hecha sino hasta el 15 de octubre. Aún después de que la prohibición de información fue levantada los detenidos podían hacer únicamente una llamada telefónica «legal» por semana. Si las líneas sonaban ocupadas o les respondían máquinas de contestar automáticas también les contaban la llamada.

Adicionalmente, el INS no fue consistente en ofrecerles a los abogados pro-bono de los detenidos del 9/11, como debería haber sucedido. A los abogados se les dijo frecuentemente que sus clientes no estaban en dichas instalaciones, cuando en realidad si lo estaban.

Como lo sugiere *El Poder del Amor,* frecuentemente éste era el mundo de cabeza en el que vivía Amalia. El gobierno federal debe accionar rápidamente para garantizar que los no-ciudadanos detenidos tengan acceso regular a representación legal designada por la corte, sin importar su clasificación.

Finalmente, hay algunos proyectos de ley para poner fin a la práctica inhumana de encarcelar a los menores de edad no-ciudadanos que no cuentan con acompañamiento adulto.[1] Es mi esperanza que los lectores de este libro sean conmovidos para apoyar este tipo de legislación diseñada a mover el país hacia una política migratoria más justa y más humana.

El Poder del Amor tocará profundamente el corazón de los lectores, pero también los informará e inspirará. Muchos de aquellos que han llegado recientemente a EE.UU. leerán esta historia como que si fuera la propia. En este sentido, este libro es una contribución única a la literatura de narrativas testimoniales sobre las experiencias inmigrantes, e ilumina tremendamente el fenómeno de la detención de no-ciudadanos.

Los que son ciudadanos, talvez especialmente aquellos que han tenido poco contacto personal con inmigrantes o personas que buscan asilo, se sentirán fascinados al conocer a Amalia y su familia, y al pasar 16 meses adentro del mundo de Amalia. Su historia tan irresistible habla por si sola, especialmente con respecto a todas las contribuciones, regalos tan grandes, que esta familia de inmigrantes trae a este país. Tengo fe que muchos de los que son ciudadanos pondrán dentro de sus corazones las oraciones de Amalia para unírsele en reconstruir lo que esta dañado en su nueva tierra.

Yo, yo soy el que te consuela. ¿Por qué tienes miedo a los hombres que mueren, a un hijo de hombre que desaparecerá como el pasto? ¿Acaso te has olvidado de Yavé, que te creó, que extendió los cielos y que fundó la tierra? Pues te lo pasas siempre asustado al ver la rabia del tirano, que trata, por todos los medios de destruirte. Pero, ¿dónde está ahora su rabia? Muy pronto saldrá en libertad el prisionero: no morirá en el calabozo, ni le faltará más el pan. Yo soy Yavé, tu Dios, que muevo el mar y hago rugir sus olas, mi nombre es Yavé de los ejércitos.

(Isaías 51: 12-16)

Introducción

Éste es un libro que trata de ilustrar en una manera sencilla: 1) La realidad que se vive en una cárcel de inmigración, 2) La consecuencia de las leyes injustas, que cuando se crean, no consideran el impacto devastador en las familias, las cuales se ven segregadas. 3) La labor de los voluntarios religiosos, los que hacen su trabajo en silencio sin esperar nada a cambio. 4) Cómo ayudando a otros te ayudas a ti mismo. 5) El poder del amor y la fe.

Es la historia de una experiencia personal vivida en el centro de detención para inmigrantes ubicado en una isla en la ciudad de San Pedro, California. A pesar de llamarse centro de detención, en realidad es una cárcel de máxima seguridad con una capacidad para albergar a 500 personas aproximadamente; pero debido a los cambios en la ley de inmigración, en algunos momentos esta cifra se ve sumamente incrementada.

El Poder del Amor

Soy una persona con bases religiosas e ingresé al movimiento carismático en el año de 1990. Ahí nací de nuevo y aprendí a vivir mi fe y me considero católica practicante que en los momentos más difíciles tuve la bendición de sentir el amor de Dios a través de sus mensajeros, unos católicos, otros evangélicos. Todos sin excepción llegaron a dar consuelo, fe y esperanza en un futuro mejor. Llegaron a unirnos en nuestro dolor, no a dividirnos de acuerdo a creencias religiosas. Esto es maravilloso; éramos un sólo cuerpo, una iglesia con un sólo pastor, en un valle de lágrimas, dolor, desesperación, injusticia y muerte.

Viaje a lo desconocido

Era un día miércoles a las 7.10 de la mañana. Mis hijos estaban apresurados para salir a la escuela, así que me puse unos pantalones color gris de mi hijo, un suéter, y salí a la carrera a dejarlos. Primero Gil y luego Amy. Era una preciosa mañana de invierno con un sol radiante, el cielo azul y despejado, y haciendo un poco de frío.

De regreso, una cuadra antes de llegar a casa, un vehículo que venía atrás de mí me encendió las luces para que me detuviera. Eran luces iguales a la sirena de los radio-patrulla, pero me percaté que era un vehículo particular de lujo y sin placas. Me detuve con calma y un hombre alto me pidió mi licencia de conducir. El hombre no tenía uniforme de policía pero yo bien obediente le mostré lo único con que contaba y era un permiso para conducir.

Me pidió que me saliera del vehículo y yo, por supuesto desconcertada, le obedecí. De pronto una mujer policía que no sé de donde salió me revisó para ver si no portaba armas y me esposó. El hombre que me detuvo me preguntó si mi esposo estaba en casa y si tenía armas. Me dio risa cuando hizo esta pregunta, pues Gil le tiene pánico a las armas y nunca hemos tenido una en casa, ni siquiera un machete. De todas maneras le contesté que si, que mi esposo estaba en casa y que no teníamos ningún tipo de armas.

Ya dentro del vehículo nos fuimos y estacionamos frente a nuestra casa y aparecieron dos vehículos similares al que anteriormente me había detenido. Se bajaron como seis hombres que usaban chalecos negros y atrás se leía FEDERAL POLICE. Tenían armas y rodearon la casa. Uno de ellos tocó el timbre. Dianita mi hija mayor de diecinueve años abrió la puerta y le preguntaron por mi esposo. Ella lo fue a llamar pero los policías ya habían entrado.

Que pasó ahí, no lo vi, pero mi hija dice que el policía preguntó:
–Hay un adulto en la casa?"
–Sí –le contestó–, mi papá. Ya le llamo.
Y de pronto estaban en el dormitorio, arrestaron a mi esposo, registraron todo y le decomisaron su pasaporte.

Mientras esto sucedía yo estaba aún en el vehículo. Se me acercó un hombre que se identificó como oficial de inmigración, y me pidió mi pasaporte. Se lo entregué y me mencionó que había violado las leyes de migración al quedarme en este país más tiempo del establecido. Recordé que tenía un comprobante de que habíamos aplicado a la ley 245 que permite tramitar la residencia sin necesidad de salir del país cuando tienes un familiar ciudadano americano. Se lo mostré, pero no le dio importancia y me mencionó que tendría que acompañarlo.

Antes de partir se acercó al vehículo en que me encontraba, otro vehículo con dos hombres americanos bien vestidos. Me llamó la atención el tipo de joyas que usaban: esclavas gruesas y cadenas que se notaba que eran costosas así como el reloj que usaban. Uno de ellos al despedirse le hizo la señal de victoria al que iba al frente del timón y se retiraron. Fue hasta en ese momento que comprendí que era un arresto bien organizado, como si ellos esperaran encontrar armas y gente peligrosa.

El oficial de inmigración que estuvo a cargo de mi arresto era una persona muy educada, y al percatarse que no me podía apoyar en el asiento, pues me incomodaban las esposas por tener los brazos hacia atrás, me las quitó y me esposó con los brazos hacia adelante para que fuera cómoda. También le pedí que me permitiera entregarle a mi hija mi cartera, y me dijo que si. Dianita, mi pobre hija, estaba asustada; lo podía leer en sus ojos.

Yo le dije –Amorcito, no se preocupe. Cuíde a sus hermanos, que todo saldrá bien.

El oficial también le dio a Diana una tarjeta con su nombre y la dirección donde íbamos a estar detenidos, y partimos.

*   *   *   *   *

Salimos rumbo a la ciudad de Los Angeles, pero yo en ese momento no tenía la menor idea del lugar al que iba. Por otro lado, mi mente estaba al lado de mis hijos, pensando en cómo iban a hacer solos en una ciudad tan grande, a la que apenas tenían unos meses de haber llegado, sin familia que respondiera por ellos y sin amigos en los que realmente se pueda contar en estas circunstancias.

Creo que no pasaron ni veinte minutos cuando llegamos a un edificio, y entramos al estacionamiento del mismo, ubicado en el sótano. Inmediatamente al llegar, lo primero que hicieron fue tomarme una foto y mis huellas digitales, pero las huellas son de los dedos completos. El lugar es un lugar cerrado, sin una ventana, como una fortaleza, un bunker, y se ve bastante movimiento de gente detenida y oficiales vestidos de civil.

Le pregunté al oficial por Gil, mi esposo, y me dijo que él también se encontraba en ese edificio. Le pedí verlo y me dijo que sólo por unos momentos. Lo pude ver; lo tenían en una celda solito, y el pobre estaba igual que yo, desconcertado. En realidad no nos dijimos casi nada. Sólo le pregunté si estaba bien, me respondió que si, y al momento el oficial me dijo que teníamos que irnos.

*   *   *   *   *

Me llevaron a una celda con más personas, todas mujeres y algunos niños. La mayoría eran mejicanas, una china, una salvadoreña y yo; en total éramos doce. Esa celda era un cuarto completamente cerrado, con una puerta metálica y una pequeña ventana en la misma puerta. Creo que no tendría más de 20 x 25 cm. Era un cuarto sucio, muy sucio, con cáscaras de naranja en el suelo, mosquitos de esos pequeñitos que atrae la fruta, cucarachas pequeñas, bancas metálicas alrededor, dos inodoros metálicos, cada uno con un mini-lavamanos. Había también dos teléfonos públicos, un termo vacío de agua con una costra de suciedad, como si nunca lo hubieran lavado, y cámaras que controlan todos tus movimientos. El aire acondicionado estaba al máximo, y me sentí como en un cuarto frío.

Las personas ahí detenidas, unas están tiradas en el suelo sobre papel periódico, otras tienen frazadas y duermen sobre ellas, otras sentadas en las bancas. Y se ven diferentes actitudes ante esta situación: 1) Las que vienen de la cárcel y prisiones están molestas, pues esperaban ver la libertad después de cumplir su tiempo. Son las más agresivas. Esperaban con ansia reunirse con su familia después de pagar su falta, pero luego oficiales de inmigración fueron por ellas, así que pasan maldiciendo y están de un humor que da miedo. 2) Las que fueron sacadas de sus casas junto con sus hijos están en un mar de lágrimas. Ellas serán deportadas con sólo la ropa que llevan puesta y por lo general sin dinero. Las llevan a Tijuana o Mexicali, y de ahí, tienen que ver como se las arreglan para llegar a su lugar de origen. 3) Las que detuvieron en su trabajo por ser indocumentadas están preocupadas por sus hijos y lloran al pensar que van a ser deportadas y los hijos se quedan aquí.

Y aquí es cuando comienza el calvario, pues sólo se escucha negativismo, enojo, malas palabras y frustración. Eso aunado a la incertidumbre que uno tiene es dañino, pues el miedo se contagia y llega un momento que tu cuerpo se siente como una bomba de tiempo, tu corazón palpita, comienza la angustia, tu estómago se siente pequeño, no toleras la comida, y si comes sabe insípido y te dan náuseas.

*   * * *   *

Pasaron como dos horas cuando la puerta se abrió y me llamaron. Era el mismo oficial que me arrestó. Me preguntó si quería salir voluntariamente del país y que firmara un papel que me entregó. Yo de inmediato le dije que tenía que hablar primero con mi esposo y que quería llamar a mi abogado. Sin contestarme una palabra me llevó de regreso a la celda.

Ahí me di cuenta que tenía que comunicarme con Diana, pero yo no contaba con dinero, así que no me quedó de otra que pedir dinero prestado. Se lo pedí a una china, pues tenía una bolsa llena con monedas de veinticinco centavos que le habían llevado un familiar. Era buena gente y les daba monedas a las que habíamos sido detenidas sin dinero en la bolsa. Hablé con Diana y le dije que llamara a la abogada para que viera en qué nos podía ayudar.

A las doce del mediodía en punto se abrió de nuevo la puerta. Era una oficial que traía una caja con sándwiches de bologna, leche y naranjas. Nos dieron uno a cada una. La leche y la naranja estaban bien, pero los sándwiches no; la carne estaba medio verde. De todas maneras no comí nada; no tenía hambre y lo regalé. A las dos de la tarde me llamaron de nuevo. Vi a Gil y decidimos pedir ver a un juez. Diana mientras tanto, contactó a la abogada. Ella fue la misma que nos tramitó, meses antes, la solicitud de permanencia legal a través de mi cuñada Tita, quien es ciudadana americana y nos ha apoyado muchísimo.

Los oficiales de deportación trataron de presionarme para que firmara la deportación y saliera del país, pero la decisión ya estaba tomada. Sólo lo que me dijera mi abogada tendría validez para mí. Mientras tanto, a hacerle frente al monstruo de INS (las siglas en inglés para el Departamento de Inmigración y Ciudadanía).

Esa tarde fue eterna; me puse a rezar el rosario, cantar alabanzas, darme ánimo, y a practicar lo que tanto he predicado: *Si tu mal tiene remedio, ¿por qué te afliges? Y si no lo tiene, ¿qué ganas con afligirte?* Parecería que el tomar esta actitud es no darle importancia al problema, pero en primer lugar: ¿Qué ganaría por preocuparme en algo que no tiene solución? Si éste es el caso lo mejor es aceptar la realidad, rendirme a la voluntad de Dios y seguir adelante. Y en segundo lugar: si el problema tiene solución, lo peor que puedo hacer es afligirme, sino por el contrario, tengo que tomar acción para salir adelante y buscar soluciones. El miedo causa aflicción y desesperación y no nos permite ver ni siquiera un rayito de esperanza, y por ende aniquila la fe.

*   *   *   *   *

Pasaron las horas, luego llegó un oficial a decirnos que teníamos que salir al corredor, y sentarnos en unas sillas metálicas colocadas en el pasillo, pues era hora de que hicieran la limpieza. Salimos y de pronto escuché silbidos, risas y voces de hombres. Ahí me percaté de que junto a nuestra celda, habían como tres más, llenas de hombres de toda raza y color.

El oficial, molesto, les ordenaba que se callaran, pues te preguntan el nombre, te dicen piropos, te preguntan si quieres ser su novia, en fin, son hombres que vienen de la cárcel y se enloquecen el ver una mujer. Por supuesto que también había en nuestro grupo mujeres que, al igual que ellos, se enloquecían al verlos y les contestaban a todo lo que les preguntan. Este pequeño recreo duró como diez minutos; luego de nuevo a la celda.

Al poco tiempo nos llevaron la cena. Eran las cinco de la tarde, y el menú era: arroz blanco cocido, masoso sin sal, zanahorias sancochadas y dos rodajas de jamón de pavo, junto con una leche. Me comí las zanahorias y fue todo. Necesitaba tomar agua y no había en el termo. Todas teníamos sed hasta que al fin, una valiente le dijo a un oficial que queríamos agua pues teníamos sed.

El oficial le respondió molesto:
–Cuando vienen cruzando los montes toman agua de los ríos, y aquí por todo protestan. Si quieren agua, tomen del lavamanos–, y cerró la puerta.

Bueno, pues ni modo, preferible del lavamanos a estar con sed. Así que tomé agua del lavamanos; la mayoría no lo hace, pues decían que el agua era sucia, pero al final la necesidad aprieta.

*   *   *   *   *

Como a las seis comenzó a llegar más gente, mujeres y niños. Los niños lloraban mucho; se veían cansados y asustados de verse entre tanta gente extraña. Todas las que llegaron en la tarde, iban a ser deportadas a México esa misma noche. Nadie sabía a qué frontera serían llevadas, así que no podían avisar a sus familiares para que las esperaran con dinero, o las acompañaran a un lugar seguro donde pasar la noche. La mayoría dice que es peligroso cuando van mujeres solas, ya que corren el peligro de ser asaltadas o incluso violadas; así que entre ellas se ponen de acuerdo para acompañarse. Por lo general no llevan dinero pero saben que existen lugares que albergan a los inmigrantes y pueden pasar la noche seguras, mientras se comunican al día siguiente con sus familias y deciden cómo llegar a su destino.

* * * * *

A las ocho de la noche, llegó un oficial con una lista y comenzó a llamar una por una, pero seis de nosotras no aparecimos en esa lista; nos quedamos ahí esperando. Yo estaba cansadísima, tenía sueño, hambre. Me sentía físicamente súper mal, y sobre todo ansiosa de saber que es lo que pasaría ahora, hasta que al fin, llegó un oficial y llamó a cinco. Yo era una de ellas. En ese momento eran las diez de la noche.

Nos condujeron a un autobús, nos sentaron en las primeras dos líneas de asientos y esperamos como diez minutos cuando comenzaron a subir a los hombres. Entre ellos venía Gil, así que me alegré mucho al verlo. No quedó atrás de mí, sino que como dos líneas después pero en un descuido de los oficiales, se cambió de puesto y pudimos tomarnos de la mano y conversar.

Le pregunté que si no era peligroso estar entre esos hombres, pues algunos tienen una cara de maleantes que asusta, y se les puede ver en su rostro el enojo y frustración. Otros se ven alegres, cantan canciones contra la migra, cuentan chistes y van piropeando a las otras mujeres. Pero Gil me dice que no, que de vez en cuando se portan groseros con los oficiales, pero así también los castigan. Gil me cuenta que lo que hace es estar apartado. Le pregunté si sabía a dónde nos llevaban y me dijo que a un lugar que es un centro de detención en la ciudad de San Pedro. Allí pasaríamos la noche.

*   *   *   *   *

Llegamos como a las 11 PM. Al llegar hicimos una fila y las mujeres fuimos las primeras en salir. Nos tomaron foto, huellas y de nuevo a otra celda. Allí esperamos como una hora, hasta que llegó un oficial. Era una mujer de aspecto latino, un poquito gruesa, morena, con el pelo rizado corto, y en su uniforme tenía una placa que decía Oficial X. Llevaba en sus manos unos uniformes amarillos y unas bolsas plásticas.

Esta ha sido la experiencia más denigrante de mi vida. La oficial nos pidió que pusiéramos nuestra ropa en la bolsa, *toda* nuestra ropa, eso incluye panties y brasier. Nos colocamos en fila, nos pidió que nos sacudiéramos el pelo, que abriéramos la boca, sacáramos la lengua, levantáramos nuestros senos, que nos diéramos vuelta y que nos agacháramos, que abriéramos nuestras nalgas y que tosiéramos tres veces.

Yo, la verdad, no podía creer que esto me pudiera pasar. Lo había visto en el cine cuando desnudaban a los presos y les dan su uniforme cuando llegan a la cárcel, pero esto no era ficción o un sueño, era mi realidad. En ese momento vino a mi mente la película *Papillón*. Me dio mucho miedo y sentí los minutos como horas mientras hacíamos este proceso. Lo peor es que lo haces frente a una cámara que controla todos tus movimientos. Se supone que esta rutina es para evitar que alguien lleve droga o cigarros. Los hombres pasan por esta rutina también.

Y mientras duró todo este ritual, ya eran las doce de la noche, hasta que finalmente nos llevaron a los dormitorios. Pero antes nos entregaron una colcha parecida a las que vi anteriormente en la celda del INS y dos sábanas. Luego nos condujeron al Pod-6 que es el área de las mujeres. Un Pod es una celda que, aparte del baño, contiene dos cuartos: una sala-comedor para actividades en el día y un dormitorio lleno de camarotes.

*   *   *   *   *

Llegamos a este lugar, nos colocamos en fila mientras esperábamos a que la puerta se abriera. Esta era metálica con una ventanita. Escuchamos el girar de una llave, y apareció una oficial afroamericana, alta y fuerte, pelo largo trenzado al estilo africano y con labios bien gruesos. Le preguntó a la oficial que nos conducía, que si éramos todas las que veníamos. Le respondió que sí, y le entregó unas tarjetas amarillas. Las tomó en su mano y comenzó a leerlas. Procedió a llamarnos por nuestro apellido, al estilo de los militares, con una voz enérgica.

Luego pasamos una por una ese cuarto que parecía un area para comer, con un televisor que por cierto a esas horas estaba encendido y había varias mujeres viendo la televisión. Vestían unas de color rojo, otras azul y otras anaranjado. Me senté en una mesa y como a los diez minutos, la oficial nos llamó para que tomáramos unas camas de plástico color azul, que en realidad son como una plataforma, duras como el piso. Nos dio una toalla, una bolsita con shampoo, un jaboncito, un cepillo de dientes bien cortito y un sobrecito con pasta de dientes.

Mis compañeras procedieron a bañarse, pero yo no tuve fuerzas, pasé al dormitorio y me acosté. Me sentía muy cansada; era ya la una de la mañana y yo por lo general me duermo a las diez. Traté de dormirme pero me molestaban las luces encendidas, el ruido del televisor y todas las voces que escuchaba de las personas que ahí se encontraban. Cerré mis ojos y me puse a rezar. No sé a qué horas me dormí, pero sentí que fueron unas pocas horas.

*   *   *   *   *

A las cinco de la mañana, sentí una patada en la "cama", y escuché en inglés:

–¡Levántense.!

Me levanté y me apresuré a bañarme, pues en media hora tienes que poner las camas una encima de otra, entregar las frazadas, sábanas y toalla, y esperar a que llegue un oficial para llevarnos de nuevo a la celda donde originalmente nos llevaron cuando llegamos la noche anterior.

Ya en esa celda, la mayoría nos acostamos en el piso pues estábamos cansadas. En ese momento me sentí como los vagabundos que duermen en la calle, con la única diferencia que ellos por lo menos tienen cartones para cubrirse y no acostarse directamente en el piso, pero yo ni siquiera contaba con eso.

Como a las seis y media llegó una oficial y nos entregó las bolsas plásticas con nuestra ropa para que nos cambiáramos y observé que una de mis compañeras se había enrollado una colcha en la cintura. Se puso su ropa, pero se dejó su camisa vaquera de fuera, para que no notaran los oficiales lo que llevaba. Mi ropa estaba mal oliente y sucia. Me tenía que poner el mismo panty, los mismos calcetines sucios, y me sentía bien incomoda. Nos llevaron rápido el desayuno, que era dos cajitas de cereal, una naranja y una leche. Yo para variar no comí; regalé mi comida pues siempre hay una comelona en el grupo.

Como a las ocho de la mañana de nuevo a los buses para llevarnos a Los Angeles. Vi a Gil de nuevo. Tenía unas ojeras bien marcadas, me imaginé que yo estaría igual o peor. Me mencionó que casi no durmió y se sentía bien cansado. Le dije que llamaría a Diana para que nos llevara ropa limpia, sobre todo suéter y ropa interior y para que me contara qué dijo la abogada.

*　　　*　*　*　　　*

Llegamos a nuestro destino, de nuevo al cuarto frió. Y que sorpresa al ver a la compañera que dejamos la noche anterior. Parece que se les olvidó llevarla a San Pedro; la pobre estaba cansada y con frío. Ya habían llevado más gente, pero me llamó la atención una señora con una bebita como de seis meses. La niña estaba enferma, tenía una tos como chiflido, temperatura y lloraba y lloraba sin parar.

Llamé por teléfono a Diana y le pedí que me trajera monedas para comunicarme con ella y un cambio de ropa. Le pregunté por sus hermanos y me contestó que fueron a la escuela y que estaban bien. Yo sabía que de ninguna manera ella iba a preocuparme, pero le pedía a Dios les diera a los niños la fortaleza para resistir este golpe. También me comentó Diana que la abogada vendría a vernos este día. Me sentí un poco tranquila y colgamos.

Invité a mis compañeras a rezar el rosario, y algunas con mucha devoción lo rezaron. La mayoría indiferente, hablando tonterías. A las diez, nos llevaron unos burritos de papa, leche y naranjas. No soportaba ver las naranjas y la leche, pero por lo visto serían mis compañeras inseparables.

A las once de la mañana me llamaron pues tenía visita. Era mi hija, Diana, con la ropa y el dinero que anteriormente le pedí. Tuvimos unos pocos minutos para hablar. Traté de darle fe y seguridad, de que todo saldría bien, y le dije que llamaría en la noche para hablar con sus hermanos. Sobre todo le pedí que no faltara a la escuela, que la vida tendría que seguir igual, aunque sus padres no estuvieran físicamente en casa. Y nos despedimos.

Mientras tanto ya en la celda, la bebé seguía llorando. Tenía hambre, estaba sucia de sus pañales, y ya nos tenía desesperadas pues no podíamos ayudar a la madre en nada. Llamamos a un oficial y le explicamos el problema pero ni siquiera nos respondió.

Eran las once y media de la mañana y la bebé seguía llorando. La madre no tenía un biberón que darle, ni pañales para cambiarle, en fin, qué barbaridad, qué injusticia con esta bebita. Así que comenzamos a darle patadas a la puerta y a gritar fuerte. Creo que fue bueno el alboroto, pues llegó un oficial. Le explicamos que la bebé estaba enferma, sin comida, sin medicina, sin pañales y para colmo

¡con el aire acondicionado al máximo! Creo que el oficial consultó con alguien superior, pues no pasaron ni cinco minutos cuando se llevaron a la señora al doctor. Gracias a Dios, por lo menos algo se había logrado. Me parecía tan injusto lo que esta bebé estaba sufriendo; era increíble la indiferencia de los oficiales. Te tratan y te ven como animales.

Llegaron las doce del mediodía y nos llevaron almuerzo. Era el menú de siempre. No tenía apetito pero me sentía muy mal. Sentía mi estómago como si tuviera un cubo de hielo adentro, así que traté de comer algo, y me recosté en una banca. Dormí un poco pues el sueño y cansancio me vencían. Me desperté cuando la puerta se abrió. Eran como las dos de la tarde y era la señora con la bebé. Nos contó que la llevaron al médico, y traía medicinas, pañales, y *diapers*, y un oficial le dijo que la llevarían a otro lugar donde detienen a las madres con niños pequeños.

*   *   *   *   *

En ese momento me llamaron, pues tenía visita; era mi abogada. Me alegré tanto al verla. Venía con un hombre afroamericano y me dijo que él tomaría nuestro caso. Él no hablaba español pero estaba más calificado para llevar el caso en la corte. Le pregunté a ella cómo veía nuestra situación, y me dijo que de momento no me podía decir nada, pero que no me preocupara, que solicitaría una fianza para poder pelear el caso en libertad, y que me comunicaría el proceso a seguir. La sentí tan segura en la manera que me hablaba, que me dio tranquilidad el saber que por lo menos habría alguien trabajando a nuestro favor. Le firmé unos papeles para que el hombre se presentara en la INS como nuestro abogado y así tener toda la información sobre nuestra detención.

Las horas pasaban lentamente, seguía llegando gente a la celda, me partía el alma ver tantas lágrimas y lamentos, mujeres que habían sido sacadas de sus casas, dejando toda una vida por detrás, hijos (ciudadanos estadounidenses), pertenencias, el compañero de su vida. En pocas palabras perdían *todo*. Nunca en mi vida había visto tan de cerca tanto dolor, tanto sufrimiento, y como madre me sentía solidaria en su sufrimiento, y era realmente difícil dar palabras de aliento en estas circunstancias.

Llegaron las cuatro de la tarde y aproveché a hablar por teléfono con mis hijos. Amy, mi hija de diez y seis años, estaba lógicamente preocupada. Lo primero que quería saber era cuánto tiempo pasaríamos en ese lugar y me preguntaba cómo veía la situación. Lamentablemente no tenía respuesta a ninguna de sus preguntas, pero le pedí que hoy más que nunca tenía que estar tranquila y estudiar, que la quería muchísimo y que gracias a Dios llegaron los del INS cuando ellos estaban ya en la escuela, porque de lo contrario el problema sería mayor.

Luego me pasó a Gilito, mi hijo menor de catorce años. Él se limitó a preguntarme cómo estaba, si estaba junto con su papá y de ahí en adelante solo me escuchó todas las recomendaciones que le di: que cuidara a sus hermanas, que no le abrieran la puerta a nadie, que si alguien tocaba la puerta en la noche que no abrieran, que por favor comieran y que no faltaran a la escuela. Cuando colgué lloré muchísimo. Mis hijos han sido la parte más importante en mi vida, y me aterraba el pensar que les pudiera pasar algo hoy que estaban solos. Volví a llamar y le dije a Diana que en mi cartera tenía las tarjetas para sacar dinero del banco. Le di mi clave para que por lo menos pudieran comprar comida, pues ya era jueves, y el viernes por lo general era el día en que hacíamos las compras. Le dije que todos los días les llamaría por teléfono a las seis de la tarde cuando ya estuvieran los tres en casa.

* * * * *

Este día nos llevaron temprano a San Pedro, salimos como a las siete de la noche y conversamos mucho con Gil sobre lo que nos podría pasar. Lo que más nos preocupaba, eran los niños. ¿Cómo se iban a sostener? Tantas preguntas y dudas pasaron por nuestra mente, como: ¿Qué pasaría con nuestra casa? La compramos hacia apenas un año y la pagábamos con mucho sacrificio. ¿Cómo se harían los pagos? ¿Qué diríamos en nuestro trabajo para justificar nuestra ausencia? Teníamos que pensar si notificábamos de inmediato a nuestra familia en El Salvador, pues sería una pena muy dura para mis suegros, y no queríamos realmente causarles un dolor tan grande. En fin, tantas decisiones que tomar y nosotros con tanta angustia e incertidumbre sobre nuestro futuro, que nos era difícil tomar decisiones en ese momento.

Llegamos a San Pedro. Pasamos por el mismo proceso del día anterior, pero gracias a Dios, en esta oportunidad, la oficial que hizo el registro nos dijo que lo hiciéramos rápido, y como éramos las mismas cinco de siempre, nos fue menos difícil. Llegamos al Pod 6, y en esta oportunidad me di un baño. Me lavé el cabello, y esperé un poco a que se me secara antes de dormirme.

Aproveché este tiempo para preguntarle a una de las detenidas porque habían uniformes de diferentes colores. Ella me explicó que las de rojo son criminales peligrosas, por lo general asesinas o con crímenes relacionados con violencia; las de azul han robado o vendido drogas; y las de color naranja son gente que capturan en los aeropuertos o la frontera y no tienen ningún record criminal en los Estados Unidos.

Me fui a acostar y en esta oportunidad no me importó la luz encendida, ni el ruido, me acosté y estaba prácticamente muerta. Sólo me puse la misma toalla con que me bañé sobre mis ojos, hice mis oraciones, y me quedé dormida. Nos levantaron temprano, la misma rutina que el día anterior, pero en esta oportunidad me llevé dos jaboncitos para lavar mis panties y calcetines, aprovechando que ya tenía un cambio de ropa extra.

*   *   *   *   *

Era ya día viernes, día de pago. En cuanto llegamos al edificio central del INS de nuevo le llamé a Diana para que fuera a recoger el cheque y dijera en la oficina que habíamos tenido que salir de emergencia a Miami a ver a mi cuñada Tita. No se me ocurrió otra excusa pues estábamos convencidos que esta pesadilla no duraría más de una semana.

Ya en la celda, llevaron una señora iraní junto con su hijita de tres años y una hindú, con su hijo de diez años. Conversé con la iraní pues hablaba perfectamente el inglés y me mencionó que tenía tres meses de estar detenida, encerrada en la habitación de un motel cercano al aeropuerto. Llegó junto con su esposo, procedente de Irán, pero en el aeropuerto cuando los detuvieron, los habían separado, y se veían sólo cuando llegaban a este edificio para ver al juez. Estaban pidiendo asilo político, pero nunca se imaginó la pesadilla que tendrían que pasar. Su hijita se veía bastante dañada psicológicamente.

Me contó que la otra señora hindú había sido capturada en el aeropuerto también, junto con su esposo y su otro hijo de catorce años y que también habían sido separados. Ambas coincidían en que nunca se esperaron que en el gran país de la democracia y respeto a los derechos humanos, fueran tratadas tan inhumanamente.

También me llamó la atención, que llevaron a una señora muy bien vestida, zapatos altos, su pelo bien arreglado y era de Armenia. La pobre lloraba inconsolablemente. Su esposo es ciudadano americano, y le llegó una cita para presentarse en las oficinas de INS para tratar asuntos relacionados son su solicitud de residente permanente. Le acompañaban su esposo y un abogado. Pero al llegar la esposaron y la detuvieron. Le dijeron que tenía una orden de deportación. Ni siquiera su abogado pudo hacer algo; simplemente le habían engañado.

Cada vez que conversaba con alguien, sólo escuchaba cosas negativas. Nadie me dijo algo positivo o me dio aliento. Al contrario, sólo escuché frustración, resentimiento y mucho dolor.

*   *   *   *   *

En la tarde, hablé con los niños, y me pareció que todo marchaba bien. No habían faltado a la escuela pero siempre estaban ansiosos de saber cuándo llegaríamos a casa.

Ese día eran las nueve de la noche y no nos llamaban para llevarnos a San Pedro. Yo estaba desesperada. Nos habíamos quedado tres. Una de ellas era la señora originaria de Armenia, su nombre es Flo. Ya el resto se había ido. Al fin como a las diez, nos llamaron. Esta vez no nos fuimos en el bus, sino que en un microbús junto con seis hombres. Entre ellos iba Gil. Todos nuestros rostros mostraban cansancio, ya era tarde. Este viaje fue diferente que los anteriores. No se escuchaban ni chistes, ni canciones. Todo mundo en un silencio total que denotaba que nuestros pensamientos estaban en otro lugar, algunos con la mirada perdida, otros casi dormidos, pero todos consientes que era viernes. Eso significaba que pasaríamos el fin de semana en detención.

Al llegar esperamos a que llegara la oficial que nos haría el registro, pero esta vez llegó una oficial gorda y alta. No vestía con uniforme azul como las anteriores sino que verde y en su chaleco se leía INS. Llevaba en sus manos tres uniformes, un rojo, un azul y un anaranjado. Fue realmente una pesadilla lo que vivimos y todo lo veía en cámara lenta. Flo estaba en su período menstrual y rehusaba desnudarse. Además era su primera experiencia ante esta situación tan denigrante. La oficial le dijo que podíamos pasar toda la noche ahí si era necesario y teníamos que hacer lo que ella decía. Al fin la pobre de Flo se rindió. Sus lágrimas corrían por sus mejías.

Todos nos sentíamos mal, pero finalmente terminamos como a la una de la mañana. La oficial empezó a repartir los uniformes. A Flo le dio el uniforme anaranjado, a mí el azul, y el rojo a la otra compañera. Me sentí tan mal ya que yo esperaba el uniforme anaranjado. Pero lo más traumatizante para mí, fue ver a Gil vestido de rojo. Ahí sí que me desmoralicé. Siempre he sido una esposa y madre protectora, pero en este caso estaba imposibilitada a hacer algo por mi esposo. Tenía que haber un error. No era posible que Gil estuviera vestido de rojo. Sólo los criminales peligrosos usan ese color. No pude más y lloré inconsolablemente. Tenía que haber un error, un terrible error. No entendía lo que estaba pasando.

*   *   *   *   *

Llegamos al Pod 6 y esta vez la oficial nos dijo que pasáramos al dormitorio y que nos acomodáramos en cualquier cama que estuviera vacía. El cuarto estaba a oscuras y tenía miedo de despertar a alguien. Así que me acomodé en el camarote de la primera fila en la parte de arriba, justo frente a la cabina de los oficiales. Esa noche comprendí que el asignarme un color significaba que me quedaría en este centro de detención hasta que viera al juez y se definiera mi caso. También significaba que ya no podría hablar con Gil y tomar decisiones juntos como familia. Estábamos incomunicados totalmente.

Por un momento me pareció estar en otro país. Había visto tanto dolor, tanta injusticia, tanto irrespeto a los derechos humanos. En fin esta realidad no concordaba con la imagen majestuosa que yo tenía de este gran país al que admiraba. Eso me preocupaba mucho, pero en ese momento lo más importante era dormir y comunicarme al día siguiente con Diana para decirle en que lugar estábamos.

Enfrentando la realidad

Me desperté al escuchar por un parlante, "El desayuno está listo". La mayoría saltaba de sus camas para ser las primeras en la fila. Yo esperé un poco y fui la última en recibir mi plato. Un oficial con el pelo rubio muy encarada que no respondía a los buenos días era la encargada ese día de entregar los alimentos. Me entregó una bandeja con una dona, leche y un poco de queso cottage. Al pasar al comedor me senté en el primer asiento disponible. Me tocó compartir la mesa con dos cubanas, una belizeña y una guatemalteca. Las cubanas al percatarse de mis intenciones de no comer, me pidieron de inmediato la comida y se la repartieron. Lo único que yo deseaba en ese momento era tomarme un café pero no tenía una taza, así que Dor, la chica guatemalteca, me cedió la suya y ese fue mi desayuno.

Al terminar de comer tienes que pasar al dormitorio mientras se hace la limpieza, así que me fui a mi cama y vi a mi compañera de la cama de abajo. Era de Sri Lanka, se llamaba Pri y tenía 18 años. También su madre estaba ahí y todas la llamaban "Mamá". A ellas las habían capturado en el aeropuerto, cuando hicieron escala para abordar un vuelo hacia Canadá, donde el resto de su familia son asilados políticos.

En cuanto terminaron la limpieza me fui a los teléfonos para llamar a Diana. Aquí sólo se pueden hacer llamadas por cobrar. Cuando logré comunicarme a casa le di a Diana la dirección y le dije que el horario de visitas era de 8 a 11 AM, de 1 a 4 PM, y de 6 a 9 PM, solamente los sábados y domingos. Al darle la dirección le dije que buscara en el mapa como llegar. También le pedí que avisara a mi amiga Ceci lo que nos había pasado y aunque ella vivía en San Diego que le llamara para cuando necesitara algo. Diana me dijo que vendría al día siguiente y colgamos.

*　　　　　*　*　*　　　　　*

Me quedé en el comedor, pues desde ahí se ve el mar y es una vista muy bonita. Me puse a rezar el rosario y a pensar en mis hijos. Me sentía tan preocupada por ellos; lo que me preocupaba era su seguridad. Eran adolescentes inexpertos e ingenuos ya que apenas tenían siete meses de haber llegado a este país. Tendría que trabajar mucho en ellos aunque a distancia. Pero necesitaba estuvieran fuertes y se unieran hoy más que nunca para cuidarse unos a otros y sobre todo no tomar el camino equivocado hoy que estaban solos y sin supervisión.

*　　　　　*　*　*　　　　　*

Llegó la hora del almuerzo, el cual sirven a las doce del mediodía. Me senté de nuevo en la misma mesa. Una de las cubanas se llama Laz. Vestía de rojo y era de raza negra, gordita y pequeña de estatura. Su paisana Mar era alta, un poco gruesa y bien comilona. También vestía de rojo. Laz me preguntó de qué cárcel venía, yo le respondí que de ninguna y que no sabía por qué me habían dado el uniforme color azul. Ambas se sonrieron dudando de mi respuesta.

– Pero tú puedes cambiar el color del uniforme si no te gustan – me respondió Laz – ¿Verdad Mar?

– ¡Claro, por supuesto! Sólo tienes que llenar una solicitud y se la entregas a la oficial, pero asegúrate de escribir el color de uniforme que tú quieres – respondió Mar.

La verdad que me pareció fantástica la idea, de por si nunca había usado el color azul. Tengo tez morena y no me gusta. Después de que comimos, pregunté quien podría darme una solicitud para pedir cambio de color en mi uniforme, y las cubanas me respondieron que se lo pidiera a la oficial que está de turno. Sólo sentí que Dor, la guatemalteca, pisaba mi pie y me hizo señas con su cabeza para que no fuera a pedir una solicitud.

En cuanto se levantaron las cubanas, Dor me explicó que el color lo asigna el INS y cada color indica lo grave del caso. Dijo que las cubanas siempre hacen lo mismo cuando llega gente nueva y que la última vez lo que habían hecho era decirle a una japonesa que podía solicitar pasar una noche con su novio y que era posible que se lo autorizaran. Así que la inocente chica escribió la solicitud, la entregó y fue el hazme reír por un rato. A las dos de la tarde, llegaron otras oficiales y se retiraron las de la mañana.

*　　　　　*　*　*　　　　　*

El resto del día me lo pasé en el comedor, hasta que escuché por el parlante: "366 Guzmán." Me acerqué a la cabina de la oficial y me dijo que me entregarían ropa y efectivamente así fue. Me dieron un suéter, un short, un pantalón, dos camisetas, dos toallas, tres pares de calcetines, tres panties, dos brasieres, un par de zapatos de lona, un par de sandalias para bañarme, un cepillito de dientes y un mini peine, todo en una caja plástica donde los guardaría. Ah, y una bolsa para entregar la ropa sucia.

Ordené todo en mi caja, lo puse debajo de mi cama y me recosté un poco. Traté de dormir pero mi mente era un torbellino de angustia y desesperación. A las cuatro de la tarde nos contaron las oficiales para asegurarse que no faltaba nadie. Éramos un total de 70 mujeres de diferentes edades y razas. La menor de todas era mi "Bunky," o sea mi compañera de la cama de abajo, Pria de diez y ocho años, y la mayor era su Mamá que tenía como 52. El 40% éramos de habla hispana y el resto en ese momento eran de China, India, Sri Lanka, Irán, Etiopia, Nigeria, Sierra Leona, Taiwán, Francia, Armenia, Jamaica y Siria.

A las cinco de la tarde nos sirvieron la cena, pero en esta oportunidad me cambié de mesa. Ahí conocí a dos salvadoreñas. Las dos vestían anaranjado y las habían capturado el mismo día en diferentes lugares pero se habían ayudado mutuamente y eran bien unidas. Eran casadas y tenían hijos. Les pregunté que cuánto tiempo tenían de estar detenidas y me respondieron que tres meses.

¡Qué horror! Me desmoralicé terriblemente. No me esperaba que fuera tanto el tiempo que uno tenía que esperar en detención, pero me dieron ánimos y me invitaron a jugar cartas con ellas. Me aconsejaron que tuviera cuidado con las cubanas pues eran terribles, especialmente Mar que tenia SIDA, y que siempre chequeara el baño y me asegurara que no hubiera sangre. También me advirtieron de la chica de Siria quien era agresiva, y con el hombre que se había hecho mujer.

– Con el hombre que se ha hecho mujer? ¿Quién es?– les respondí. Sólo eso me faltaba, me dije a mi misma.

Me lo enseñaron y era una mujer jamaiquina, alta, raza de color y sus manos eran bien grandes. Tenía una cara tan amargada y vestía de color azul. A las compañeras les agradecí sus recomendaciones y de ahí en adelante me acerqué a ellas pues me sentía en confianza.

* * * * *

En la noche hablé a casa. Los niños se escuchaban bien, optimistas de que todo se solucionaría y me prometieron ser fuertes, estudiar, y cuidarse mutuamente. Me contaron que Gil, mi esposo, ya se había comunicado con ellos y que se sentían tranquilos, pues al menos íbamos a estar en un solo lugar y no en esa viajadera e incomodidad de pasar en el edificio central del INS.

A las ocho de la noche hicimos otra fila, nos dieron un snack, y a las diez nos contaron y cambiaron el turno de las oficiales. Qué diferencia de turno a turno. Las de la mañana son pesadas, irrespetuosas y mantienen la disciplina a puro grito. Las de la tarde son lo contrario, te saludan, te tratan como persona, platican contigo, te sonríen y mantienen la disciplina y el orden sin abusos de autoridad. Las de la noche son igual que sargentos en el cuartel, gritan y te transmiten temor; te intimidan.

Invité a unas compañeras a rezar el rosario y aceptaron. Éramos solamente tres, pero hicimos el compromiso de rezarlo todas las noches para pedir a la Virgen María que cuidara de nuestros hijos. Todas tenemos esa pena en común y al finalizar, me acosté de inmediato. Otras se quedaron escribiendo cartas o viendo televisión, pero yo no tengo deseos de nada. Quisiera dormirme y despertar en mi casa con mi esposo y mis hijos, y pensar que esta es una pesadilla, que no es realidad lo que estoy pasando por estos momentos. Deseo volver a mi hogar. Quiero abrazar a mis hijos, darles un beso de buenos días y decirles que los quiero mucho.

*　　　　*　*　*　　　　*

El día siguiente era domingo. A las nueve de la mañana, si tú quieres, puedes salir al patio a tomar aire fresco y un poco de sol. Este recreo dura una hora, así que me animé, pues estaba desesperada de estar sin hacer nada. En cuanto salimos observé que había un tablero para jugar basketball y una mesa de ping pong. Había dos máquinas, una para comprar sodas y otra para comprar golosinas y también una máquina para hacer ejercicio. Alrededor se observaban unas mesas.

Me puse a caminar alrededor de la cancha cuando observé que llegó un sacerdote. Era alto y delgado, llevaba un portafolio en sus manos, y nos invitó a celebrar la santa misa. Limpiamos una mesa y el abrió su portafolio y sacó un mantelito blanco impecable, un cristo, una cajita con hostias y los misales para celebrar la misa. También sacó su sotana blanca y una estola verde preciosa que reconocí de inmediato pues era tejida con diseños guatemaltecos. Celebramos la misa y lloré cuando comulgué.

Al terminar la misa me acerqué al sacerdote, que antes ya se había presentado con nosotros como el padre Robert y le pregunté que si la estola era de Guatemala. El me dijo que si, que como lo sabía. Le dije que era salvadoreña y estaba familiarizada con ese tipo de tejidos. Conversamos un poco y me mencionó que el era un sacerdote jesuita y parte de su tiempo lo había dedicado a visitar comunidades en Guatemala y El Salvador. Cuando el me dijo eso, sentí como un rayo de luz en esas tinieblas, pues hablaba perfecto español y su homilía fue buenísima, de mucha reflexión. Y para cerrar con broche de oro: sacerdote jesuita que conocía mi cultura.

Sentí como un nexo con mi Patria, pues yo me eduqué en la universidad jesuita en El Salvador y todo el tiempo de mi niñez y adolescencia estuve en internados, donde las monjas y los sacerdotes son las personas en las que hay que confiar. Hablamos de los mártires jesuitas asesinados en mi país y de los logros alcanzados a raíz de su muerte. Al despedirnos me mencionó que vendría todos los domingos a celebrar la misa con nosotros. Antes de retirarse nos regaló un rosario y una Biblia y a partir de ese día invité a mis compañeras a formar grupos para rezar el rosario todas las noches. Llegamos a formar tres grupos, el hispano, el filipino, y el de inglés. Nunca antes se había visto algo similar, según las oficiales.

El conocer a un sacerdote como el padre Robert fue trascendental para mí. El no me dio una charla de evangelización o arrepentimiento sino que simplemente me dijo:

– Amalia, aquí hay mucha necesidad. Recuerda que tu espíritu es libre.

La verdad que esas palabras fueron mi inspiración para no dejarme vencer y ser libre, libre de espíritu. Mi cuerpo estaba en prisión, pero yo tenía vida; podía reír, soñar y luchar por el día en que vería mi libertad y lograr para mis hijos un futuro mejor. Mientras este momento llegaba, tendría que aprender a vivir dignamente en prisión. Esta sería mi nueva casa, la cual estaba decorada con dolor, frustración, enojo, ira, maldad, injusticia, indiferencia, y desamor. Era un ambiente terrible, así que el reto de redecorarla no sería fácil.

Pero estaba dispuesta a tomar este reto, no dejaría que el sistema aniquilara lo más precioso que tenía en este momento, mi libertad espiritual, el tener fe de que Dios no abandona a sus hijos, tener la esperanza de que este momento era pasajero, que este sería mi nuevo mundo. Era un mundo hostil lleno de injusticia y dolor, un mundo que Dios no ha creado sino que los hombres para destruirte espiritualmente, pero contra el que yo lucharía, ayudando a mis compañeras a vencer el miedo, fortalecer su fe y encontrar el amor de Dios en este lugar.

*   *   *   *   *

En la tarde me llamaron, pues tenía visita. Estaba ansiosa de ver a Diana y cual sería mi sorpresa cuando la vi junto con sus hermanos. Me alegré mucho, pero tenía unas inmensas ganas de llorar. No los podía abrazar y mucho menos besar, pues nos separaba un vidrio. Puse mi mano en el vidrio y ellos automáticamente pusieron la suya como queriendo tocarme. Pasamos así unos minutos, nadie derramó una lágrima, y comencé a hablarles con mucho entusiasmo aunque sólo yo sabía en mi interior lo que estaba sufriendo en esos momentos.

Sentí que no podía correr el riesgo de preocuparlos, pues sería peor el que ellos se dieran cuenta que no podían ayudarme. ¡Así que la obra de teatro tenía que ser perfecta! Les dije que era un lugar precioso, del cual se podía ver el mar y que había un salón para hacer ejercicios. También les dije que la comida era buenísima y en fin ya ni recuerdo que tantas mentiras les dije, pero lo principal era que había logrado mi objetivo. Ellos se comprometieron a estudiar duro, no faltar a la escuela, y a comportarse lo mejor posible. Les dije que ese sería mi aliciente para seguir adelante. Nos despedimos y quedamos en vernos la siguiente semana.

En cuanto regrese al Pod me fui directo a mi cama. Estaba desvastada. Había tanta incertidumbre respecto al tiempo que duraría en este lugar. Lo que me atormentaba era la situación de los niños. ¿Cómo harían para sostenerse en nuestra ausencia? El poco dinero que teníamos les duraría al máximo un mes. Pero también había que pagar al banco la cuota sobre la casa, así que tendríamos que decidir si pagar la casa o comprar comida para ellos. Por otro lado los gastos ahora se habían duplicado. Las llamadas telefónicas son carísimas, pues sólo puedes llamar por cobrar y no sólo se paga un cargo por conexión sino que también la tarifa es bien alta. Yo hablaba todos los días al igual que Gil. De esa manera nos asegurábamos que los niños estaban bien. Por tanto, la cuenta de teléfono quién sabe de cuánto llegaría.

No hay dolor que se compare al que se siente cuando uno está imposibilitado de ayudar a sus seres queridos, ya no se diga cuando estos son tus hijos, por los cuales has dado toda tu vida y esfuerzo para educarlos, darles amor y corrección, pero sobre todo que tengan una niñez mejor a la que tu viviste. Es un dolor que te oprime el pecho, que te desgarra el alma y sientes que mueres lentamente, pues no hay opciones de nada. Yo luchaba diariamente para recordar que tenía que ser fuerte para exigirles fortaleza. Tenía que hablar con ellos muy optimista para que tuvieran fe de que esto pasaría pronto y sobre todo decirles que yo confiaba plenamente en ellos, de que no me fallarían pues. Sabía que me amaban así como yo a ellos, y fue así como me di cuenta que el amor sería mi más grande aliado.

Comenzando la batalla

Mi compañera salvadoreña me consiguió trabajo. Me pagaban $1.00 al día por hacer la limpieza. Eso alivió mucho mi ansiedad, pues estaba ocupada. Aunque sólo era una media hora, mi mente descansaba de toda preocupación. También aprovechaba a doblar ropa, aunque no me pagaban. Lo único que quería era estar en actividad. La mayoría de mis compañeras pasaban acostadas, pedían medicamentos para la ansiedad, y pasaban drogadas todo el día. Sólo se levantaban a comer; eran un desastre. Preferían medicarse a afrontar sus problemas y buscar solución al futuro que tendrían que afrontar.

Ese día lunes observé que a las seis de la tarde se reunía un grupo para cantar y estudiar la Biblia, así que compartí con ellas y eso me ayudó muchísimo. Era una hora de reflexión, de orar unas por otras, especialmente las que tenían corte el día siguiente y éramos solidarias en nuestros problemas.

Me sentía fuerte y optimista al leer las promesas de Dios para sus hijos. Me encantaba leer Isaías 43, especialmente los primeros siete versículos; me aferraba a esa lectura. Tantas veces que había leído la Biblia y había predicado su palabra en mi grupo de oración pero ahora lo sentía tan cerca. Es algo que no se puede explicar, hay que vivirlo. Dios estaba ahí conmigo. Cuando me sentía sola y abandonada, cuando tenía mucho miedo de lo que pudiera pasarle a mis hijos, en mis momentos de incertidumbre y dolor, El estaba ahí.

*   *   *   *   *

En esa semana me entregaron un papel en que se me notificaba que tenía corte en dos semanas. Le avisé a Diana para que se comunicara con la abogada. Me alegré muchísimo con esa noticia. Los días pasaban lentamente y yo seguía luchando por no dejarme vencer por la depresión y angustia. Me propuse ser útil porque era inconcebible pensar que me limitaría a estar encerrada desperdiciándome, habiendo tanta necesidad entre nosotras.

Había trabajado toda mi vida. Soy bien activa, y el encierro y la inactividad estaban aniquilándome. Así que decidí empezar a servir de traductora con las oficiales, pues la mayoría no habla español. Cuando alguien necesitaba algo me pedían ayuda, fuera de llenar un papel, pedir ver al doctor... lo que fuera. Yo lo hacía con gusto. Esto hizo que la mayoría me llamara Madre Teresa. Mis compañeras no entendían el por qué yo ayudaba tanto a cambio de nada, pero en realidad yo necesitaba ser yo misma y no perder mi identidad.

Necesitaba vivir aunque sea en esas precarias condiciones, sentirme útil. Todas estábamos sufriendo. Compartíamos tristezas, frustración, hasta alegría al ver que algunas eran liberadas, y dolor al vernos en esta situación. La verdad que yo necesitaba más de ellas que ellas de mí, pues al permitirme ayudarlas y consolarlas encontraba una razón valida para estar en ese lugar. Esa era mi motivación para seguir luchando con lo poco que yo tenía, mi ser. De lo contrario para mi hubiera sido un infierno.

* * * * *

Una semana antes de la corte nos visitó la abogada, y nos explicó en detalle la razón de nuestra detención. Los oficiales que nos detuvieron eran de INTERPOL (Policía Internacional), e INS (Departamento de Inmigración y Ciudadanía), ya que se les había solicitado nuestra captura. Según ellos éramos criminales que habíamos hecho una estafa por el valor de $ 650 millones de colones en nuestro país, El Salvador. Yo no lo podía creer, pero de inmediato sabía de donde venía esta denuncia.

Antes de venir a Estados Unidos me dedicaba al comercio y Gil era un arquitecto dedicado a la construcción. Yo era propietaria de pequeñas boutiques de ropa, y al cerrar operaciones hubo en especial un prestamista, un usurero con él que no pude negociar el pago de la deuda. El plan de pagos que le proponía no le parecía, a pesar que durante 5 años le estuve pagando el 5% de interés mensual sobre el préstamo y ya se había cobrado tres veces la deuda. El no tuvo ninguna consideración y nosotros habíamos salido del país sin poder pagar lo que el exigía. Efectivamente este señor era el responsable.

Pero para mi sorpresa no sólo él, sino que también la ex-secretaria de mi esposo, quien junto con él, habían hecho todos los movimientos necesarios para que esto sucediera. Pusieron demasiadas demandas contra nosotros en El Salvador, nos reportaron con la embajada estadounidense, y listo. Darme cuenta de esto me dolió más, pues mi matrimonio estuvo a punto de fracasar por esta mujer. Gil se sentía súper mal al darse cuenta de esto, pero la verdad que nosotros éramos los únicos responsables de lo que estaba pasando por confiar demasiado.

La abogada nos informó que tendríamos que probar que estas acusaciones no eran verdaderas para salir de las acusaciones criminales. Pero también había problemas con nuestro estatus migratorio y por lo tanto aconsejó que pidiéramos asilo político porque habíamos sido afectados por la guerra civil en nuestro país. Nos explicó que sería un juicio difícil y que tendríamos que proporcionar todas las pruebas que tuviéramos al respecto. El tiempo se fue volando y la reunión no duró más de quince minutos cuando un guardia le notificó a la abogada que tendría que retirarse.

Ya de camino al Pod sentía mis pies muy pesados. Mi mente estaba en blanco y mis esperanzas de reunirme lo más pronto con mi familia se habían esfumado. Me sentía tan impotente y tan preocupada por el futuro de mis hijos que era frustrante el pensar y pensar para encontrarme en un camino sin salida. Tendría que resignarme a enfrentar esta situación y estar lista a soportar lo que fuera. Por otro lado, tendríamos que avisar a nuestra familia en El Salvador y ocasionarles esta pena tan grande.

El fin de semana cuando vinieron los niños a visitarme, le pedí a Diana que le avisara a su tía Musi de lo que estaba pasando. ¿Por qué a ella? Bueno, la verdad que siempre que la he necesitado ha estado ahí, a mi lado, solidaria, dándome ánimos, pero sobre todo dándome fe, recordándome que para Dios no hay problema tan grande que no se pueda resolver. Cómo la extrañaba en estos momentos. Cómo hubiera querido tenerla a mi lado aunque fuera por unos minutos.

*   *   *   *   *

El tiempo pasaba lentamente, pero al fin se llegó el día de mi audiencia en la corte. Esa noche casi no pude dormir. Me levanté temprano para estar lista a tiempo. Mi corazón palpitaba a mil y tenía miedo, mucho miedo, a pesar de que la sala de corte es en el mismo edificio. No tenía ni idea de lo que iba a pasar ese día, pero estaba nerviosísima y mis manos sudaban. La oficial nos llamó a las que teníamos audiencia. Todas estábamos ansiosas y nerviosas. Yo comencé a repetir en voz baja la oración de Santa Teresa de Ávila, *"Que nada te turbe. Que nada te espante. Quien a Dios tiene, nada le falta."* Esa fue mi letanía hasta que me calmé y pude controlar mis nervios hasta que llegamos.

Era una sala pequeña. A las mujeres nos sentaron en las primeras bancas y al poco tiempo llevaron a los hombres. Entre ellos pude ver de reojo a mi esposo, pues es prohibido intercambiar la mirada con una persona masculina, independientemente que sea tu esposo, padre, o familia. Éramos en total como veinte inmigrantes, todos con uniformes de diferentes colores. Cuando apareció la juez, todos nos pusimos de pie. Era un ambiente de orden y respeto, todo mundo en completo silencio. La juez era de aspecto joven y en su escritorio tenía los expedientes de todos los que nos encontrábamos en ese momento. Primero pidió que levantaran la mano los que querían ser deportados a su país. Muchos levantaron la mano, especialmente los hombres. Les tomaron sus nombres y los retiraron de la sala.

Al llegar nuestro turno nos llamaron al frente. Nos preguntaron nuestro nombre, si necesitábamos interprete, y que juráramos decir la verdad y sólo la verdad. Nos leyeron nuestros derechos y a continuación el juez intercambió unas palabras con nuestro abogado. Eran palabras técnicas, así que no entendí a lo que se referían y para desilusión mía, se cerró nuestra audiencia y nos dieron cita hasta dentro de quince días.

Yo no podía creerlo. ¡Qué frustrante! Tanta espera para nada. Me sentía tan molesta. No entendía como esto era posible; me parecía una burla. Oh Dios, ¡qué frustración tan grande! Todas las que fuimos a corte regresamos peor que como salimos, algunas llorando, otras molestas porque, como siempre ocurría, el abogado no se presentaba a la audiencia y ya sus familias le habían dado cuantiosas sumas de dinero.

En fin sólo cosas negativas habían pasado ese día, nada positivo. Llegué al Pod e inmediatamente lo primero que hice fue dirigirme a mi cama. No tenía ganas de hablar con nadie. Mi desesperación y frustración crecían incontrolablemente. No quería ni pensar que justificación les daría a mis hijos, para que comprendieran que tendríamos que permanecer más tiempo separados. ¿Cómo explicarles que soy un número más y que no hay prisa en la corte?

Esa noche hablé con ellos y por supuesto que estaban muy tristes al saber la noticia. Ellos habían estado escuchando de mi parte sólo cosas positivas y optimismo de que esta separación no sería por largo tiempo, pero hasta el momento, todo indicaba que faltaba un difícil y largo camino por recorrer.

*　　　　*　　*　　*　　　　*

Los días después de mi audiencia pasaban lentamente, pero un día miércoles en esa semana, llegaron a visitarnos al pod, un señor y una señora de edad avanzada. Eran como las nueve de la mañana y nos invitaron a compartir una lectura bíblica. Me acerqué al grupo de la señora, pues ella hablaba español. Su nombre era Alice. Y el señor, que se llamaba Donald, formó un grupo en inglés.

Comenzamos y oramos, leímos y compartimos las escrituras y en un momento dado Alice me preguntó por qué estaba triste y qué era lo que me preocupaba. Yo le respondí con voz entrecortada y conteniéndome para no llorar, que estaba triste por que me preocupaban mis hijos, y me atormentaba la idea de que algo malo les pudiera pasar y yo no estar a su lado.

Ella tomó mis manos y con una voz muy dulce, mirándome fijamente a los ojos me dijo – ¿Ha cuidado Dios de ti en estos años y te ha hecho milagros?

– Por supuesto – le respondí. – Mi hija Amy es el milagro más grande que El me ha hecho. Le salvó la vida y como ese hay muchos más.

– ¿Entonces por que te preocupas? – me respondió. – ¿No te das cuenta que hoy que lo necesitas es cuando El está más pendiente de ti y de tu familia? ¡No te mortifiques y confía! Entrégale tus hijos y verás que no te va a fallar.

Esas palabras fueron mágicas para cambiar mi actitud, a partir de ese instante mi vida en detención tomó otro rumbo. Me dediqué de lleno a colaborar con todos los grupos religiosos que nos visitaban. No importaba la denominación de iglesia de que fueran. Todos llegaban a darnos aliento, a consolarnos, a llenar ese gran vacío de amor y comprensión que teníamos, cuando ellos nos visitaban. Eran momentos de gozo, los únicos momentos en que yo personalmente sentía que no estaba sola y abandonada. Por lo contrario me sentía amada, apoyada, pero sobre todo sentía que era un ser humano. Fortalecía mi fe, fe en que el mal jamás triunfaría sobre el bien.

*　　　　*　*　*　　　　*

Llegó por fin la semana de mi audiencia en la corte. Estaba un poco nerviosa pero no como la primera vez. ¡Ah! y por supuesto con mucho entusiasmo de que en esta oportunidad todo se aclararía. Pero que desilusión. En esta oportunidad mi abogado le dijo a la jueza que solicitaríamos asilo político, y eso fue todo. La jueza fijó la próxima audiencia hasta dentro de un mes.

Yo no podía creerlo. Todo indicaba que este proceso sería larguísimo y que tendría que quedarme en este lugar quien sabe por cuanto tiempo. Todo parece indicar que hay demasiados detenidos, y los jueces no dan abasto. No pueden dedicar mucho tiempo a un caso. Solamente hay dos jueces y somos como 700 inmigrantes detenidos en este lugar.

En esta oportunidad, igual que en la anterior corte, pude ver a Gil de cerca. No podía hablarle ni mucho menos tocarlo, tampoco verlo directamente a los ojos, pero pude observar que había perdido mucho peso y se veía anímicamente decaído.

*   *   *   *   *

La situación de los niños era cada vez más preocupante. Una noche que hablé a casa Amy estaba llorando. Me decía que no aguantaba más. Se sentía muy sola. Diana tenía novio y la relación entre ellos había cambiado mucho. Como era lógico y normal, ella dedicaba parte de su tiempo a salir con su novio, un compañero suyo de la universidad. Pero sus hermanos se sentían relegados a un segundo plano.

Para mi era una situación difícil de controlar, ya que no podía esperar que Diana desempeñara el rol de mamá, y a la vez comprendía lo importante que era para sus hermanos el sentirse apoyados y atendidos por su hermana mayor. Ellos veían en ella el salvavidas que tenían a mano en ese mar turbulento de inseguridad, de miedo y de frustración al ver que sus padres no regresaban a casa en el tiempo esperado.

Yo no podía hacer absolutamente nada para resolver esta situación, sólo pedirle a mis hijos que trataran de salir adelante, que se unieran hoy más que nunca, pues divididos sería más difícil salir adelante. Les dije que se cuidaran uno al otro y que el mejor regalo que podían darme era que se comportaran como si sus padres estuvieran en casa.

Lo peor de todo es que no podía compartir mi preocupación respecto a los niños con mi esposo, así como tampoco tomar juntos una solución a este problema. Por lo pronto tendría que resignarme y aceptar que mis hijos ya no estaban bajo mi supervisión, y que ellos tendrían que valerse por si solos para resolver sus propios problemas.

Tenía que aceptar la realidad. El futuro de mis hijos no estaba bajo mi control. No tuve control ni sobre mi propio futuro. Tendría que aprender a vivir día a día, sin expectaciones de nada a futuro. Inmigración me había quitado la libertad, mis hijos, mi trabajo y mi esposo. Había perdido todo.

Es como estar muerto, pero en vez de llegar al paraíso te enfrentas a un mundo hostil, sin amor, sin esperanza, sin privacidad, sin recursos, un mundo creado por Inmigración para romper tu espíritu ,en el que tu no vales nada; eres una persona indeseable, eres tratado como un criminal. Es un infierno.

Y aquí comenzó la batalla más difícil. Tendría que salir adelante en honor a mis hijos. No quería que me vieran derrotada, sin deseos de vivir un futuro mejor. Y si ellos estaban luchando afuera por salir adelante, yo lo haría en detención.

Una historia triste

Y así pasaron los días. Comencé a dibujar, y me relajaba mucho. Aprendí a colorear usando dulces M&M, y por supuesto todos los días a las seis de la tarde teníamos grupo de estudio bíblico. Cantábamos y compartíamos nuestras experiencias. Orábamos unas por otras y a pesar de que algunas veces teníamos diferencias, las católicas con las evangélicas, recordábamos que la Biblia era para unirnos, no para desunirnos.

Y recordábamos sobre todo que teníamos que apoyarnos para darnos ánimo y comprender que había un futuro, que habían hijos y familia esperándonos, que estaban luchando desde fuera con o sin recursos y si decaíamos era un problema más para ellos. Si llorábamos cuando hablábamos por teléfono con ellos, no era justo, pues estaban imposibilitados para ayudarnos y les dábamos un sufrimiento más. Esta era mi doctrina.

*   *   *   *   *

Recuerdo que en una oportunidad un oficial de inmigración me llamó y me pidió que hablara con una señora que habían detenido. Pidió que la convenciera que entrara al Pod, pues de lo contrario usarían la fuerza. Ella se rehusaba a entrar. Pensaba que su vida estaría en peligro con tantas mujeres para ella peligrosas, ya que eso es lo que esperas encontrar en una cárcel. Hablé con ella. Estaba en un mar de lágrimas, completamente descontrolada. Finalmente accedió a entrar, con la promesa de que no me apartaría de su lado.

Comenzamos a platicar y me contó su historia. Su nombre era Luci, era peruana de una provincia lejos de Lima, llamada Arequipa. Tenía como 50 años y decidió dejar su país porque su esposo era alcohólico y además tenía problemas en su trabajo. Prestó el dinero para viajar a los Estados Unidos y partió a Bolivia junto con el coyote. Ahí se unió con otra mujer en este viaje y de ahí, los tres tomaron un vuelo hasta Los Ángeles usando el pasaporte de otras personas parecidas físicamente a ellas y con visa de turista.

Cuando llegaron al aeropuerto el oficial de inmigración descubrió el engaño y las capturó junto al coyote. Fueron trasladadas a una cárcel y permanecieron detenidas hasta que declararon como testigos contra el coyote con la promesa de que serían liberadas si testificaban y lo identificaban. Esta detención duró como tres meses, pero tuvo que contratar a un abogado y pagar una fianza, contando con la ayuda económica de su hermana que vivía en Maryland.

Un día le llamaron y le dijeron que podía irse, que estaba libre. Al salir, ella reclamó su maleta y le dijeron los oficiales de la cárcel que había quedado en Inmigración. Como necesitaba sus pertenencias, se dirigió a las oficinas del abogado que llevó el caso y le explicó que le faltaba su maleta. Este hizo una llamada a Inmigración para averiguar al respecto y luego le dijo a Luci que se esperara pues le llevarían la maleta a la oficina.

Ella esperó pacientemente, cuando para su sorpresa, en vez de su maleta llegaron los oficiales de inmigración y la arrestaron para llevarla a San Pedro. Ella les enseñó sus documentos en que constaba que ella había pagado una fianza para su libertad, pero se limitaron a decirle que eso no tenía validez para ellos.

Ahí comprendí el porqué del nerviosismo y la angustia de Luci. Sólo le pedí que se calmara, que nadie le iba a hacer daño, y que lo mejor que podía hacer era controlarse para de esta manera pensar como podría contactar a su hermana y hacerle saber que estaba detenida de nuevo. Luci nos acompañó ese día en nuestro estudio bíblico y no le fue difícil acomodarse a nuestro grupo, pues se sentía apoyada y lo más importante de todo es que sabía que no era la única que estaba sufriendo, y que tendría que sacar fuerzas de sus flaquezas.

* * * * *

La situación de mis hijos cada vez peor. Ya teníamos tres meses en detención y el dinero se acabó. Les cortaron el teléfono por falta de pago, así que ahora tendríamos problemas en comunicarnos regularmente. El único medio para comunicarnos eran las visitas semanales, a las que ellos siempre acudían sin fallar. Algunas veces hacían colas de hasta dos horas para poder vernos sólo por 10 o 15 minutos. Pero era a través de estas visitas que yo podía comunicarme con mi esposo, intercambiando correspondencia. De otra manera era imposible.

Recuerdo que en una oportunidad le envié una carta a través del correo, pues teníamos un buzón donde poner la correspondencia. No necesitábamos estampillas, pero las cartas llegaban a su destino. La primera vez, la carta la recibió Gil. Creo que se les pasó por alto que era correspondencia interna. La segunda vez que lo intenté me llamaron la atención, pues me informaron que no puede haber correspondencia entre los detenidos. Dijeron que lo hacían por razones de seguridad, no importaba que fuéramos esposos.

– ¿Qué tal que planeen un escape? – me mencionó la oficial.

Yo no podía creerlo pero así es la regla, así que enviábamos nuestro correo a través de los niños.

Diana dejó de estudiar en la universidad y tenía que buscar un trabajo para poder mantenerse y aunque siempre vivían en la misma casa, eso duraría mientras el banco no los desalojara. En una carta hablamos con Gil que tendríamos que ver como hacíamos dinero para darles a los niños por lo menos $50 semanales para su comida. Así que nos tuvimos que rebuscar. Yo dibujaba, hacia tarjetas de felicitación, de cumpleaños, de todo y las vendía. Gil aprendió a hacer unas bolsas para guardar dinero; Diana le compraba el hilo y se lo entregaba cuando nos visitaba.

Así emprendimos nuestro negocio. Yo comenzaba en la tarea de cortar y preparar el papel después de hacer la limpieza. Paraba a la hora de almuerzo y continuaba al terminar mi tarea. En la noche no trabajaba mucho pues soy un poco ciega así que a las diez de la noche me acostaba. Lo importante de todo era una gran satisfacción entregarle a mis hijos lo poco que podía reunir y siempre llevaban a casa los $50 que nos comprometimos con Gil a entregarles.

*   *   *   *   *

Llegó al fin el día de mi corte. La verdad es que ya no sabía ni que pensar ni en que esperar. Los nervios me traicionaban. *Que nada te turbe, que nada te espante. Quien a Dios tiene nada le falta,* solía repetir. ¡Oh! que poderosa es esta oración. Ya no quería hacerme falsas ilusiones ni dárselas a mis hijos. Así que cambié mi estrategia y ahora ya les hablaba de ser pacientes para esperar el resultado.

Esa corte fue la mejor para mí, pues al entrar vi a uno de los hermanos de Gil en la sala. El había llegado para testificar en la corte. Me sentí tan bien cuando lo vi. Me dolió no poder hablar con él ni abrazarlo, pero me sentía contenta y feliz con tan sólo verlo. El básicamente le pidió a la jueza que nos concediera el asilo político. Y le explicó la persecución y pérdidas económicas que sufrimos durante y después de la guerra. La juez le hizo muchas preguntas para entender un poco mas de nuestra situación. La sesión de la corte se cerró y nos dieron otra cita hasta dentro de un mes.

Al llegar a mi Pod, todo mundo me preguntó que había pasado, pero al igual que las cortes anteriores no había una respuesta, no había algo concreto, sino que a seguir viviendo en la incertidumbre. Me desilusionaba al ver que algunas compañeras recibían fianza para pelear el caso en libertad y algunas con unos historiales criminales que daban miedo. Pero si algo aprendí era que nunca se puede saber el resultado final. Lo cierto es que todas las que pedían asilo no eran sujeto de fianza. Había quienes ya tenían un año esperando el resultado. Pero en mi interior yo tenía la esperanza de que yo no pasara por esta situación, sino que por lo contrario, que todo se aclararía y ganaríamos el asilo político.

* * * * *

A medida que pasaba el tiempo, el número de detenidas aumentaba, pero especialmente las que venían de la cárcel o la prisión, así que el ambiente era cada vez más tenso y más difícil de sobrellevar. Eran muchas peleas y lenguaje obsceno; la ley del más fuerte se hacía sentir y no todas eran fuertes para lidiar con este ambiente.

Recuerdo a Martha, una salvadoreña de treinta y seis años de edad. Ella había vivido en este país 12 años, con permiso de trabajo y ya había ganado su asilo político. Era una de las miles de víctimas de la guerra; su esposo y dos de sus hijitos murieron acribillados a balazos por hombres armados que irrumpieron en su casa. Sólo le quedó un hijo mal herido pero vivo.

Volviendo a su historia, resulta que su mamá estaba muy enferma y ella es su única hija. Solicitó permiso a Inmigración para salir del país y se lo concedieron por 60 días. Antes de salir, ella consultó que podría pasar si no llegaba en la fecha establecida, y le indicaron que tenía quince días máximo después de vencido el plazo para ir a la Embajada de Estados Unidos en El Salvador para que le dieran una ampliación.

Partió hacia su país, cuidó de su madre enferma, pero esta no se recuperaba, así que se le venció el plazo y fue a la embajada a pedir una ampliación y le dijeron que esa ampliación no existe y que si se le venció el plazo, simplemente no puede volver a los Estados Unidos. No conforme con esta respuesta viajó a Honduras, el país vecino, y obtuvo la misma respuesta. Desesperada pues su único hijo estaba aquí en los Estados Unidos, solicitó una visa de turista y se la concedieron y en cuanto su mamá se recuperó, regresó vía el aeropuerto de Los Ángeles donde fue detenida de inmediato, arrestada y enviada a San Pedro. Ella lloraba mucho. Estaba traumada de tanta violencia y le afectaba muchísimo el ambiente, especialmente cuando había peleas. Tenía problemas cardíacos.

En una ocasión estábamos en el almuerzo y justo en la mesa contiguo a la nuestra, se inició una pelea. Fueron segundos pero como el espacio es reducido, es un alboroto de gente. La mayoría quieren ver la pelea, la disfrutan. Otras como Martha se afligen y se ven afectadas emocionalmente. No están acostumbradas a este ambiente, sobre todo cuando llegan los oficiales a separar a las involucradas, porque las esposan y se puede ver el uso de la fuerza. En esta oportunidad Martha se desmayó y estuvo hospitalizada por tres días.

A su regreso del hospital estaba más desesperada que nunca por salir de este lugar. Contrató un abogado para que pidiera una corte lo más pronto posible, pero el abogado le mencionó que su caso no era difícil y que le daba un 90 % de que ganara, por tanto accedió a intentar pelear su caso de asilo político. Llegó el día de su corte y era la misma historia de todas; le dieron otra corte en quince días. Su desesperación era cada vez mayor y perdió mucho peso.

En la segunda corte no hubo ninguna decisión a su caso y tuvo que esperar un mes más para que al final le dijeran que le negaban el asilo político. Le dieron salida voluntaria con derecho a apelar la decisión del juez ante una corte superior. Pero ella renunció a todos sus derechos, pues no soportó el ambiente que estaba viviendo.

Ella fue una de mis mejores amigas. Había sufrido mucho en la vida y quizás por eso tenía una mirada triste y melancólica todo el tiempo. Era calmada y reservada, pero al hablar con ella se veía que era una buena mujer, una mujer sufrida que llevaba mucho dolor por dentro. Cuando se fue me sentí feliz por ella, pero me hacía mucha falta. A los meses de haber salido ella a El Salvador, recibí una carta en que se lamentaba de su poca valentía por luchar por su futuro. Tenía un sentimiento de culpabilidad enorme, pues estaba separada de su único hijo, y como ella me lo decía en su carta, su vida había perdido sentido.

Aceptando el veredicto

Por fin llegó el día de mi audiencia en la corte. "Un paso más para mi libertad," me repetía a mi misma. Me levanté temprano y para variar los nervios me traicionaban. Nunca sabes lo que puede pasar.

Caminé a la corte comencé con mi letanía, a repetir y confiar en lo que decía: *"Que nada te turbe, que nada te espante, quien a Dios tiene nada le falta."* Tenía que vencer este miedo que hacía que mi estómago lo sintiera como un cubo de hielo y que mi corazón palpitara a mil.

Mi fe se quebrantaba por momentos, y olvidaba que tengo que ser paciente y no perder la esperanza en que Dios actuará a su tiempo. En estos momentos era cuando me daba cuenta que mi fe era frágil y tenía que trabajar mucho para fortalecerme, confiar y vencer este miedo.

En esta ocasión, venían dos personas de El Salvador, una el abogado que me representaba y defendía ante mi acusador, el usurero, y la otra persona era el mismo usurero que había interpuesto una demanda de fraude en mi contra. Todo indicaba que esta sesión sería tensa e importante pues el fiscal de inmigración tenía al usurero como su as, para demostrarle a la jueza que no merecíamos el asilo político pues éramos unos criminales.

Por el otro lado, mi abogado contaría con el testimonio del abogado que estaba llevando el juicio en El Salvador, y que declararía que eran acusaciones falsas, pues estábamos hablando de una deuda comercial por la que se había pagado el 60 % anual en intereses y por lo tanto sus acusaciones de fraude no eran verdaderas.

La sesión duró tres horas, pero lo más importante de todo para mí fue que el usurero declaró que la deuda se había originado por un préstamo. Mintió al decir que no habíamos intentado negociar la deuda, pero ya eso no era importante para mí. Lo importante era que él pronunciara con sus propias palabras que era una deuda por un préstamo otorgado, y no un fraude como anteriormente lo había declarado.

Al terminar la sesión, la jueza fijó la próxima audiencia dentro de un mes. Ya estábamos en el mes de junio, ya teníamos cuatro meses en detención, y hasta la fecha, nada concreto en relación a nuestro futuro. Lo único que era seguro era que en la próxima sesión nosotros seríamos interrogados y que la jueza entonces tendría los argumentos necesarios en que sustentar su decisión respecto a nuestra petición de asilo político.

*　　　　*　*　*　　　　*

El mes de junio fue bien difícil para mí. Mi hija, Amy, cumplió diez y siete años. Ella era la que estaba más desesperada por nuestra ausencia. Se sentía sola y en una ocasión me llamó para decirme que ya no aguantaba más. Las relaciones con su hermana iban de mal en peor y Amy quería salirse de casa e irse a vivir a otro lugar, pero no sabía a donde ir. También me preocupaba mi hijo que por ser el menor, él sólo se limitaba a observar y estar callado.

Sabía que las cosas no iban bien entre ellos, pues aunque se esforzaran siempre en las visitas de los domingos, discutían por tonterías. Veía la frustración y el distanciamiento entre ellos y en esta oportunidad les pedí que hicieran el máximo de esfuerzo para entenderse y que si en realidad me amaban como decían, tenían que probármelo comportándose lo mejor que pudieran, y siempre que tomaran una decisión pensaran si yo me sentiría orgullosa de ellos.

Yo sabía que era una gran presión, un chantaje, pero tenía que hacerlo. El amor que existía entre nosotros era mi único aliado.

Lo que yo ignoraba era que mis hijos estaban viviendo en realidad un infierno, el novio de Diana se movió a casa con el pretexto de ayudarles, y adoptó el papel de jefe de familia. Amy y Gil sintieron que estaba usurpando el lugar que pertenecía a su padre. A esto hay que agregar que comenzaron a sentir que en realidad estaban solos y que su familia se había desintegrado. Para colmo, al novio le molestaba que hablaran español. Había problemas cuando ellos lo hacían, y era motivo de discusión y maltrato verbal entre ellos. Además, el novio no entendía el porqué Diana se preocupaba por sus hermanos, ya que consideraba que ellos eran los suficientemente grandes para valerse por si solos. Comenzó a presionarla para que cambiara su actitud protectora.

Yo estaba ignorando estos aspectos, y me dolía verlos tan distantes entre ellos y con mucho resentimiento, sin poder entender la razón para esta actitud. En alguna ocasión les llamé la atención y les dije que eran unos desconsiderados al darme este tipo de problemas, que mi sufrimiento al estar encarcelada no era nada si yo los veía unidos y luchando por salir adelante.

*   *   *   *   *

El tiempo seguía su curso. Cada día era insoportable. Había demasiadas detenidas; algunas tenían que dormir en el suelo en camas plásticas pues no había espacio disponible en el dormitorio. El comedor estaba lleno en su alrededor de este tipo de camas. Había mucho ruido y por supuesto muchas peleas. Yo me entretenía haciendo mis manualidades, trabajando, y coordinando el grupo de oración, pero estaba cansada de tanto encierro.

Por otro lado se me comenzó a caer el cabello, tenía mucha caspa, pie de atleta, y mi piel se comenzó a resecar tanto que se veía escamosa. Decidí ir a visitar al doctor para que me ayudara y me diera algo, así que hice una petición para ver al doctor, y en tres días me llamaron.

Fue bien interesante esta visita y la disfruté al principio. Nos llevaron a la clínica que queda en el mismo edificio pero al menos salíamos de nuestro ambiente. Ahí había unas sillas igual que en cualquier clínica y esperamos nuestro turno. Los oficiales que nos llevaron en esta oportunidad eran bien amables y jocosos. Nos trataron súper bien y sentíamos el alivio de salir de la rutina en la que pasábamos las 24 horas del día.

El doctor me vio, me preguntó el porqué de la visita y le expliqué, así que me dio un champú y una crema para la infección de hongos. Pero después le pregunté que es lo que me recomendaba para mi piel.

El me miró fijamente a los ojos y me dijo – Aquí es una cárcel, y no damos tratamiento cosmético. El problema de su piel es por su edad. Usted ya tiene 43 años, no espere tener la piel de una quinceañera. Retírese, que no puedo seguir perdiendo mi tiempo.

Me sentí tan molesta. No sólo me dijo vieja sino que estaba perdiendo el tiempo conmigo. Ni modo. Me retiré y me senté de nuevo a esperar a que terminara de atender a las demás, pero tenía unas terribles ganas de llorar. Me sentía humillada y siempre que me enojo, lloro, pero en esta vez tuve que aguantarme.

Mi compañera Luci, la peruana, también fue en esta oportunidad. Ella tenía algo en su seno. Se sentía una masa dura y siempre se quejaba del dolor, pero al igual que mí, no la atendieron como ella esperaba y le dieron Tylenol, que debe ser la medicina milagrosa para todas las enfermedades ya que eso es lo que te dan siempre que vas al doctor.

* * * * *

Cada día que pasa entiendo más el sistema. Aquí somos un inventario de personas. Hay un control estricto del número de detenidas; nos cuentan tres veces al día, nos dan de comer lo necesario, nos dan analgésicos para el dolor, nos lavan la ropa y nada más. No se invierte ni un centavo más en nosotras. Nos dan lo mínimo necesario para no tener problemas con Detention Watch Network, la organización que vela por las condiciones en las cárceles de inmigración. Así que aquí no me voy a morir de una enfermedad pues cuando es algo serio de peligro de muerte, rápido te llevan al hospital. Pero nada de medicina preventiva.

Todo te lo hacen difícil. Te proporcionan teléfonos pero sólo para hacer llamadas por cobrar. No hay a la mano un directorio telefónico, ni siquiera en la biblioteca. Lo único bueno que recibimos es la visita de los voluntarios religiosos, que la verdad los admiro, pues los guardias no los tratan bien y algunas veces los dejan parados hasta quince minutos antes de dejarlos entrar a nuestro Pod. A ellos les damos todas las quejas que tenemos; son los únicos en los que confiamos, y sabemos que de corazón se preocupan de nosotras y sufren al verse imposibilitados de ayudarnos y al ver tanto dolor e injusticia.

Siempre me pregunto que les motiva a visitarnos si aquí los guardias les hacen las cosas tan difíciles. Los tratan con rudeza, les registran de pies a cabeza y ellos siempre están aquí cada semana, con una sonrisa radiante llenos de amor, sin importar si llueve, hace frío o es día feriado... *siempre.*

* * * * *

Ha terminado el mes de junio y el 21 cumplió cincuenta años Gil. Le pude enviar una tarjeta con los niños pero es difícil estar separados y tan cerca a la vez. Ya tengo más de tres meses en este encierro y creo que ya paso la etapa de adaptación e incertidumbre. Ya conozco las reglas del juego. Ya no estoy con falsas expectativas de que voy a salir pronto de este lugar. Ahora tengo que ser paciente y comprender que no tengo control de mis hijos ni de mi futuro, que tengo que vivir un día a la vez. No debo preocuparme por el mañana pues no puedo esperar nada concreto.

Gil siempre me escribe y sus cartas me irritan pues me escribe pasajes de la Biblia. Creo que toma la Biblia, escoge una lectura, y se pone a copiarla, así que en la carta que le envié esta semana le dije que yo no necesito que me escriba pasajes bíblicos, pues yo tengo mi Biblia y la estudio todos los días. Yo quiero saber lo que él siente, cuáles son sus preocupaciones, qué piensa respecto a los niños, todo lo que respecta a la familia. Y sobre todo lo que pasa en su Pod, si se siente seguro, si no es peligroso, en fin tantas cosas.

Por suerte mi querido esposo no se resintió por la dureza de mi carta y la siguiente carta que me envió fue totalmente diferente. Me contó que iba a comenzar a trabajar en la cocina y que le pagarían un dólar diario, que tendría más tiempo para escribirme y de tomar el aire fresco pues almorzaban en el patio.

También me pidió perdón por lo que había pasado, y se sentía responsable de nuestra desgracia. Pero le expliqué que yo no veía las cosas así, pues todo lo que pasa tiene un propósito y la clave es no buscar responsables, sino que afrontar la realidad, vivirla lo mejor que se puede, viendo lo positivo en vez de lo negativo, pero sobre todo aprender la lección. Así que desde la ventana de mi Pod procuraba verlo aunque fuera un minuto cuando salía al patio a comer y escribir; lo veía siempre tan pensativo y aislado pero me sentía muy feliz de verlo.

*   *   *   *   *

Un día miércoles cuando tenemos la visita de los voluntarios religiosos, vino un pastor. Nunca había venido al Pod a visitarnos y preguntó por mí. Se identificó y me dijo que se llamaba Ron. Dijo que el acostumbraba visitar a los hombres, que había conocido a Gil, y que él le había pedido que me visitara. Conversamos unos minutos y después nos reunimos varias en una mesa y escuchamos su mensaje.

Me gustó muchísimo la manera en que lo condujo. En esta oportunidad el habló del perdón y especialmente nos mencionó que tenemos que quitarnos nuestros sentimientos de culpa y perdonarnos por los errores cometidos, que tenemos que entender que si Dios nos perdona por nuestros errores y faltas ¿quienes somos nosotros para pasar recriminándonos y culpándonos por tantos errores del pasado? Dijo que tratáramos de vivir en paz con nosotras mismas, pues de lo contrario no podríamos ser nunca felices y por ende hacer felices a nuestras familias.

Y él tenía razón al decir esto, pues la carga es muy pesada cuando guardas en tu interior el sentimiento de culpa y ese sentimiento te impide iniciar una nueva vida en paz, viendo el presente y el futuro con mucha esperanza. Hubo muchas lágrimas en esta oportunidad, pero al terminar con nuestra reunión, mucha paz. Yo hasta ese momento no me había perdonado por el dolor causado a mis hijos, por el sufrimiento y angustia en que estaba toda la familia para sacarnos de este lugar y por tantas cosas que pasaron por mi mente en ese momento de reflexión.

Que privilegio y que bendición el poder contar con los voluntarios que nos visitan. Son los que vienen a darnos fuerza y esperanza para seguir en este infierno. Es increíble pero cuando ellos vienen hay más paz en el Pod; es un día diferente. Francamente es un privilegio el recibir este tipo de visitas. Me hacen tanto bien. Me siento viva cuando veo su sonrisa y escucho palabras llenas de fe y de amor. Creo que me sería difícil vivir en este encierro sin ellos, y no sólo a mí me pasa esto sino que a la mayoría. Creo que Dios los usa y siempre tienen palabras adecuadas al momento que estamos viviendo.

*   *   *   *   *

Esta semana es mi corte final, se supone que el juez dará su decisión a nuestra petición de asilo político. Sólo tenemos dos posibilidades: o nos lo da o lo niega. Yo trato de no pensar en ello, pues me pongo tensa. Sin embargo una noche le pedí a Dios me revelara lo que iba a pasar, y que así como en los años antes de su venida se revelaba a través de los sueños, le pedí que me adelantara el resultado de mi corte, y efectivamente así sucedió. Soñé que iba en un avión junto con otras personas, pero iba un oficial de inmigración cuidándonos. El avión hizo varias escalas, pero no me bajé en ninguna, permanecía siempre en el avión.

Al día siguiente les comenté en el grupo de oración que iba a perder mi asilo político y que me iban a deportar, pero que no me importaba pues sabía que estaba en las manos de Dios y que si esa era su voluntad, yo la aceptaba. Y así sucedió en la corte. La jueza nos denegó el asilo y fijó 30 días para apelar la decisión ante una corte superior si nosotros pensábamos que su decisión no era la correcta. De regreso al Pod, yo iba tranquila; no me sentía molesta ni preocupada por el veredicto. Creo que ya estaba preparada y por eso no me afectó.

Esa noche hablé con los niños, y ellos sí estaban desmoralizados e inquietos. Ninguno de los tres quería regresar a El Salvador. Los tres me decían que querían seguir estudiando aquí. Eso era inconcebible de aceptar para mí, pero por otro lado me ponía a pensar que mal o bien estaban establecidos y lo que menos quería era darles más inestabilidad. Así que les expliqué que teníamos un mes para decidir lo que haríamos y que necesitaba hablar con Gil para saber lo que pensaba al respecto.

*   *   *   *   *

Estoy en una etapa de resignación. Ya superé la de adaptación e incertidumbre. La decisión del juez está tomada y ahora tengo que resignarme, poner los pies sobre la tierra y hacerle frente a esta nueva etapa. Me preocupa la actitud de mis hijos; los veo tan decididos y convencidos de que este país es el mejor lugar para ellos y no entiendo como pueden decirme esto si yo veo las penalidades que están sufriendo. Pero nada puedo hacer por el momento, sólo pedirle a Dios que me dé la fuerza para tomar la decisión adecuada.

El fallo de la corte en mi contra ha bajado la moral de varias en el grupo de oración. La fe se rompe cuando los resultados no son los que esperamos, cuando no se ve el fruto de nuestras plegarias, pero la verdad que cuando pedimos siempre decimos, *"que se haga tu voluntad, no la mía."* Por otro lado el orar y hacer el bien no garantizan un milagro. Eso mis compañeras se niegan a entender y esta es la prueba de fuego, aceptar la voluntad de Dios.

Este fue el tema en nuestro grupo de oración: si de verdad confiamos que nuestro futuro está en las manos de Dios, no tendríamos que preocuparnos si las cosas no salen como lo esperamos, pues no hay mejor lugar que el que Dios decida para nosotros. Yo, la verdad, quiero confiar. Sé que Dios está en control de mi futuro y el de mi familia, y creo que este resultado tenía que darse pues hay mejores planes para mi, planes que desconozco pero serán para mi bien y el de mi familia.

Al fin una victoria

Recibí carta de Gil y me dice que la abogada nos recomienda que hagamos una apelación ante una corte superior, alegando que la jueza dio un fallo equivocado pues se presentaron pruebas evidentes de persecución. No nos garantiza que ganemos el caso pero cree que vale la pena intentarlo. Esto implica que tendríamos que quedarnos en detención de seis meses a un año, hasta que la corte superior dé su fallo.

Bonita decisión la que tenemos que tomar, y en este momento no tengo ni la menor idea de que hacer. Lo único de lo que estoy segura es que no quiero alejarme de los niños. Puedo soportar todo menos el dejarlos solos aquí en este país sin supervisión y yo sin poder verlos.

*   *   *   *   *

Esta semana mi compañera Luci de Perú ha estado con mucho dolor en su seno. Tiene una bola inflamada. Todas esperamos que no sea un tumor. Fue nuevamente al doctor y le dio otra vez Tylenol. Estamos preocupadas pues llora mucho del dolor. Además su corte se aproxima, no tiene abogado, no tiene dinero, en fin, está sola completamente y, para colmo, enferma sin posibilidades de ver a un buen médico. Ofrecí ayudarle y le sugerí que pidiera asilo político. Estaremos pendientes de lo que le diga el juez, si le da la oportunidad de escuchar su caso o no.

También vino una señora religiosa de la orden de misioneras Maryknoll. Es alta, elegante y muy bonita, una americana que infunde mucha confianza y se interesa en tu situación. Me encantó como dirigió su charla; nos puso a que pensáramos en los momentos más felices de nuestra vida, y al final dimos gracias a Dios por esos momentos.

Nos hizo ver que este momento es pasajero, que no estaríamos prisioneras toda la vida, y que teníamos familia esperando por nosotras para comenzar una nueva vida. Comulgamos y cerramos con una oración de acción de gracias. Esta religiosa se llama Molly y además, trajo una bolsa con rosarios y estampitas, así que todo el mundo feliz con los regalitos. Antes de que se retirara, le explicamos el problema con Luci y dijo que vería que podía hacer al respecto. Tomó nota de su nombre y número, y se retiró.

*   *   *   *   *

El correo siempre viene a las tres de la tarde. Yo ni me preocupo en buscar mi nombre pues recibo pocas cartas. Pero en esta ocasión yo tenía una carta. No me imaginaba quien me había escrito, así que fui de las primeras en la línea y tuve una gran sorpresa al recibir una carta de Martha, mi compañera que renunció a sus posibilidades de quedarse aquí con su hijo por no aguantar este encierro. Bueno pues, me cuenta que se viene de regreso. No puede estar separada de su único hijo. Se va a venir por tierra, y va a pagarle a un coyote en Tijuana para que la pase. Me dice que tiene mucho miedo, pues tiene que caminar por el desierto y pasar por muchas penalidades, pero está decidida, así que me pide que oremos para que pueda llegar a su destino sana y salva.

Esta carta fue una señal para mí. Yo la comprendía en su sufrimiento al estar separada de su hijo. Me veía en ella pasando el desierto, aguantando hambre, pasando sed y expuesta a arriesgar mi vida con tal de reunirme con mis hijos que tanto amo. Definitivamente estoy decidida a apelar la decisión del juez. No tengo idea del tiempo que tendré que estar en este infierno, pero lo prefiero pues por lo menos veo a mis hijos todas las semanas. Son unos pocos minutos pero son lo suficiente para darme aliento y seguir luchando por un futuro mejor.

*   *   *   *   *

Luci fue a corte y la jueza le dio una solicitud para asilo político, y le dijo que se podía representar por ella misma si no tenía abogado, así que esa misma noche manos a la obra y comenzamos a llenar la solicitud. La clave para ganar el asilo era probarle al juez que era perseguida en su país. Ella es bien insegura pues ha sufrido tanto, pero después de conversar por largas horas con ella le pedí que me contara su historia y si veíamos que tenía posibilidades de ganar, llenaríamos la solicitud. A Luci le daba pavor el pensar que iba a regresar a su país ya que había prestado dinero equivalente a $8,000 para hacer este viaje, y si la deportaban era imposible pagar esta deuda.

Esta es su historia: vivía en un lugar llamado Asentamientos Humanos que queda en la región de Arequipa; era un pueblo en que habían muchos indígenas. Luci hablaba el dialecto quechua y había conseguido trabajo en un comedor popular en donde repartían alimentos a los indígenas, y ella se comunicaba con ellos en su dialecto. Pero para variar la gente se aprovecha del más débil y en este lugar los indígenas beneficiados firmaban que habían recibido cierta cantidad de alimentos, pero la realidad era que siempre recibían una cantidad menor a la que firmaban.

Luci comenzó a explicar a los indígenas la cantidad que tenían que recibir y que se aseguraran que esa era la cantidad por la que firmaban. De esta manera se comenzó a ganar enemigos y comenzó a tener problemas con aquellos que quedaron al descubierto de que estaban robando a los indígenas. Fue a tal grado que en una ocasión uno de ellos la persiguió con un machete para matarla. Por suerte fue auxiliada por unos vecinos pero desde ese día su vida era una zozobra.

Para colmo no tenía apoyo en su esposo pues era un alcohólico que a menudo la maltrataba, a tal grado que en una ocasión ella puso una demanda en la comandancia de la policía. Pero no hubo ningún resultado positivo, sino que por el contrario su esposo se sintió engrandecido al ver que ella no había logrado nada. Fue después de escuchar su historia que decidimos pedir asilo por razones étnicas y por el abuso de su esposo. Escribió a su país y pidió que le enviaran las pruebas necesarias, entregó su aplicación y en un mes tendría su corte final.

*   *   *   *   *

Este día me llamaron por los parlantes. Me dijeron que tenía una sesión de consejería. Yo no sabía de qué me estaban hablando pero me preparé, y que grata sorpresa. Me llevaron a un cuartito y ahí se encontraba el Pastor Ron.

Tenía una gran sonrisa y me dijo: – Te tengo una sorpresa. He conseguido una sesión junto con tu esposo. Vamos a estar los tres y podrán platicar. Habrá un guardia vigilando por la puerta, así que tenemos que esperar a que venga.

Al momento venía Gil y nos saludamos sin abrazo ni nada, pues no es permitido. Lo vi más delgado y se había dejado crecer el bigote y la barba. No lo vi bien; había perdido mucho peso y se veía tan descuidado y enfermizo. Pero me imagino que él me vería de la misma manera. Le comenté que mi decisión era la de apelar el caso. No me importaba el tiempo que tendría que esperar pero prefería hacerlo a vencer o morir, pero no quedarme con remordimientos y dudas de que no llegue al final por miedo y cobardía. Gil me apoyó y me dijo que hablaría con la abogada para que comenzara la apelación.

Fue una bendición el poder conversar y ponernos de acuerdo acerca de nuestro futuro porque había sido bien frustrante estar sin poder comunicarnos en absoluto, más frustrante aún porque Gil estaba en el Pod 5, separado de mí en el Pod 6 por una sola pared de concreto. El pastor Ron nos pidió que renováramos nuestros votos matrimoniales y que nos perdonáramos por los errores del pasado. Así lo hicimos, oramos, y nos dimos un abrazo los tres a la vez para no levantar sospechas.

Fue una sesión corta, como de veinte minutos y me sentí tan agradecida con este buen hombre por su compasión ante nuestro dolor y por todo lo que tuvo que hacer para que las autoridades del centro de detención autorizaran esta entrevista. Esa noche me sentí bien tranquila. Tenía cuatro meses de no hablar con Gil personalmente y mucho menos tocarlo y abrazarlo. Al día siguiente les conté a los niños mi experiencia y estaban felices.

* * * * *

Este mes de julio han venido muchas personas detenidas y la mayoría de este grupo tiene antecedentes criminales. Llamó mi atención una boliviana de 18 años (Jessica) y una chino-filipina (Chin-Chin). Con ellas me llevo súper bien porque les gusta el deporte. Jugamos ping-pong y siento que el tiempo vuela cuando salimos al recreo. Estos partidos me hacen mucho bien; siento que no estoy detenida. Nos reímos y jugamos. También jugamos al básquetbol y siempre convencemos a otra más para que seamos cuatro y podamos jugar en equipo.

Cada día que pasa es terrible. Ya parece un campo de concentración. No cabemos en el dormitorio y en el comedor hay gente comiendo en el suelo. Hay muchas peleas por la televisión ya que sólo hay una y a pesar que hay un horario para ver programas en español e ingles, siempre hay alguien con la mentalidad de la cárcel, o sea que vale la ley del más fuerte. Pero aquí no funciona así la cosa; todos somos tratados por igual y hay que tener respeto por los demás. Esto no toda la gente lo entiende, especialmente las pandilleras que quieren hacer de este pequeño espacio su territorio y quieren hacer lo que les da la gana y es aquí cuando la guerra explota y los oficiales tienen que hacer uso de la fuerza para restablecer el orden.

* * * * *

Esta madrugada me despertó el llanto de varias compañeras. Están recogiendo lo poco que tienen, pues les han llamado para trasladarlas quien sabe a que lugar. Todo es tan rápido, todas lloran y piden que les den información de lo que está pasando y adónde serán llevadas. Pero es como hablar con una pared. No hay respuesta. Lo único que se escucha es la voz fuerte y exigente que dice:

– ¡Muévete! ¡Rápido! ¡¡¡Empaca tus cosas ahora!!!"

Todas lloran de angustia. Hay varios oficiales en el dormitorio y saben que tienen que obedecer lo más pronto posible. No se les permite usar el teléfono para informar a sus familiares. (Esto es terrible! Siento angustia al ver esto; lloran de miedo.

Yo también tengo mucho miedo. Esta escena me recuerda a la película La lista de Shindler cuando los nazis usaban su poder contra los judíos y los separaban del grupo para ejecutarlos. Es una angustia indescriptible y ruego a Dios que mi nombre no sea mencionado. Se llevaron como a veinte compañeras. Ya no hay muchas camas en el suelo pero a la mañana siguiente se respira un ambiente de tristeza.

*　　　*　*　*　　　*

Me parece increíble que en este país no se escuchan realmente fuertes protestas ante este tipo de injusticias. En El Salvador mi país natal y en muchos países hay ciudadanos estadounidenses luchando, protestando, y exigiendo respeto a los derechos humanos. A muchos les ha costado la vida el luchar por los marginados, los desprotegidos, los que no tienen voz ni derechos, pero... ¿Dónde están ellos ahora? ¿Será que ignoran lo que está pasando en estas cárceles o es que tienen miedo de hacer esta denuncia en su propio país? Ojalá algunos estén en esta lucha también.

Es irónico. Estados Unidos se quiere presentar ante el mundo como el país donde la injusticia no se conoce, pero aquí la estoy viviendo cada día. A nivel de gobierno mandan tropas supuestamente para llevar la libertad a otros países, pero la realidad es que ellos están muriendo y gastando su dinero por arreglar otros países y descuidan de su propio país.

*　　　*　*　*　　　*

Esta tarde como a las 3 PM, me llamaron por los parlantes. Me reporté con la oficial y esta me dijo que preparara mis cosas. Le pregunté que a donde iba y me dijo que no sabía. Mi corazón comenzó a palpitar a mil por hora. No podía creer lo que me estaba pasando. Sólo pensé en mis hijos y anoté el número de teléfono en un papel para que alguien avisara a mis hijos de que me habían trasladado quien sabe a dónde y ellos le avisaran a mi abogado. Todas mis compañeras estaban sorprendidas. Luci la peruana lloraba porque yo le estaba ayudando para su corte que sería en unos pocos días. Era un caos. Yo sentía mis movimientos tan pesados; creo que estaba paralizada. Me despedí de todas y les pedí que siguieran el estudio bíblico. Nos abrazamos y muchas lloraron, me sentí muy triste pero contuve mis lágrimas.

Me llevaron al mismo cuarto en que me pusieron cuando llegué por primera vez. Pasé como media hora encerrada sin que nadie llegara a decirme algo, hasta que al fin apareció un oficial con mi pasaporte en su mano y me dijo que esa noche saldría a El Salvador. Traté de explicarle que mi caso no estaba cerrado, pero cerró la puerta en mi nariz. Me sentí mucho más confundida y angustiada pues nuestro caso estaba a la orden de una corte superior, e Inmigración no podía decidir algo así sin una orden de esta corte. Pero ni modo yo en el fondo sabía que los de la Inmigración hacen lo que les da la gana. Simplemente usan su poder.

Me angustiaba la situación en que quedarían mis hijos. No me los imaginaba solos en este país. A pesar de que estábamos detenidos y no podíamos estar físicamente presentes, ellos sabían que estábamos siempre apoyándolos y proveyéndolos de dinero para su comida y sobre todo dándoles ánimo y consejo. Creo que esto era demasiado para poder soportarlo. Me sentía tan poca cosa, sin armas ni defensa, sin una voz ni mucho menos voto para decidir ante esta situación. Para colmo, Diana cumplía años la próxima semana el 19 de agosto. Esto me puso mucho más triste.

Me puse a orar y a darle gracias a Dios por lo que había logrado con mis hijos hasta este momento, y le pedí que me los cuidara, que si tenía que irme de esta manera está bien, ni modo, pero en el fondo de mi corazón El sabía que sería como morir. Pasó una hora y yo en la misma angustia. Hacía un silencio sepulcral y nadie se asomaba hasta que al fin apareció de nuevo el oficial y me dijo que iba de nuevo al dormitorio.

* * * * *

Cuando regresé al dormitorio mi cama ya estaba ocupada por otra compañera y ni modo que decirle que me la diera de nuevo, así que a buscar una cama vacía y a comenzar de nuevo. Mis compañeras estaban contentas al verme de regreso pero todo era hasta ese momento un misterio para mí. Sentía mi cuerpo tan pesado. No cené sino que no pude más y me acosté. Di gracias a Dios por permitirme estar siempre cerca de los niños, y le pedí por mis compañeras que se habían llevado esa madrugada y quien sabe adónde estarían.

Al día siguiente llamé a mi abogada le comenté lo que había pasado. Ella ya lo sabía. Parece que Gil le llamó de inmediato y le dijo que a él lo iban a mover. En ese mismo instante ella envió por fax el documento de la apelación y de inmediato Inmigración suspendió la operación. Que alegría me dio el saber que Gil si había sido inteligente y había hecho lo que se necesitaba en el momento apropiado. Si él no hubiera llamado a la abogada, estoy segurísima de que nos hubieran deportado.

* * * * *

Luci tiene su corte en dos días. Está nerviosa, más bien nerviosísima. Hemos estudiado y repasado su historia, pero siempre necesita un abogado, así que ya consiguió uno para que venga a su corte. Lo único malo es que él no le ha llamado para confirmar que vendrá a representarla. Eso la tiene como león enjaulado, pero aprovechando que es día miércoles y vienen los voluntarios, después de nuestro estudio bíblico le dio a una de ellas un papelito con el nombre y teléfono del abogado y se arrodilló llorando y pidiéndole el favor de que lo llamara y le recordara que se presentara en su corte final. La voluntaria le dijo que con mucho gusto pero que no era necesario que se arrodillara.

Al instante una oficial de las peores llamó a la señora voluntaria y al supervisor de seguridad quien la condujo al pasillo. Desde el comedor podíamos ver que le reclamaban algo. Le registraron la Biblia y su bolsa, se veía que le estaban haciendo pasar un mal momento, y después se retiraron.

* * * * *

Esta noche pedimos mucho en el grupo de oración para que Luci pueda salir de este lugar. Todo parece indicar que tiene un tumor y tiene mucho dolor, y aquí no le dan atención médica apropiada, sólo Tylenol y Tylenol. Nunca le hacen un mamograma. Son tan indiferentes al dolor.

Hace unas semanas, la Hermana Molly se preocupó tanto al verla llorar cuando estábamos reunidas en oración, que trató de ayudarle preguntando a un oficial que cuando sería llevada al doctor. ¡Pero esta pregunta le costó muchísimo! Le llamaron la atención y le dijeron que ella estaba autorizada a visitarnos para ayudarnos en asuntos religiosos, no en problemas médicos. Y esta es la triste realidad en este lugar. Si no fuera por la labor de los voluntarios me atrevo a decir que nos tratarían como animales. Pero ellos no se dejan intimidar y con amor y dedicación nos visitan y oran por nosotros y son nuestros ángeles guardianes.

* * * * *

Gracias a Dios, Luci ganó su petición de asilo y al día siguiente se fue feliz. Ya había terminado esta pesadilla para ella y nosotros celebramos su victoria, pues era nuestra victoria también.

Viviendo sin control

Ya he pasado siete meses en detención. Cada día tengo más preocupaciones por los niños. La casa tiene que entregarse al banco. Ellos tienen que moverse; la pregunta es ¿adónde? Cuando vienen a visitarme, los veo tan distantes entre ellos. Sólo viven peleándose, y no quieren moverse a un apartamento y que el novio de Diana viva con ellos.

Es tan difícil para mí. ¿Pero qué puedo hacer? Sólo los veo 15 minutos a la semana y apenas me alcanza el tiempo para saber como están. Y lo peor es que me dicen verdades a medias. El fondo del asunto sólo ellos lo conocen, pero me aman tanto que no me dicen los problemas para no preocuparme. Esta noche no pude más y lloré. Me sentía tan impotente y sentía que mi familia se desquebrajaba, que el control se escapaba de mis manos y que no podría garantizar que se mantendrían unidos así como yo lo quería.

Pero mis deseos salían sobrando. Las circunstancias por las que estaban pasando a esa edad en un país extraño eran bien dolorosas, y tendría que dejar que las cosas siguieran su curso. Tenía que aceptarlo por más doloroso que fuera.

*　　　　　*　　*　　*　　　　　*

Lo único que podía hacer era tratar de darles más dinero a la semana para sus gastos, aliviarles un poco este problema de cómo mantenerse. Nos pusimos de acuerdo con Gil y definitivamente tendríamos que hacer más dinero.

Yo por mi parte aprendí a hacer con las bolsas en que vienen las papas unos adornos bien bonitos. Las chinas me enseñaron este arte tan delicado. Para eso sólo necesitaba tiempo, una carta plástica de naipe, una aguja, hilo, y un libro para aplastar las partes que se iban a ensamblar.

Al principio fue difícil, pero tenía tiempo. Me regalaron una carta de naipe, conseguí un libro grueso para poder aplastar las piecesitas ya dobladas y busqué en los basureros las bolsas de papas. Pero aguja no se puede encontrar fácilmente, así que tenía que conseguir una grapa y de ahí tendría que formar una aguja. Fui a la biblioteca, y ahí encontré una revista. Le quité la grapa, la escondí en mi calcetín y la llevé al dormitorio. En lo que respecta al hilo, aprendí a quitarlo de la costura de mi pantalón.

Ya con los materiales listos, manos a la obra. Los dedos me dolían muchísimo, y pasaba trabajando un promedio de diez horas diarias, pero en esa semana me gané 30 dólares. Hice tres corazones y me los compraron rápido. Mi pobre esposo seguía haciendo bolsas para guardar el dinero, vendiendo parte de su comida y entre los dos podíamos darles un poquito más de dinero.

* * * * *

Los voluntarios que vienen a visitarnos están orando mucho por mis hijos. Alice y Donald me dan mucho aliento y tienen a toda su congregación orando por ellos. Sister Molly y padre Robert igual. Eso me da mucha confianza y me hace sentir que no estoy sola en este lugar. Ellos me dan esperanza y aliento cuando siento desfallecer. Por otro lado la familia en El Salvador y mi cuñada Tita están pendientes de ellos.

Pero ellos ignoran lo que está pasando; los niños son bien discretos en sus problemas y por tanto todo parece como que va de maravilla. Pero una madre percibe los problemas al ver la mirada de sus hijos y eso es algo que Gil no entiende y me dice que me encanta preocuparme por gusto. Pero yo siento en mi corazón que están pasando una crisis familiar.

* * * * *

Es ya el mes de octubre y escuchamos en las noticias que hubo un huracán muy fuerte en Centroamérica, que hay muchos muertos y desplazados. Aquí es un caos completo. Hay muchas mujeres que han dejado a sus hijos en sus países y no saben como están. No se pueden hacer llamadas internacionales en estos teléfonos y son momentos bien dolorosos para todos. El miedo y el dolor son contagiosos así que se respira en el ambiente mucho dolor.

Esta semana Sister Molly ofreció que podía investigar el paradero de los familiares que vivían en las áreas mas afectadas. Ella pidió los nombres y la ciudad en que vivían estas personas para que a través de las hermanas de la orden Maryknoll seguir el rastro y poder traer noticias. Este día hicimos mucha oración por las víctimas del huracán.

* * * * *

Desde que comencé a trabajar en estas manualidades, me he acercado con las chinas. No podemos comunicarnos mucho por la barrera del idioma, pero le pedí a Chin Chin que pensara en formar un estudio bíblico con las chinas, y así lo hizo. Así que ahora en el estudio bíblico cantamos en chino, español e inglés. Somos como 25 en total y me encanta pues cuando vas al estudio bíblico dejas tu carga a Jesús y pasas mucho mejor. Le encuentras sentido a tu sufrimiento y tienes paz en tu corazón, no importa cuan difícil sea lo que tienes que enfrentar. Es una paz que sólo Dios te puede dar. Sabes que tu futuro está en buenas manos.

* * * * *

Jessica, la chica boliviana, fue a corte y le dieron una solicitud de asilo político. Ella no cuenta con medios para pagar a un abogado. Vino sola a este país, tuvo problemas, fue a la cárcel, y de la cárcel la trajeron a inmigración. Así que me pidió ayuda para presentar su caso al juez.

Comenzamos con su historia, la de una joven llena de vida que vive con su madre, hermanos, y su padrastro. Pero con el paso de los años y en su transformación de niña a mujer, su padrastro la ve con otros ojos y la comienza a acosar sexualmente. Su madre no la apoya y termina huyendo de la casa. Se va a vivir con su abuelita, pero aun allí el padrastro la vigila y su obsesión no la deja en paz. Se va de casa de la abuela y a la edad de 15 años llega a Brasil para comenzar una nueva vida pero su inmadurez y falta de guía la llevan a cometer errores y regresa a Bolivia embarazada.

Vive con su abuela, da a luz a una niña, y esta vez el acoso de su padrastro es peor. Ya no la respeta y en una discusión acalorada en que el quería abusar de ella a la fuerza, Jessica toma una pistola y lo hiere en una pierna. Su vida fue un tormento desde ese momento. Su padrastro no puso cargos en su contra pero ella decidió salir de su país, dejó a su hija, y se vino a este país en busca de un futuro mejor.

Llenamos su petición de asilo, le escribió a su abuelita para que le enviara las pruebas necesarias, y cuando fue a corte la juez le adjudicó una fianza para que pudiera presentar su caso en libertad. Todas estábamos felices pues ella tenía apenas 18 años. Era bonita con buena figura y había sufrido desde pequeña. Ahora venía lo más difícil; la fianza era de tres mil dólares y ¿cómo podría reunir este dinero? Ella decía que su mamá tenía negocios y que tenía dinero así que le escribió pidiendo ayuda.

*　　　　　*　*　*　　　　　*

Ya es el mes de octubre y sigo en este lugar. Las cosas no han cambiado mucho. Mucha gente ha entrado y salido pero algunas ya somos inventario. Por ejemplo Mar y Laz (Cubita), siguen sin oportunidad de salir. Tienen record criminal y Cuba no las recibe. Ellas están en una posición tan difícil pues vienen de la prisión y han estado presas por muchos años, y aquí están sin oportunidad de ver la libertad.

May, la jamaiquina tiene cuatro años de estar en este lugar, su problema es complicado pues cambió de sexo y ahora es una mujer y no hay registro de ella en su país. Me parece algo injusto que ella siga en este lugar por tanto tiempo. Sufre muchísimo pues algunas detenidas la maltratan y ofenden diciéndole que ella debería estar en el dormitorio de los hombres, que ella nunca será una mujer, y le dicen groserías desde culero, culo roto, marica y otras más. Me he acercado mucho a ella pues está muy herida y siempre a la defensiva ya que ha sido victima de discriminación y rechazo, pero es una linda persona y la admiro por su valentía. Ella es el hombre del que tenía que tener cuidado cuando llegué a este lugar; pero ¡¡que va!! Es una excelente persona.

Hay una china que ya tiene un año esperando que le den su asilo político y una señora de Etiopia está en la misma situación. Tengas record criminal o no lo tengas, el tiempo de espera es igual. Parecería que no es importante el record que tu tienes y eso me extraña muchísimo y me desanima pues he visto pasar gente con record de delincuencia bien graves y el juez les ha dado fianza, algunas veces de $ 1,500 o bajo palabra. Por ejemplo a Jessica le piden $3,000 a otras hasta $5,000 y no tienen record criminal, así que el criterio que el juez utiliza siempre ha sido una incógnita para mí.

Escuchamos en la televisión que no van a haber deportaciones para Centroamérica debido a la crisis y los problemas ocasionados por el huracán Mitch, así que todo el mundo está contento pues esperamos que varias puedan salir libres.

* * * * *

Estamos planeando hacer una fiesta para el día de las brujas pero tenemos que pedir permiso pues queremos tomar sodas y comer papitas o nachos. La haríamos en la noche de 7 a 10 PM. Solicitamos el permiso a la oficial de la tarde y ella nos dijo que si, pero que tenía que hablar con el supervisor. Todo parece indicar que podremos tener nuestra fiestecita.

La verdad que el turno de la tarde es especial; son estrictas pero te respetan y te tratan como ser humano. Cuando tienes un problema tratan de ayudarte en lo posible y sobre todo siempre tienen una sonrisa. El ambiente que se respira en la tarde es más tranquilo. En la noche es un ambiente de temor. Te gritan, te tratan como en un campo de concentración, y no te resuelven un problema. Las de la mañana no son tan mal a excepción de dos que te hacen la vida de cuadritos. Quieren silencio total y siempre están demasiadas ocupadas para atenderte.

* * * * *

El problema de hacinamiento es cada vez peor; han venido muchas detenidas y como las deportaciones están suspendidas para Centroamérica, hay un gran malestar pues ya no cabemos de nuevo. Se está organizando una huelga de hambre.

La causa me parece justa pues quieren que se deporte a las de Centroamérica que ya han terminado su proceso legal y ya tienen orden de deportación. ¿Por qué seguir deteniéndolas? Quieren ir a sus países para saber algo de sus familiares y poder estar con ellos en estos momentos después del huracán. Es mejor que las repatrien pues la angustia que están pasando por no saber de sus familias las vuelve muy temperamentales y estallan a la mínima provocación. Entiendo que los hombres harán huelga de hambre también pues hay alguien que llama de afuera indicando las instrucciones.

Me han pedido que forme parte del grupo pero no quiero, pues las organizadoras son las buscapleitos y problemáticas y no estoy de acuerdo con la violencia. Además yo pierdo peso con mucha facilidad y ya estoy suficientemente delgada para quitar otra librita. Pero sí las apoyaría en la parte de consejería. No hay un acuerdo en quien es la líder. Todas tienen miedo de dar la cara, pero al fin escogieron a una señora mejicana.

Casi todo el dormitorio se ha anotado para participar, y muchas vienen a preguntarme que hacer y si yo voy a participar. Yo lo único que les digo es que si se incorporan a la huelga que sean responsables y la hagan de verdad para que el grupo tenga fuerza. Por supuesto siempre hay un informante pues los guardias ya saben de esto. La huelga va a comenzar en dos días. Se están preparando comunicados para las autoridades de INS dirigidas especialmente a G.K. que es la oficial encargada de todo este centro.

* * * * *

Esta mañana comenzó la huelga, no se levantaron a desayunar unas 30 personas. Las guardias van a despertarlas y les piden que se levanten pero no obtienen respuesta. En el almuerzo ya eran como 20, y en la cena también. Se envió un comunicado explicando lo de la huelga al periódico, *La Opinión*, y parece que alguien llamó al canal de televisión KMX.

El segundo día las guardias comenzaron a decir que si no comían, las iban a llevar al hospital para que les pusieran suero y comenzaron a anotar el nombre de las huelguistas. Esto hizo que muchas ya no siguieran en la huelga por el miedo a que INS tomara represalias. Al mediodía ya eran unas 15 y a eso de las tres de la tarde llegaron oficiales de inmigración preguntando quien era la líder. Hubo un silencio total. La supuesta líder tuvo demasiado miedo para explicar las peticiones hasta que al fin dijo el oficial que en media hora querían saber quien representaría al grupo cuando se reuniera con G.K..

Se eligió a una panameña de nombre Eloy, una señora de unos 56 años que se daba ínfulas de ser una vendedora mayorista de drogas. No era nada sencilla y tenía facilidad de palabra. Era un poco enferma pues padecía de asma y le hacían daño los químicos con que trapeábamos el piso, pero sí tenía cualidades de líder. Fue a la reunión con G.K. y regresó una hora después de haber entregado el pliego de peticiones, las cuales eran:

1.- deportación inmediata para las centroamericanas con orden de deportación.
2.- acelerar el proceso de deportación para las demás que también tienen orden de deportación.
3.- mejorar la comida.
4.- acelerar las audiencias con el juez.
5- mejorar la atención médica.

Al regresar mencionó que la señora G.K. fue muy amable y se comprometió a estudiar las peticiones.

La huelga siguió adelante pero con muy poco apoyo, como a las cinco de la tarde vino el dietista encargado de la alimentación de este centro y preguntó que nos gustaría comer. Era un alboroto. Nunca nos había visitado nadie para preguntar sobre la comida. Al siguiente día Eloy fue llamada de nuevo y a su regreso dijo que si la huelga continuaba se suspendería la deportación del grupo que saldría esa semana. Así que la huelga terminó; únicamente duró dos días. Una semana después se fueron dos de nuestras compañeras, una de Guatemala y otra de El Salvador. Hubo una gran desilusión. Eso no era lo esperado; había 15 mujeres ya con orden de ser deportadas esperando regresar a sus países y todas esperaban ser escogidas.

Al mes de que ellas se fueron, recibimos una carta en la que nos contaban que se fueron en un avión militar esposadas a los asientos junto con varios hombres y escoltadas con policías que no las dejaban ni moverse y las llevaron a una cárcel en El Paso, Texas. Allí no les daban buena comida ni ropa limpia; pasaron quince días en esa cárcel hasta que al fin las enviaron a sus países de origen.

*   *   *   *   *

Jessica fue a la biblioteca y estaba un oficial joven en turno. Se intercambiaron papelitos comunicándose, así que ella está bien emocionada, y va a ir mañana de nuevo para verlo y seguir con su coqueteo. Su mamá no le ha enviado el dinero para la fianza y el tiempo pasa y puede perder esa oportunidad, así que sin dudarlo le pidió ayuda a este oficial, pero todo bien discreto pues no es permitido. Pero para el amor no hay imposibles así como dice el dicho, pues en la noche cuando traen la medicina, el enfermero le entrega cartas sin que la guardia se de cuenta.

Las envidiosas no faltan y ya comienza el chisme, así que se le dificulta comunicarse con él como antes, pero lo importante es que él le ha prometido sacarla de este lugar pagándole la fianza y así lo hizo. Meses después contrajo matrimonio con este oficial.

* * * * *

El tiempo sigue su curso. Ya es el mes de noviembre y siguen llegando más y más personas. Hay gente durmiendo en el comedor y en medio de los camarotes he llegado a contar 125 personas y sólo hay capacidad para 70. Están haciendo redadas en los trabajos pues viene mucha gente que dice que la migra llegó y allí los capturaron.

También ha venido un grupo de la cárcel que son pandilleras y para colmo son centroamericanas, jóvenes con futuro que deciden tomar el camino equivocado. Ayer atacaron a una rival porque "les vio feo." Le dieron de patadas cuando estaba acostada sin darle oportunidad a que se defendiera. No me explico esta mentalidad. Creo que también contribuye el hacinamiento en que estamos. El ambiente es inaguantable.

Todas las que vienen de la cárcel o prisión dicen que aquí es el peor lugar, pues de donde vienen les permiten usar su propia ropa, maquillarse y hay programas para estar ocupado, hacer deportes al aire libre. Cuando tienen visita pueden abrazar a sus familiares y dura horas esa visita. Se puede ir a la escuela y aprender algo, pero aquí sólo estamos encerradas entre cuatro paredes sin espacio a donde ir, sin privacidad, con muchas restricciones, y las visitas que sólo duran 15 minutos.

* * * * *

En el grupo de ayer vino una colombiana que tiene escondido maquillaje. En realidad es un lápiz de ceja y pinta labios. Así que se dieron cuanta los oficiales al ver que algunas se habían maquillado y nos llevaron a todas al comedor. Comenzaron a registrar nuestras camas tratando de encontrar el bendito lápiz y como no lo encontraron nos dijeron que nos iban a desnudar hasta que apareciera.

Hubo un malestar y enojo en general contra las que se pintan, pues no es justo que todas paguemos por las indisciplinadas. En todo esto transcurrió como una hora hasta que al fin se llevaron a las que andaban pintadas para hacerles una revisión. Hubo intercambio de palabras entre varias debido a esta situación.

Hasta ahora no entiendo cual es el problema en que uno se pinte. Me parece que quieren hacernos sentir sin derecho a nada. Yo entiendo que es deprimente ver tu rostro en el cuasi espejo; en lo personal evito hacerlo, pues me deprime verme tan envejecida en tan pocos meses, tan demacrada y con ojeras pronunciadas, la piel reseca. En fin no es nada agradable.

Al regresar el grupo que registraron, la colombiana dueña del lápiz y pintalabios dijo que pondría una demanda, pues las desnudaron, las pusieron en fila. Una oficial de INS se puso un guante y les reviso la vagina y el ano, pero nunca se cambió de guante. Fue un alboroto, y efectivamente ella puso una demanda y la reportó a Washington.

Todas estaban criticando a las policías... y es cierto que fue una violación, una humillación, y un atentado contra la salud de ellas. Yo estoy de acuerdo. Pero a veces pienso que si sabemos las reglas del juego, ¿porqué quebrarlas? Bien sabemos que vamos a tener que afrontar alguna consecuencia y que aquí siempre se les va la mano.

* * * * *

Llegó el día de acción de gracias. Al mediodía nos dieron una excelente comida: codornices, puré de papas, ensalada abundante, en fin fue un verdadero banquete. Cuando estaba orando antes de comer no pude contener las lágrimas. Yo disfrutando de esta comida y mis hijos ¿quién sabe cómo la estaban pasando? Lo más probable es que con limitaciones. Yo con mis amigas riendo y recordando buenos tiempos pero... ¿ellos? ¿Con la angustia de buscar a donde ir a vivir? Estarían solos sin pavo en su mesa y mucho menos amor de familia.

El resto del día lo pasé bien triste, pero a pesar de todo di gracias a Dios por tanto que me ha dado, pero especialmente por su amor y el valor de no dejarme vencer y seguir adelante confiando en que pronto me reuniría con mis hijos para ser una familia de nuevo, cuidarlos y guiarlos como siempre lo había hecho y poder devolverles su felicidad.

Navidad en Pod 6

Hoy más que nunca siento que he caído en el lodo y que mi vida es miserable. El problema de las lesbianas se ha agudizado. No soporto verlas besándose o en la noche una encima de otra. Cada quien es libre de hacer su vida pero este no es el lugar para estas prácticas. Mis compañeras de Sri Lanka, India y China son las más afectadas. En su cultura esto no es permitido y puede causarles la muerte por estas prácticas.

Yo tengo aquí amigas que son lesbianas y por la confianza y el cariño que les tengo les explico que tienen que respetar al resto, que hagan sus cosas en la madrugada discretamente pero que no lo hagan tan abierto. De todas maneras se ven en problemas pues siempre hay alguien que avisa a las guardias y las sancionan.

Gracias a Dios hablé con el padre Robert, y le comenté todo lo que estaba pasando y como me sentía. Y él como siempre con sus palabras sabias y con tanta paz, me pidió que pensara que ellas también eran hijas de Dios y que orara mucho por ellas para que encontraran el camino. Eso me ayudó mucho para no sentir tanta rabia y repulsión.

También me afecta mucho el ambiente bélico que se respira. Sólo se escucha intercambio de palabras soeces, amenazas, y al rato un pleito de nuevo. Y como aquí no hay nada que hacer y el espacio es tan pequeño, se puede observar como la gente disfruta y se emociona al ver peleas. Disfrutan con la violencia. Es tan difícil no contagiarse.

Estoy más vulnerable al enojo y a ver sólo lo negativo de este lugar. Pero estoy consciente que de seguir así pasaría a ser parte de este grupo que tanto detesto, pues nos roban la paz. Pero no voy a permitir que esto me pase. Sería lo peor. Tengo que trabajar a cada minuto para recordar mis principios y la educación que con tanto esfuerzo me dio mi madre y seguir adelante.

* * * * *

Ya es principios de diciembre. Tendré que pasar aquí la navidad, así que decidí organizar un acto conmemorando el nacimiento de Jesús. Lo primero era escribir el libreto, así que con Chin Chin nos pusimos de acuerdo y ella lo escribió. Luego lo corregimos y organicé el programa incluyendo canciones y una parte de testimonios a manera que todas participáramos.

Fue difícil conseguir actores. En estas circunstancias todo el mundo es apático y no comprende que podemos celebrar la navidad, que hay un lugar en nuestro corazón para vivir, reír, y recordar bellos momentos como el nacimiento de Jesús. No obstante el negativismo, logramos reunir como a quince personas. Las chinas serían los ángeles, pues no hablan inglés. Los pastorcitos serían las hispanas que no quieren decir ni una palabra pues les da pena. Y por supuesto no podían faltar los reyes magos, María, y José.

Ensayamos todos los días con mucho entusiasmo y, para bendición, las hermanas de la congregación de la Madre Teresa nos visitaron y apoyaron en este proyecto, prestándonos el vestuario. También trajeron colores y dibujos alusivos a la navidad para que decoráramos la pared del comedor y así dar un ambiente navideño a este lugar. Las hermanitas se retiraron y nos ingeniamos a usar pasta de dientes como pegamento y decoramos el comedor bien bonito. Eso nos hizo sentir en un lugar diferente, pero como a la hora justo cuando recién habíamos terminado, llegó la oficial y nos dijo que quitáramos esas tonterías porque eso no era permitido.

Todas estábamos de mal humor, pues ¿como es posible que una cosa tan mínima les moleste? Pero se nos olvida que la idea en este lugar es hacerte la vida imposible de cualquier manera. Ni modo.

Tuvimos que quitar la decoración pero decidimos ponerla en nuestra cama, pues queríamos tener una navidad. Este mes es bien tenso. Hay muchas lágrimas y peleas. Las centroamericanas ya deportadas aún siguen aquí en su mayoría. En fin es bien difícil.

*   * * *   *

El padre Robert como siempre viene a visitarnos, y ahora ha venido otro padre que se llama Peter. El habla perfecto el español y sus misas son bien campechanas. Habla en un lenguaje bien sencillo y a todas les gusta como conduce la misa, pues explica el significado de ella. Nos habla mucho de que antes los cristianos íbamos a la iglesia sólo a recibir, pero es tiempo de dar, que hay que colaborar con la iglesia. Hay mucha necesidad y no tenemos que ser indiferentes a las necesidades de los demás. Aunque sea en este lugar podemos hacer buenas obras, dice él.

Desafortunadamente no todas captan la idea pues aquí aunque no lo parezca, hay quienes son implacables al cobrar por una pequeña ayuda. Sin llegar muy lejos hay quienes piden rosarios y después los venden a dólar. Venden todo lo que pueden, inclusive medicinas.

*   * * *   *

En esta semana los voluntarios nos trajeron tarjetas de navidad para que enviemos a nuestros familiares y amigos. Nos dieron un promedio de seis a cada una, pero para las chinas no tenían mucho valor ya que no celebran la navidad en esa fecha pues son budistas. Así que mis queridas cubanas fueron las que acapararon casi todas las tarjetas y comenzaron a venderlas.

Yo estaba súper enojada, así que comencé a regalar mis tarjetas y comencé a motivar a las que tenían todavía a que las regalaran cuando alguien necesitara. Esto no le agradó a las del negocio, así que sin darme cuenta me robaron mis tarjetas para evitar que yo las siguiera regalando. Este incidente hizo que hubiera malestar en el dormitorio y alguien les dijo a las oficiales lo que había pasado. Cuando salimos a recreo hicieron un gran registro y confiscaron todas las tarjetas de navidad para que aprendiéramos a no pasarnos de listas.

* * * * *

Este 17 de diciembre cumplo 23 años de casada. No lo podía creer. Se sienten tantos años, pero al ver atrás siento que el tiempo ha corrido. Ha pasado tan rápido. He compartido tanto con Gil: triunfos, fracasos, alegrías, tristezas, desilusiones... En fin, creo que hemos vivido un matrimonio verdadero, lleno de todo, y a pesar de los sin sabores y malos ratos, estamos unidos. Hemos triunfado en mantener nuestra unión, hasta que Dios lo permita. En mi caso creo que nuestro matrimonio ha permanecido porque ambos hemos aceptado que no somos perfectos. Hemos reconocido nuestras fallas y sabemos que el convivir significa aceptar lo bueno y malo de tu pareja, pero sobre todo tratar de cambiar para mejorar.

Una tarde me llamó la oficial y me dijo que me preparara pues iba a tener confesión. Al momento pensé ¿confesión? Yo no me anoté para confesarme. Pero que bueno pues, veré al padre Robert y conversaré un rato con él. Me preparé y al momento me llamaron. Al llegar al cuartito, vi al padre Robert y a Gil esperándome.

El padre nos explicó que había pedido permiso a migración para tener un momento de consejería matrimonial, y nos pidió que renováramos los votos que hicimos ante el altar cuando nos casamos. Fue un momento bien emotivo para ambos. Sentí el tiempo tan corto, pero fue maravilloso que a pesar de tanto dolor tuviéramos nuestro espíritu inquebrantable para seguir adelante como familia.

Ya me imagino como le ha de haber sido de difícil al padre conseguir este tiempo para que estuviéramos juntos, probar que estábamos legalmente casados, y no sé que tantas mil cosas y firmas, pero fue tan valioso para nosotros pues sanamos muchas heridas y, sobre todo, nos perdonamos el uno al otro.

* * * * *

La obra esta lista y vamos a hacer tres presentaciones. En la semana de navidad el miércoles, vamos a hacerla en honor de los hermanos evangélicos que nos visitan como lo son el pastor Ron, Alice, y Donald. El sábado lo haríamos para los hermanos evangélicos chinos que siempre vienen, especialmente para Albert. Albert nunca falla un sábado con su guitarra. Nos deleita con su música y tenemos un servicio religioso de alabanza maravilloso con él. El domingo sería para los católicos, comenzando con el padre Robert, Sister Molly, Padre Peter, Padre John, Vicente y Josefina, Kent y las hermanas de la congregación de la madre Teresa. Y en este día, tendríamos una visita importante como lo era el arzobispo Torres quien oficiaría una misa.

Estábamos emocionadas. La verdad que no teníamos nada que regalarles para navidad y eran todos tan espléndidos con nosotros, tan amorosos, tan comprensivos, siempre dándonos aliento y consejo trayéndonos alegría y esperanza a este lugar. Ellos eran lo único bueno que teníamos, y queríamos decirles lo mucho que apreciábamos su trabajo.

* * * * *

Todo salió de maravillas. Gozamos y fuimos felices, muy felices, al ver a nuestros amigos voluntarios sentados en una silla escuchándonos, riendo, cantando, disfrutando y sintiéndose amados por nosotros. Hubo lágrimas en algunos ojos, especialmente los más emotivos como el pastor Ron y Alice, pues sabían que lo habíamos hecho con mucho amor.

Todas las que participamos coincidimos en que revivimos nuestros tiempos de escuela cuando había un acto en honor de la madre o del padre. Por un momento nos desconectamos del ambiente encarcelario en que vivíamos. Por supuesto había quienes nunca fueron a la escuela y fue su primera experiencia, pero igual, se sentían muy felices. Y yo en lo personal estaba muy emocionada al ver que nos habíamos unido por fin, diferentes razas, sin prejuicios de quien es el mejor, sin rivalidades ni resentimientos.

Todas teníamos un solo objetivo: homenajear a quien se lo merece, dar una pequeña muestra de agradecimiento por la labor y la entrega que dan a favor de los inmigrantes, acompañándonos en este calvario. Aquí se vive la pasión de Cristo, y ellos son la Verónica y el Cirineo, tratando de aliviar nuestro sufrimiento. Para algunas chinas fue algo extraordinario, pues eran budistas y aquí en este lugar se han convertido al cristianismo. Por primera vez en su vida han celebrado el nacimiento de Jesús, y cuando una de ellas (Hong Chi Chi) dio su testimonio, con lágrimas en sus ojos dijo que si la deportaban siempre agradecería a este país porque conoció a Cristo.

*   *   *   *   *

Llegó el día de navidad y organizamos un intercambio de regalos, pero casi nadie participó. Muchas no esperaron las doce para darse un abrazo sino que la mayoría quedó en su cama pensando en su familia y llorando. Mis hijos me visitaron ese día en la mañana. Fue una visita corta. Les pregunté que si tenían planeado algo, pero me dijeron que no. No había mucho que hablar y en esta oportunidad estábamos tristes. Y así pasó la semana hasta fin de año.

Los días se sienten más largos de lo normal. No hay cortes pues los jueces están de vacaciones. Viene mucha gente detenida y nadie sale, así que el hacinamiento es insoportable. Somos 125 personas en este lugar tan pequeño. Hay mucho ruido y la televisión está encendida las 24 horas del día. Es más difícil mantenerse en paz, pero no hay otra salida que seguir adelante, tener mucha paciencia, y sobre todo tolerancia.

Comenzando el Y2K

Ha comenzado el año. En mis cuentas la apelación tiene que durar seis meses. Eso significa que al final de este tiempo tendremos la resolución de la corte, así que me mentalizo que sólo faltan dos meses para salir de este lugar. Eso me ayuda a soportar este ambiente pues siento que la hora se acerca. Una noche de estas, como a las 2 de la mañana, había humo en el dormitorio.

– ¡Fuego! ¡Fuego! – se oía que gritaban.

Me levanté y seguí al resto que corrían despavoridas al comedor. No entendía lo que había pasado. Mi sueño es bien pesado gracias a Dios. Al instante llegaron los oficiales de INS y los de seguridad. Yo tenía mucho frió y estaba medio dormida y el oficial dijo que quería saber quien había encendido unas revistas pegadas a la pared. Preguntó que si no sabíamos que el edificio se puede incendiar y que moriríamos quemadas pues esa puerta no se iba a abrir.

La mayoría no sabíamos de lo que hablaba pues ya estábamos dormidas a esa hora, pero siempre existen los búhos. (Así les llamamos a las que duermen de día y se levantan en la noche.) Ellas si tendrían que saber. Pasaron como 20 minutos. Yo tenía frío y sueño y me quería dormir. Y el oficial estaba grita que grita tratando de encontrar a la culpable.

Al final se llevaron a Zad, una chica de Etiopía, problemática, de las que más pelea. Ella tiene problemas mentales pues siempre la tienen con medicamentos para calmarla. Todas estábamos impresionadas sólo de imaginar la tragedia que pudo haber pasado.

Ya eran casi las cuatro de la mañana cuando nos permitieron ir a acostarnos.

Al día siguiente nos enteramos de toda la historia. Zad fue al doctor y se robó un encendedor. Al regresar lo introdujo al dormitorio, y las oficiales no lo detectaron. Estuvo despierta hasta muy tarde. Parece que no se tomó los medicamentos que le dan para dormir y al menor descuido encendió unas revistas junto a una columna en el dormitorio. Afortunadamente alguien se dio cuenta cuando estas comenzaban a incendiarse y dio la alarma. Después de este incidente se nos prohibió tener revistas en el dormitorio, ni siquiera el periódico Vida Nueva con noticias de la Iglesia. Así que hubo un registro al día siguiente y sólo nos dejaron la Biblia y nos decomisaron el resto de libros y revistas; tuvimos un buen susto.

Conversando con Zad, me dijo que estaba molesta con el INS pues pasó seis meses en una cárcel de inmigración en Phoenix, Arizona y ya tiene aquí más de ocho meses. No la deportan ni le dicen nada respecto a su situación. La quieren deportar sin su hija, y ella quiere llevársela. Lamentablemente ella no está mentalmente capacitada para cuidarla y eso Zad no quiere aceptar.

*　　　*　*　*　　　*

Cada día que pasa siento desfallecer. Siento una gran carga. Por un lado está el problema de mis hijos; definitivamente se van a separar. Diana consiguió trabajo en un valet parking. Los dos menores no se van con Diana sino que una señora les ofreció casa y comida a cambio que cuiden a sus dos hijos, una niña de siete anos y un varón de cinco. Esta señora vive a tres cuadras de la escuela donde mis hijos estudian. Es mamá soltera y conocida de una de las mejores amigas de mi hija Amy, así que le apoyé en su idea, al fin que no me quedaba de otra. Pero en el fondo me dolía tanto este rompimiento entre ellos, la única condición que les puse es que siempre estarían en contacto y que Diana los traería para la visita. Y por supuesto hice énfasis en que tenían que apoyarse unos a otros.

Por otro lado, al ser líder tenía que dar el ejemplo de fortaleza y fe, de paciencia de esperanza y tantas cosas que yo les decía a mis compañeras cuando las veía con problemas similares a los míos. Tenía que predicar con el ejemplo, así que tenia que hacer un doble esfuerzo, fingir algunas veces que estaba bien, cuando en realidad estaba destrozada.

Gracias a Dios, siempre recibía de mi familia en El Salvador (cuñadas y cuñados) libros y oraciones de fe, cartas preciosas que hacían que sin quererlo derramara mis lágrimas al sentirme amada. Sentía que tenía a ellos atrás de mí, dándome ánimos, trabajando durísimo por nosotros, tocando puertas y haciendo hasta lo imposible para presentar todas las pruebas necesarias para sacarnos de este lugar.

Sin embargo estaba entrando en un estado de incomodidad ante este ambiente, estaba harta de ver tanta injusticia, tanto dolor, tanta maldad, tanta degeneración y violencia y tenia una lucha interna terrible. Habían pasado ya diez meses y había usado todas mis herramientas para ver algo bueno en este lugar. Le encontré sentido al encarcelamiento ayudando a las más necesitadas. Le hacía de consejera, confidente, abogada, y pastora, pero sentía que nadaba contra corriente y me faltaban las fuerzas para seguir adelante.

Comencé a jugar cartas. Aprendí un juego que se llama espadas y me encantó. Pasaba horas jugando con Chin Chin, Blondie y May, pues éramos de las veteranas en este lugar. Nos divertíamos y nos desconectábamos. Nos imaginábamos jugando en un casino en Las Vegas, apostábamos, y pasábamos un buen tiempo.

Esta nueva rutina en mis quehaceres dio mucho que hablar. ¡Que horror! ¡La madre Teresa jugando cartas! La verdad es que yo no veía nada de malo, pero muchas no lo veían así. Sin embargo al transcurrir unos días, mis compañeras comprendieron que yo seguía siendo la misma y que cuando me necesitaban, suspendía mi juego para atenderlas. Y por supuesto siempre teníamos nuestro estudio bíblico.

*　　　　*　*　*　　　　*

Estamos en febrero y no he podido conseguir una cita con el dentista. Las encías me sangran mucho y no nos permiten usar hilo dental. Me duele una muela y no sé si tengo caries o qué. Además mis compañeras dicen que cuando te llevan al dentista los oficiales son bien atentos y hasta te regalan un cigarro. Yo me moría de ganas por tener esta experiencia y por fin conseguí que me autorizaran a ir a una consulta.

Yo esperaba que cuando me tocara mi turno también fuera una de las cubanas, pues son bien alegres y hablan con los oficiales de tu a tu, y efectivamente así sucedió. Fui con Cubita, (cariñosamente le decíamos así porque es la mas pequeña de estatura) y Pachi. Nos llevaron en un microbús y Cubita pidió un cigarro a uno de los oficiales y le dieron uno para cada una. Me lo fumé despacio y nos íbamos riendo y conversando.

Era la primera vez que veía el mundo exterior después de 10 meses y qué precioso veía todo. Disfruté las flores y los árboles. Que bello panorama. La gente caminaba a sus labores pues nos llevaron temprano; eran como las ocho y media de la mañana. Nunca había disfrutado de tanta belleza. Pasamos por un restaurante de comida rápida y ¡que aroma! Dios mío, como añoraba vivir en libertad.

Llegamos al dentista. Nos atendieron rápido; me tomaron una radiografía, y me prepararon para sacarme la muela. Cuando yo vi esto, le dije al doctor que yo no permitiría que me sacaran la muela pues la radiografía no mostraba caries, así que me limpiaron la muela a regañadientes pero me dieron un papel que decía que necesitaba una limpieza dental. A mis dos compañeras le extrajeron una muela a cada una.

Cubita iba de regreso como siempre chistando y de buen humor, pero Pachi iba llorando. Nunca le habían extraído una muela y apenas tiene 28 años. Le dije que por que no pidió que le hicieran un relleno y ella me contó que no hay dinero para rellenos, que lo único que hacen es sacarte los dientes o muelas porque eso es lo más barato. Pero en la mayoría de las veces, el dolor es insoportable y prefieres perder la pieza aunque tú sabes que con un simple relleno el problema termina.

De regreso creo que los oficiales tomaron otra ruta y podíamos ver el mar y respirar la brisa marina. Fue un viaje maravilloso. De regreso al Pod, antes de entrar nos registraron minuciosamente para evitar que ingresáramos artículos peligrosos así como sucedió con Zad.

*   * * *   *

Pero no siempre es una buena experiencia cuando te llevan al doctor. Recuerdo que Jamaica (le llamábamos así por su país de origen) estaba feliz cuando le autorizaron la compra de anteojos. Ya tenía un año en la cárcel y no le habían hecho ese examen aunque tenía dificultades para leer. Después de pedir y pedir, le autorizaron una visita al oculista.

El día de su cita se arregló lo mejor que pudo. Pagó $5.00 a otra detenida para que le trenzara su rizado cabello y se puso vaselina en los labios para verse diferente. Soñaba con fumarse un cigarrito. Para su sorpresa la subieron a una minivan con cadenas en los pies, manos y cintura, escoltada por dos oficiales. Así tuvo que caminar hasta la clínica del doctor ubicada en un centro comercial. Dijo que toda la gente la veía con espanto y ella se sintió tan mal que caminó con la cabeza viendo al suelo todo el tiempo. Fue una terrible humillación, y al regreso al dormitorio estaba muerta en llanto y no paraba de quejarse y ultrajar a los de la migra que la llevaron al doctor.

*   * * *   *

Pedí de nuevo otra cita con el doctor y le dije que necesitaba que me llevaran de nuevo al dentista. También quería una cita con el ginecólogo pues ya llevaba un año detenida y tenía que hacerme el examen rutinario para prevención del cáncer. Esto no le agradó mucho al doctor y me dijo que por qué no pedía que me deportaran así no tenían (INS) que estar gastando en mi persona. Me contuve para no responderle y solamente le recordé que tenía derecho a medicina preventiva, que hiciera su trabajo, y solicitara ambas autorizaciones.

Aproveché la oportunidad para escribirle a Gil y pedirle que hiciera lo mismo, que solicitara un examen médico. Yo lo veía tan delgado y deteriorado pero parece que a Gil no le interesa este aspecto. Es más, me contó que fue al dentista y le extrajeron dos muelas. La corona que él tenía en su muela se quebró y al ver que definitivamente no se la reemplazarían prefirió que le extrajeran las muelas a aguantar el dolor insoportable que tenía.

* * * * *

Ya han pasado doce meses y yo sigo en este lugar. Han pasado cientos de mujeres por aquí y muy pocas se han quedado en este país. La mayoría han sido deportadas. Siento que ya no soporto más. Ahora además de la frustración y el dolor por estar en este lugar, hay pleitos entre pandilleras. Este ambiente me enferma; estoy harta de tanta pelea y es más, he decidido intervenir en la próxima pelea que haya.

Siempre son las mismas personas: Mina y Rosa, las dos salvadoreñas jóvenes, pandilleras que al principio eran íntimas amigas pero hace unos meses son enemigas acérrimas. La otra vez se intercambiaron palabras y se amenazaron. Hay un ambiente muy tenso; este grupo no nos deja en paz. Cuando tenemos estudio bíblico hacen ruido. Nos hacen burla porque estudiamos la Biblia. En fin, están dando muchos problemas, tanto que he solicitado que me lleven a las celdas que están en segregación. No me importaría con tal de que por un momento pueda escuchar silencio. Estoy harta de este ambiente. Siento que ya no puedo más.

Chin Chin está igual que yo y ella también ha solicitado que nos encierren en celdas de segregación. Hemos hablado con muchas oficiales pero sólo les da risa, hasta que al fin la oficial Willy llamó a un capitán de INS y este aceptó hablar con nosotras. La verdad es que ambas somos líderes: ella de las chinas que son el 30 % de la población y yo de las hispanas que somos el 50 %. Así que nos llevaron a nuestra entrevista con el gran jefe. El se portó muy amable, pero en pocas palabras nos dijo que no nos llevaría a segregación, que en ese lugar es horrible pues están los reos mas problemáticos y violentos y los enfermos mentales. En ese lugar todo el día se escuchan gritos, malas palabras, maldiciones contra la migración, y gente llorando. El consideraba que sería mucho más dañino para nosotras.

Yo le pregunté porque no hacían nada si ellos sabían quienes eran las problemáticas. Le dije que el ambiente era cada día más tenso en nuestro pod y que pagamos todas por un grupo reducido de bochincheras. Le dije que sabiendo que existían problemas serios de odio, si ellos no actuaban, iba a pasar lo mismo que pasó hace unos días en el dormitorio de los hombres, cuando uno de ellos murió al ser atacado por otro. El no nos respondió sino que se retiró y fuimos llevadas de nuevo al dormitorio.

*   *   *   *   *

Las cosas no cambiaron. Yo estaba con una gran ansiedad de que hubiera otra pelea, y así ocurrió. Al poco tiempo, Mina atacó a Rosa cuando esta descansaba en su cama. De inmediato se formó una rueda alrededor de ellas; la mayoría disfrutaba al ver como estaban en el suelo dándose duro. Sin sentirlo corrí y agarré a Mina de su pelo y la jalé con todas mis fuerzas como si fuera un saco de papas. No sé quien se encargó de Rosa pero las separamos cuando de pronto llegaron los oficiales corriendo y se las llevaron. Mina iba sangrando de la cara. Rosa logró ensartarle sus uñas en el rostro. Yo me sentía como nueva. Descargué toda mi frustración y enojo en esa jalada de pelo.

A los pocos minutos llegó una filipina y me dijo:
– ¡Qué vergüenza, Madre Teresa! ¿Cómo es posible que hayas intervenido? ¡Tendría que ser cualquiera menos tú!

– Esto tiene que terminar–, le respondí. – Ya no aguanto más. Este lugar que antes era pacífico se ha convertido en un infierno y ya no puedo más. No lo voy a permitir.

Me retiré a mi cama y lloré. Me sentía mal por haberme dejado llevar por mis impulsos, pero lo hecho estaba. Las peleoneras pasaron en segregación tres días. A Rosa la trasladaron a otra cárcel para ver si el ambiente mejoraba.

A su regreso Mina comenzó a preguntar que quién la había separado jalándole del pelo, y le dijeron que fui yo. Así que al segundo día de su regreso, estaba yo en el comedor haciendo mis trabajos manuales cuando ella se sentó en la mesa de en frente. Por suerte nunca me encontraba sola en esa actividad sino siempre acompañada de gente que estaba aprendiendo o de quienes deseaban platicar.

Ella dijo, – ¿Quién fue la estúpida que me jaló del pelo?

Yo de inmediato le respondí – Fui yo, y lo volvería a hacer si peleas de nuevo.

Ella se levantó de la mesa con una actitud amenazante y de inmediato a mi alrededor había como ocho personas protegiéndome. Ay, Dios mío, ¡qué susto! La oficial en turno de inmediato sacó a Mina. Llamaron a un supervisor y se la llevaron. Nunca más la volvimos a ver. Fue trasladada a otra cárcel para evitar problemas futuros. El ambiente cambio de inmediato. Todo volvió a la normalidad.

*   *   *   *   *

Los voluntarios religiosos siempre vienen. Estamos atendidas espiritualmente a cuerpo de rey. Qué amor más grande, Dios mío. Nunca les podremos pagar todo lo que hacen por nosotros. Yo creo que ellos no se dan cuenta de la importancia de su labor, pero son el rayo de luz en las tinieblas. Si me preguntan como los puedo describir lo único que se me viene a la mente es la canción Vienen con alegría, pues siento que los describe:

Vienen con alegría, Señor
Cantando vienen con alegría, Señor

Los que caminan por la vida, Señor
Sembrando tu paz y amor.

Vienen trayendo la esperanza
A un mundo cargado de ansiedad,
A un mundo que sufre y que no alcanza
Caminos de amor y de paz.

Vienen trayendo entre sus manos
Esfuerzos de hermanos por la fe
Deseos de un mundo más humano
Que nacen del bien y la justicia.

Ellos han cambiado la vida de muchas personas que han pasado por este lugar. Nos hacen ver que este tiempo es importante para reflexionar sobre nuestra vida, que este tiempo es valioso. Cuando estamos en libertad los afanes diarios por lo general no nos permiten ver nuestros errores. Aquí, en cambio, tenemos tiempo suficiente para pensar, reconocer nuestros errores, enmendarlos y planear nuestro futuro, así que es importante aprovechar este tiempo.

El padre Robert se especializa en hacer que pensemos en cosas positivas, siempre que viene nos dice:

– Es un gusto venir a visitarlas al hotel San Pedro. Vean a través de la ventana y observen que bello se ve el mar. Piensen cuanta gente paga miles por tener un apartamento que les ofrezca este panorama. Recuerden su cuerpo está en esta cárcel pero su espíritu es libre.

* * * * *

Escuchamos en las noticias que han aprobado una ley que dice que es injusto e inhumano detener una persona indefinidamente por problemas migratorios. Eso nos ha dado tanta alegría pues hay cubanas y vietnamitas en esta situación. No las pueden deportar pues sus gobiernos no las reciben y no saben que hacer con ellas. Mientras tanto se están pudriendo en cárceles de inmigración.

Cubita y Mar se verán beneficiadas con esta ley, gracias a Dios, pues Mar cada vez está más enferma. Tiene mucha tos y se escapa a asfixiar cuando duerme pues tiene mucha flema. La atención que ella tiene no es la adecuada para alguien que tiene HIV. No nos deja dormir y esta perdiendo peso. En la clínica no le dan importancia a sus achaques pues dicen que es normal. La última vez que fue al doctor le explicó que salía sangre de uno de sus pechos y el doctor le dijo que no se olvidara que tenía SIDA. Vino bien desmoralizada llorando.

Yo escribí una carta dirigida al jefe de la clínica pidiéndole que por humanidad le atiendan pues tenemos miedo que se pueda asfixiar. Por momentos se queda sin respiración cuando tose. La firmamos todas y la enviamos. La respuesta no se hizo esperar; la doctora a cargo la atendió de inmediato y esperamos que por lo menos tenga una mejoría.

*　　　*　*　*　　　*

Hoy estamos de fiesta. ¡¡May se va!! Es la que más se merece la salida, pues, son cinco años en este lugar. Me alegro tanto por ella. La admiro mucho, pues no cualquiera soporta todo lo que ella ha sufrido. Llegué a conocerla y es una excelente persona. Nunca la vi involucrada en un pleito o conversando tonterías, sino que siempre reservada y triste.

Dolor de madre

Mis hijos están "bien". No fallan en visitarnos. Amy se gradúa en junio. Me duele que no voy a poder acompañarla y mucho menos ayudarle en sus preparativos ni disfrutar de la emoción de su triunfo pues se va a graduar con honores. Siempre están viviendo con esta señora a cambio de cuidarles a sus hijos. Me duele tanto que estén pasando tantas penalidades.

Mi cuñada Tita quiere que se los mande a Miami. Allí ella los cuidaría, irían a la escuela y tendrían una familia. Pero en realidad creo que no es conveniente para ellos pues van bien en la escuela. Si es cierto que están pasando muchas penalidades y muchas limitaciones pero tienen a sus padres cerca y nuestros lazos de amor son tan fuertes que sólo el hecho de vernos mutuamente nos da ánimos para seguir adelante.

Además yo siempre les he dicho que cuando se hunde el barco las ratas son las primeras en salir y que el amor se prueba en estos momentos. Por supuesto si los viera en peligro no hubiera dudado en enviarlos con su tía.

*　　　　　*　*　*　　　　　*

Este mes de mayo con el día de las madres es un mes muy triste. Yo lo pasaré por segundo año separada de los seres que más quiero en esta vida. Soy muy afortunada en tener a mis hijos, pero algunas de mis compañeras están sufriendo mucho pues perderán a sus hijos definitivamente o ya los perdieron. Los casos más difíciles son cuando deportan a los padres y los niños tienen que enfrentar diferentes situaciones:

1. Se quedan con su madre o padre y regresan a su país de origen, pero los padres tienen que trabajar y los niños están mal atendidos. No tienen los cuidados y la nutrición adecuada pues su padre a duras penas puede manejar la situación.

2. Se quedan con un familiar. Esta es la mejor opción, pero siempre hay dolor y angustia en si serán tratados bien y si los familiares tienen la solidez económica para mantenerlos y cuidarlos. Por lo general tienen que pedir asistencia al gobierno para poder mantenerlos.

3. Los niños están en una casa de cuido y las madres no pueden acudir a las citas de la corte juvenil para recuperar la custodia de sus hijos pues inmigración no autoriza esta salida. Esto hace que pierdan sus derechos como madres al no presentarse.

Este último caso es el más doloroso pues muchas veces los niños son dados en adopción, pues la madre no se presentó a atender la corte de sus hijos y no puede probar que se puede hacer cargo de ellos. El sufrimiento y la frustración respecto a los hijos sobrepasa todos los límites. Es algo espantoso, terrible.

Yo viví el sufrimiento de una filipina que fue deportada de por vida a su país natal. Tenía dos hijos, un niño de seis y una niña de tres años. Ella recibió una carta que los niños serían dados en adopción, pues ella era madre soltera. Sabía que no los volvería a ver en su vida y fue un golpe muy duro para ella. No había palabras para consolarla.

Dor, mi compañera de Guatemala que me libró de hacer el ridículo con la broma de las cubanas, tuvo mejor suerte. A ella la deportaron y tenía a un hijo de cuatro años que estaba a cargo de su esposo. Pero este señor era taxista, así que se llevaba al niño en el taxi cuando trabajaba porque no tenía quien se lo cuidara. Dor le pidió al esposo que le trajera al niño para verlo por última vez, pues sólo habían estado en contacto telefónico.

La vinieron a visitar y cuando regresó de la visita era un mar de llanto. El niño estaba bien delgado y se veía pálido y descuidado. Y la verdad es que no podía culpar al esposo pues este estaba haciendo lo máximo posible por cuidar al niño pero su trabajo no se lo permitía.

Llegó el día en que deportarían a Dor. Se fue con $ 400 que sería el dinero con que comenzaría una nueva vida en Guatemala. Pero al siguiente día la trajeron de regreso. Nos sorprendimos al verla y nos contó que se rehusó subir al avión sabiendo que dejaba aquí a su hijo. Se puso histérica gritando y llorando, pidiendo piedad al oficial de la migra que la llevaba para que le permitieran llevarse a su hijo. En esas condiciones la línea aérea no la aceptó y la trajeron de regreso. Dor logró llevarse a su hijo pero tuvo que pagar el boleto así que se fue sin un cinco en su bolsa.

Y así como ella hay muchas más. Mima dejó a su hija de 13 años con una señora que no conocía. La niña hacia trabajos en la casa a cambio de comida y un pedazo de alfombra en que dormir.

*   * * *   *

Es increíble que estos niños, ciudadanos americanos, tengan que sufrir todo esto, y todo a raíz de la ley IIRIRA *(Illegal Immigration Reform and Immigrant Responsibility Act de 1996)* que dice que todas las personas no ciudadanas americanas que hayan tenido problemas con la ley tienen que ser deportadas, sin importar que el crimen se cometió hace muchos años. Y esa es la razón por la que cada vez viene más gente a este lugar. Y esta es la horrible y cruel realidad que están sufriendo muchos ciudadanos americanos, ver su familia separada.

Me parte el alma como mujer y como madre ver estas situaciones. Yo me imagino la cantidad enorme de niños sin madre, algunos con sus familiares, otros a cargo del estado con familias adoptivas, pero la mayoría viviendo de la generosidad del estado. El estado se encarga de que no les falte nada material ¿pero qué pasa del aspecto sentimental y psicológico de estos niños? ¿Cómo les afectará en su formación? ¿Serán adultos resentidos por haber sido su familia desintegrada? Tantas preguntas e interrogantes y tan pocas respuestas en este aspecto.

Se viene a mi memoria Victoria. Ella nació en Perú pero sus padres, ciudadanos americanos, regresaron a Estados Unidos cuando ella apenas tenía dos meses de haber nacido. Hoy a sus 38 años y por problemas de drogadicción fue detenida por la inmigración, y se ha enterado que no es ciudadana americana y la van a deportar a Perú. Y es risible pues no habla ni papa del español, es rubia, ojos claros, y de peruana no tiene nada. No conoce la cultura y tampoco existe un familiar en ese país. Si deportan a Victoria, sus padres tendrán que hacerse cargo de su hija o entregarla al estado pues ellos ya están viejos. Y como este caso hay cientos más que me parecen de película.

Mar la cubana con HIV fue puesta en libertad. Le dieron salida con supervisión. Cubita está triste pues esperaba que salieran juntas, pero a la semana le dieron también su salida siempre con supervisión. Con ellas compartí trece meses en este espantoso lugar, pero me queda el gozo que al menos Cubita lleva en su mente que cambiaría su vida y lucharía por un futuro mejor. Las voy a extrañar pues cada vez viene gente rara y sólo quedamos Chin Chin, Blondie, y yo como veteranas.

* * * * *

Esta semana me llamaron para ir al doctor. Me extrañó pues no había solicitado últimamente una visita. Fui y me hicieron un físico. Me pusieron la prueba de la tuberculosis y ya. También me confirmaron que en una semana iría por fin al ginecólogo. Todo estaba bien hasta que al día siguiente observé mi brazo y vi una mancha roja en el lugar en que me hicieron la prueba de la tuberculosis. Ay ¡Dios mío! Esto fue como un tiro de gracia. La prueba dio positivo.

De inmediato sentí mucha rabia. ¿Cómo era posible que esto me hubiera pasado? A mis 45 años jamás había estado en contacto con la enfermedad y ahora ¿que pasaría? Me tomaron una radiografía para ver si la tuberculosis estaba activa o si únicamente tenía el basilo en mis pulmones, pero afortunadamente no había desarrollado la enfermedad.

Pregunte si había tratamiento para esto y me dijeron que si pero que por mi edad no podían darme este medicamento pues los daños hepáticos son muy severos. ¡Así de simple! Me sentí tan impotente, tan poca cosa para cambiar las circunstancias.

Me vino a la memoria cuando meses atrás trajeron detenida a una joven de china con una mascara. Siempre nos preguntábamos por que la usaba. La mayoría de las veces se la quitaba pero cuando iba al doctor le exigían que se la pusiera. Entonces vi a mi alrededor y vi mucha gente que tosía, pálidas, enfermas. Pero como aquí sólo te dan Tylenol, te acostumbras a vivir en estas condiciones.

¿Cuántas veces vi compañeras con esa mancha roja tan horrible en su brazo y nunca se me cruzó por la mente que podian estar infectadas? Jamás vi que les dieran tratamiento.

La falta de atención médica es un grave problema. Unos meses atrás vino una mejicana que la habían operado de cancer en el estómago. Por alguna razón que desconozco, en la herida se le había hecho un agujero del cual supuraba pus. Ella solo pasaba acostada con dolor y el doctor le decía que no era nada, que tomara Tylenol y esperara su corte pues la iban a deportar.

Una noche me dijeron que estaba llorando y sin dudarlo me acerqué a ella para ver en que podía ayudar. Me explicó que tenía miedo que la deportaran pues iba a morir lejos de sus hijos. Su corte era el día siguiente. No tenía abogado, venia de la cárcel, y su deportación era inminente.

Me sentí tan impotente. ¿Qué mensaje de esperanza podría darle? Oramos, lloramos, y al final le sugerí que le escribiera al juez y le pidiera una oportunidad. Ella accedió pues no tenía nada que perder, y me pidió que le escribiera la carta pues no hablaba inglés. Redacté una carta de cuatro líneas solicitando al juez la oportunidad de vivir sus últimos días al lado de sus hijos. Al día siguiente fue a su corte y la juez le concedió su libertad. ¡Fue un milagro!

* * * * *

Padre Eterno, ¿cómo puede haber tanta crueldad en esta gente? ¿tanta maldad? ¿Cómo es posible que te hagan tanto daño espiritual y físico? Nos tratan como seres indeseables y miserables. Nos sentimos abandonados y olvidados, un criminal en una prisión tiene mejor atención que nosotros. ¿Y cuál es nuestro delito? Ser indocumentados o residentes legales que cometieron una falta por la cual ya pagaron.

Siempre me he preguntado si el pueblo americano sabe lo que está pasando en estas cárceles. Si se dan cuenta que las familias están siendo desintegradas y hay una nueva generación de ciudadanos americanos que se quedaron sin padre o madre y son potenciales candidatos a la delincuencia y a no sentir la menor gratitud a su país, a su gobierno. Así comenzó la guerrilla en El Salvador, al ver la participación del Gobierno ante la injusticia e irrespeto a los derechos humanos.

* * * * *

Hablé con mi abogada para decirle lo que me estaba pasando respeto a la prueba de tuberculosis. Lamentablemente ella no podía hacer nada pues la enfermedad no se había desarrollado. Ni modo. De nuevo a resignarme y a seguir adelante. Mis hijos estaban preocupados por mi salud y averiguaron todo lo relacionado con esta enfermedad.

Le escribí a Gil contándole lo que me había pasado y le pregunté como había sido su resultado. Pero a él no le habían hecho ningún examen físico. Le pedí que lo solicitara y que pidiera sus records médicos pues con esta gente es imposible saber la realidad de lo que está pasando. Yo pedí los míos para ver el reporte escrito de mi radiografía. Quería asegurarme que en realidad no estuviera infectada con tuberculosis.

Por fin me llevaron al ginecólogo y el doctor me dijo que estaba todo bien pero que recomendaba un mamograma. Le pregunté al doctor que cuando me lo harían y sólo se sonrió y me dijo:

– Lo mejor es que pidas la deportación para que puedas atenderte con tu médico.

Solo eso me faltaba para confirmar que el mamograma nunca me lo harían.

Una victoria con dolor

Ya es el mes de junio. Siento la necesidad de preparar a alguien para que continúe con el estudio bíblico. Mis hijos dicen que viene de El Salvador uno de mis cuñados que trae unos documentos para presentar al INS y lograr que nos den una fianza para esperar el resultado de nuestra apelación en libertad. También me dicen que Diana se ha separado de su novio y que los tres están viviendo juntos de nuevo en el apartamento de Diana. Esto me alegra mucho.

Pero la vida encarcelada es cada dia más difícil para mí. En el fondo siento que ya no soporto más. Chin Chin, mí más cercana compañera, ¡tiene novia! Me siento tan desilusionada de ver como este ambiente te corrompe y si tú no te aferras de Dios es bien difícil salir adelante. Puedes cometer locuras y romper tus principios morales porque necesitas un escape a tanto dolor e incertidumbre. Por suerte ella tiene su corte final en una semana y espero que pueda irse a casa junto con su esposo y su bebe.

Recibí carta de Gil y me cuenta que su prueba de tuberculosis salió positiva y le han tomado ya tres radiografías pues no salen bien.

Le ha preguntado al doctor que es lo que está pasando y el doctor le dijo:

– Si no tienes noticias, son buenas noticias. No hay de que preocuparse.

Dice Gil que ya tiene todo arreglado pues vamos a salir en una semana. La noticia me alegró mucho pero a estas alturas después de 16 meses, no quiero hacerme ilusiones de la fecha, pues sentiría los días eternos. Le pido a Dios hoy mas que nunca me de fortaleza para seguir adelante.

*   *   *   *   *

El estudio bíblico sigue pero ya no soy yo quien lo dirige sino que Ani. De esta manera les quiero dejar preparadas para que luchen por su fe, que recuerden que no están solas, Dios está aquí acompañándonos en este calvario y necesitamos de El para dar a nuestros hijos y familia la fe y fortaleza que muchas veces nos falta.

Chin Chin logró que le dieran fianza así que se va en tres días, gracias a Dios. Estoy feliz, pero ahora si quedo completamente sola. Todas mis amigas se han ido, y este lugar está cada vez mas lleno de gente.

*   *   *   *   *

Este día 26 de julio de 1999 a las cinco de la tarde me llamó la oficial y me dijo que podía irme, que me preparara. Tenía un sentimiento de alegría y de tristeza, mucho dolor al ver ese mar de gente en desesperación y frustración. Parte de mi quedaba en el Pod 6. En este lugar experimenté el amor de Dios a plenitud y no soy la misma persona. Mis prioridades han cambiado.

Con mis compañeras compartí tristezas, alegrías, frustración y fortaleza para seguir adelante, pero especialmente amor. ¿Qué hubiera sido de mí sin amor? No quiero ni pensarlo. Hubiera sido peor que un infierno.

El amor tuvo un rol muy importante en estos 16 meses. Por amor mis hijos lucharon solos para salir adelante, demostrándonos a su padre y a mí que nos amaban al salir en sus estudios con excelentes notas y seguir en el buen camino así como les habíamos enseñado.

Por amor vienen los voluntarios a visitarnos, a darnos las fuerzas necesarias para luchar por nuestra familia, por nuestro futuro, por nuestra fe. Ellos vienen a enseñarnos que Dios nos ama enviándolos como mensajeros de su paz, amor y esperanza. Ellos son los héroes de mi historia, fueron mi inspiración, el modelo a seguir.

Por amor nuestra familia en El Salvador, Guatemala y Miami estuvieron a nuestro lado apoyándonos, siendo solidarios económica y espiritualmente en nuestro sufrimiento, haciéndonos llegar su amor a través de cartas y libros de crecimiento espiritual.

Por amor pude sobrevivir en este infierno, por amor a Dios, a mi esposo, a mis hijos, a mi familia, amor a mis compañeras que al igual que yo en los momentos más difíciles se dejaron amar, consolar, y aconsejar, haciendo que mi sufrimiento tuviera una razón de ser.

*　　　*　*　*　　　*

Después de 16 meses pude tomar a Gil de su mano y caminar juntos hacia la salida. No hubo un abrazo, ni palabras, pues una oficial nos acompañaba y nos advirtió que no quería ni abrazos ni besos ni nada. Pero podía sentir su mano apretando la mía. Al llegar al portón vi a Amy que corrió hacia nosotros así como solía hacerlo cuando estaba pequeña, diciendo ¡Papi!.... ¡Mami!

La abrazé fuertemente y volví mi rostro al centro de detención. Parte de mi quedaba allí. Tenía un sentimiento de alegría y tristeza. Diana y Gilito nos esperaban en la casa y nos habían preparado una suculenta cena. Por fin unidos como familia. Qué felicidad tan grande el poder estar todos unidos de nuevo.

*　　　*　*　*　　　*

Lamentablemente seis meses después de ser liberados, Gil empeoró de su salud y se le diagnosticó un tumor canceroso en su pulmón izquierdo. ¡Qué frustración más horrible! Esa era la razón por la que le tomaban tanta radiografía en inmigración, pero nunca fue notificado de esta enfermedad. Y en lo que se refiere al cáncer, el tiempo sin tratamiento médico significa vida. Perdimos seis meses de tratamiento...seis meses de vida.

Gil perdió su batalla contra el cáncer el 20 de junio del año 2001. Al morir dijo claramente a sus hijos que no quería que regresaran a El Salvador, pues su futuro estaba en este país, y no quería que su sacrificio fuera en vano.

El realizó su sueño de llevar a su familia al país que creía ser la tierra de oportunidades de estudio y de progreso, pero no logró el sueño americano. No le dieron la oportunidad de vivir. Con una simple carta notificándole su condición médica, hubiera sido diferente.

* * * * *

Pero esa es la dura realidad del inmigrante. Tu vida no tiene importancia. No tienes valor. ¿O acaso se hace algo para evitar que miles de inmigrantes mueran en el desierto tratando de llegar a este país?

Mi plegaria es que algún día, los norteamericanos se darán cuenta de lo que en realidad está pasando en su casa y se dediquen a reconstruirla en vez de estar arreglando la casa del vecino.

Sobre el Autor

Nacida en San Salvador, El Salvador en 1955, Ana Amalia Guzmán Molina recibió su titulo como Contador Público Académico en la Universidad Centroamericana, UCA. Posteriormente, recibió su maestría en Finanzas en la Universidad Tecnológica.

Actualmente es volutaria Católica para el Ministerio de Detención en Los Angeles y colabora con el Servicio Jesuita a Refugiados visitando niños inmigrantes encarcelados por el Servicio de Inmigración, ofreciendoles apoyo y orientación pastoral. Ha sido invitada por diferentes organizaciones en los Estados Unidos para hablar a favor de los inmigrantes detenidos en cárceles de Inmigración a travéz de su experiencia.

Amalia reside en California junto a sus tres hijos y sus otros dos hijos adoptados, "Chiqui" y "Lucy" Molina, y su perro y su gatita.